The Influence of *Star Trek* on Television, Film and Culture

CRITICAL EXPLORATIONS IN SCIENCE FICTION AND FANTASY
(a series edited by Donald E. Palumbo and C.W. Sullivan III)

1. *Worlds Apart? Dualism and Transgression in Contemporary Female Dystopias* (Dunja M. Mohr, 2005)

2. *Tolkien and Shakespeare: Essays on Shared Themes and Language* (edited by Janet Brennan Croft, 2007)

3. *Culture, Identities and Technology in the* Star Wars *Films: Essays on the Two Trilogies* (edited by Carl Silvio and Tony M. Vinci, 2007)

4. *The Influence of* Star Trek *on Television, Film and Culture* (edited by Lincoln Geraghty, 2008)

5. *Hugo Gernsback and the Century of Science Fiction* (Gary Westfahl, 2007)

6. *One Earth, One People: The Mythopoeic Fantasy Series of Ursula K. Le Guin, Lloyd Alexander, Madeleine L'Engle and Orson Scott Card* (Marek Oziewicz, forthcoming 2008)

7. *The Evolution of Tolkien's Mythology: A Study of the History of Middle-earth* (Elizabeth A. Whittingham, 2008)

8. *H. Beam Piper: A Biography* (John F. Carr, forthcoming 2008)

The Influence of *Star Trek* on Television, Film and Culture

EDITED BY LINCOLN GERAGHTY

CRITICAL EXPLORATIONS IN
SCIENCE FICTION AND FANTASY, 4
Donald E. Palumbo *and* C.W. Sullivan III, *series editors*

McFarland & Company, Inc., Publishers
Jefferson, North Carolina, and London

Library of Congress Cataloguing-in-Publication Data

The influence of Star Trek on television, film and culture /
edited by Lincoln Geraghty.
     p.   cm.— (Critical explorations in science fiction and
    fantasy ; 4)
    Includes bibliographical references and index.

ISBN-13: 978-0-7864-3034-5
softcover : 50# alkaline paper ∞

    1. Star Trek television programs.   2. Star Trek films—History
and criticism. I. Geraghty, Lincoln, 1977– II. Title. III. Series.
PN1992.8.S74I54   2008
791.45'72—dc22   2007028357

British Library cataloguing data are available

Cover image ©2007 Comstock

Manufactured in the United States of America

McFarland & Company, Inc., Publishers
  Box 611, Jefferson, North Carolina 28640
    www.mcfarlandpub.com

For Becky, Diane and Malcolm

Acknowledgments

Special thanks go to Donald Palumbo for at first suggesting submitting a proposal on *Star Trek* to the Critical Explorations in Science Fiction and Fantasy series, and then offering to contribute a chapter. Of course, mention must be made of the support given by my colleagues at the University of Portsmouth.

To my parents, Malcolm and Diane, I offer my love and gratitude as always. My final and most heartfelt love and appreciation goes to my partner, Becky Janicker, whose endless patience in putting up with me and my fascination for *Star Trek* continues well beyond what I deserve.

Contents

Acknowledgments   vi
Introduction: The *Star Trek* Effect
    Lincoln Geraghty   1

PART I: THE FRANCHISE

1. Eight Days That Changed American Television: Kirk's
   Opening Narration   11
       Lincoln Geraghty
2. The Accidental Apotheosis of Gene Roddenberry, or,
   "I Had to Get Some Money from *Somewhere*"   22
       Dave Hipple
3. Franchise Fatigue? The Marginalization of the Television
   Series after *The Next Generation*   41
       Ina Rae Hark

PART II: THEMES

4. Crossing the Racial Frontier: *Star Trek* and Mixed
   Heritage Identities   63
       Wei Ming Dariotis
5. Save the Whales and Beware Wilderness: *Star Trek* and
   American Environmental Views   82
       Elizabeth D. Blum
6. Batter Up! The Mythology and Psychology of Sports and
   Games in *Star Trek: Deep Space Nine*   100
       Barbara A. Silliman

PART III: FILM AND TELEVISION

7. The Monomyth in *Star Trek* Films   115
       Donald E. Palumbo

8. "Blow Up the Damn Ship!": Production Redesign and
   Special Effects Reuse in the *Star Trek* Films   137
   Michael S. Duffy
9. *Star Trek*: Popular Discourses—The Role of Broadcasters
   and Critics   153
   Paul Rixon

PART IV: THE FANS

10. *Star Trek*: The Franchise!—Poachers, Pirates, and Paramount   173
    Sue Short
11. Fan Culture and the Recentering of *Star Trek*   186
    Justin Everett
12. Locating the "*Star Trek* Experience"   199
    Angelina I. Karpovich
13. A Very *Trek* Christmas: Goodbye   218
    Karen Anijar

Notes on Contributors   235
Index   239

Introduction

The Star Trek Effect

LINCOLN GERAGHTY

> When I didn't have any friends, it made me feel like maybe I did.
> —Philip J. Fry on *Star Trek*, "Where No Fan
> Has Gone Before" (2002), *Futurama*.

The May 30, 2004, issue of *TV Guide* voted *Star Trek* the "top cult show ever" out of 25 lucky hopefuls. The reason, according to the small write-up, was that "the series (and its spin-offs) all but created fan obsession, conventions and an enduring link between science fiction and geekdom that has given countless outsiders the will to get out of bed every day for 38 years" (40). In other words, *TV Guide* has deemed that *Star Trek* changed the face of television programming. Not only has the series created the concept of the fan convention (a multimillion dollar enterprise for collectors and fans across the globe) but it has also given people a unique space within which to express their personal identities. As *TV Guide* sums up rather crudely, *Star Trek* has become an inspirational text for those fans who consider Gene Roddenberry's utopian vision something worth living for. However, as well as providing fans a creative space in which they can fulfill their own desires and fantasies, *Star Trek* has set the benchmark for subsequent television franchises which strive to attract and maintain an audience in a multimedia, multichannel age. Only *Doctor Who* has achieved a longer life span, having recently returned to British screens after a long, self-imposed hiatus. *Star Trek*'s narrative text and the commercial images that have been built around it for the last 40 years have become a pervasive part of the cultural environment, so much so that they have become part of the identity of the millions of people who watch, read and consume the films, television episodes, network specials, novelizations, and fan stories. Chris Gregory, in *"Star Trek" Parallel Narratives*,

1

considers it "to be one of the most valuable 'cultural properties' in the world" (2000: 2). *Star Trek* then is not just a television series: it has become part of who we are as individuals living and working in a global culture. It has had an effect on us as people living through the twentieth century, and there is no doubt, even after *Star Trek: Enterprise*'s (2001–2005) recent cancellation, it will continue to do so well into the twenty-first century.

This book examines *Star Trek* from various critical angles in an attempt to record and analyze the effect the franchise has had on popular culture. The essays in this collection provide vital new insights into the myriad ways that the franchise has affected the culture it represents, the people who watch the series, and the industry that created it. These particular discourses are synonymous with the world's largest television franchise, one that is now entrenched in both the American and global psyches. Consequently, this study moves on from the idea of *Star Trek* as purely a televisual text to account for the successful movie series and other related cultural phenomena including fan groups, novels, games, toys and merchandise, conventions, the Las Vegas Experience, world exhibition tours, the Internet, music, and Paramount's use of branding and advertising in the marketing of their multibillion dollar franchise. There are four sections in this collection, each examining the particular effects *Star Trek* has had on four different areas: television, American culture, the film industry, and the fan community. Throughout these sections, authors have taken care in treating the series as a whole, examining themes and trends that encapsulate the entire franchise. Previous studies of *Star Trek* have tended to focus on one particular series—most often the original *Star Trek* (1966–1969) or *Star Trek: The Next Generation* (1987–1994)—or a selection of related episodes, which in the long term has a detrimental effect on our understanding of the entire *Star Trek* product. This collection intends to look at the franchise through a wider lens and as such follows the ethos expressed by *Star Trek* executive producer Rick Berman in an interview with *TV Guide* in 1994:

> Gene taught me a new language, and now I have become relatively fluent. We've bent his rules a little, but we haven't broken them. *Star Trek: The Next Generation* [*TNG*] is not a series about my vision of the future or Patrick Stewart's or anybody else's. It's a series about Gene's vision of the 24th century. As a result, I will continue to follow his rules as long as I'm connected with *Star Trek* in any way [Berman, 1994: 2].

Rick Berman, the man who took over the mantle of maintaining *Star Trek*'s image following Roddenberry's death in 1991, explains that he was taught how to understand *Star Trek* and how to write stories that kept within the boundaries of the original concept. In the interview celebrating the final season of *TNG*, Berman explains that he had to become fluent in a language created by Roddenberry in order to continue his vision; rules were in place to keep *Star Trek* on course with its mission to promote liberal humanism in an entertaining fashion. Berman's choice of words hints at the existence of a formula or blueprint to which *Star Trek* must adhere lest it depart from Roddenberry's vision and lose its ability to entertain the audience. Whether the series are set on a space station or starship, in the future or the past, they are all part of Roddenberry's tradition. This means that the entire franchise, including all five series and ten feature films, can be looked at as one: as a gestalt entity greater than the sum of its parts. Quite literally, Berman was given the task of continuing to effect both Roddenberry's vision and that of the millions of fans who watch the series. *Star Trek*'s power to entertain is both textual and expressive, and through the next thirteen chapters it will be reexamined so that we can begin to understand the effect it has.

The Franchise

In the first section of this book Dave Hipple, Ina Rae Hark and I explore how the franchise was created, how *Star Trek* grew from obscurity to worldwide popularity, and how Paramount has allowed the franchise to decline by failing to adapt and develop alongside current trends in American television scheduling. My chapter, "Eight Days That Changed American Television: Kirk's Opening Narration," critically looks at the famous "Space the Final Frontier" opening narration spoken by Captain Kirk on the original *Star Trek* television series. In particular, I take issue with recent academic discourse that contends that *Star Trek* cannot be defined by one coherent reading, instead arguing that perhaps such a reading is possible through an understanding of how the series was presented to and received by its audience—both American and international—in the sixties through to the present day. The opening narration can be seen as a clarion call for sixties audiences and a symbol of the new "high concept" that would define television science fiction and dictate the format for such popular programming well into the 1990s.

Dave Hipple's "The Accidental Apotheosis of Gene Roddenberry" continues with this examination of the fledgling franchise by analyzing Gene Roddenberry's creative input. Whether we can attribute the rise of *Star Trek* to one sole author, or see it as an amalgamation of incidents and accidental moments that gave it an air of inevitability, the franchise became a success. Hipple looks at these developments in an attempt to chart Roddenberry's and Paramount's contributions to the longevity of the popular franchise. While both Hipple and I examine the positive aspects of the series' creation, Ina Rae Hark looks at the current downturn in *Star Trek*'s popularity. "Franchise Fatigue? The Marginalization of the Television Series after *The Next Generation*" looks at how Paramount has "mishandled the franchise by not responding to radical changes in the way science fiction television was produced and marketed." Hark posits that in the face of competition from series such as *Buffy the Vampire Slayer* and *Battlestar Galactica, Star Trek* tried to return to the tried and tested format of the starship adventure seen in *Enterprise.* In doing so, the franchise failed to attract new viewers and even alienated some of its most ardent fans. As a result, Hark questions whether the franchise has truly adapted to life in the twenty-first century.

Themes

For Michèle Barrett and Duncan Barrett, "the underlying issue around which *Star Trek*, in all its manifestations, revolves is that of the qualities and morality of humanity" (2001: 57). *Star Trek* has a particularly positive view of the world and of the future; it is a vision of utopia that sits in stark contrast to many of the filmic visions of dystopian futures seen in *Planet of the Apes* (1968), *Blade Runner* (1982), or *The Matrix* (1999). Humanity is on a constant voyage of discovery on which it can learn from mistakes of the past and continue to improve and achieve the fairytale utopia: "In this sense *Star Trek* acts much like a Jeremiad, as a moral guide to humanity's progress in life, making obvious what needs to be done but not providing its audience with all of the answers" (Geraghty, 2003: 235). With these observations in mind, chapters four, five and six in this second section focus on the theme of humanity, more particularly, how notions of the individual and the formation of personal identity ties in with the overarching themes of self-improvement and self-discovery already identified in the *Star Trek* narrative.

Wei Ming Dariotis's "Crossing the Racial Frontier: *Star Trek* and Mixed Heritage Identities" investigates the transgressive sexuality manifested in the franchise's more peculiar characters, Spock and Seven of Nine, who, as "outsiders," have been able to cross between identities, whether they be personal, national, sexual or racial. As transgressive figures, Spock and Seven have forced audiences "to confront the central question of all science fiction: What is human?" Throughout *Star Trek*'s history it has tested notions of identity and humanity through embodiment of the alien or android "other": Spock, Data, Odo, Seven of Nine.

Elizabeth D. Blum's "Save the Whales and Beware Wilderness: *Star Trek* and American Environmental Views" sets *Star Trek*'s view of humanity in a wider context—examining how the franchise has balanced notions of technology and the environment. For Blum, *Star Trek* "provides an excellent avenue to look at the impact of a social movement on popular culture"; through all the series, we can see how the future might look if we followed the lessons set by Captain Kirk and others over their concern for the environment. In several episodes and movies Kirk often goes to great lengths to prevent environmental destruction: in *Star Trek IV: The Voyage Home* (1986) he goes back in time to show humanity (and remind viewers of) the cost of species extinction. Concerns for the environment in *Star Trek* highlight the franchise's didactic tendencies.

The third chapter in this section emphasizes the role of sport in *Star Trek*'s narrative. Barbara A. Silliman's "Batter Up! The Mythology and Psychology of Sports and Games in *Star Trek: Deep Space Nine*" examines the use of baseball to bring characters together and help form supportive friendships. Humans and aliens cohabit and learn understanding through the camaraderie and mythology of America's favorite sport. Silliman's argument suggests that *Star Trek* not only uses the futuristic settings of the twenty-third and twenty-fourth centuries to tell its moralistic stories, but it also uses familiar sports and games (human contests) to show how people can learn to develop meaningful relationships.

Film and Television

Although they span four decades and have been recognized by many film critics and fans as the epitome of *Star Trek*'s ethos, the six original cast movies followed by the four with the cast of *TNG* have received little critical attention. One might suggest that even though the franchise films have been predictable movie blockbusters, the fact that they are from the silver screen instead of the television screen has somehow obscured them from essential debates surrounding the *Star Trek* text and thus left them alienated from the larger picture. However, the films are important to the understanding of the "*Star Trek* effect" since they can be described as "high concept" imaginings of Roddenberry's simple yet significant vision. Justin Wyatt sees the "high concept" movie as an important part of the New Hollywood film industry. Films that are high concept are ones that are conceived as highly marketable, and therefore highly profitable, as well as being visually striking and stylistically innovative. High concept films, for example *Star Wars* (1977), are different through their "emphasis on style in production and through the integration of the film with its marketing" (Wyatt, 1994: 20). In terms of the *Star Trek* features, we can describe them as "high concept" since they are comprised of what Wyatt labels "the look, the hook, and the book": "The look of the images, the marketing hooks, and the reduced narratives" (22). Chapters seven, eight and nine in this section of the collection consider each of the three cornerstones of the high concept franchise, enabling us to understand for the first time how the *Star Trek* movies are both integral contributions to the fictional *Star Trek* narrative and highly sophisticated enhancements of the original *Star Trek* televisual format.

Donald E. Palumbo's "The Monomyth in *Star Trek* Films" examines the overarching mythic narrative that links the first six movies with the last four, in connection with Joseph Campbell's theory of the "monomyth" in his work *The Hero with a Thousand Faces* (1949). The monomyth, when the hero is called to adventure, endures tests and trials, and returns to bring redemption to his people, is essential to the narrative structure of the *Star Trek* films. Palumbo posits that, pared down, the films represent the most basic of Campbell's definitions of the monomyth, and are therefore "profoundly engaging because each of us is the monomythic 'hero' and the hero's adventure is our adventure." Enabling us to identify Wyatt's notion of the "reduced narrative" as part of high concept filmmaking, Palumbo's chapter shows us how both Kirk and Picard can symbolize the monomythic hero. Willing to undergo extreme tests, they overcome adversity and save whole planets and colonies in order to continue *Star Trek*'s positive re-visioning of humanity's future.

Alongside the narrative aspects of the films, Michael S. Duffy's "'Blow Up the Damn Ship!': Production Redesign and Special Effects Reuse in the *Star Trek* Films" analyzes the significant developments in movie special effects made by the *Star Trek* franchise to bring the famous USS *Enterprise* to the big screen following *Star Wars*' blockbuster impact. As Wyatt maintains about the "look" of "high concept" movies, Duffy describes how the *Star Trek* films were produced on modest budgets yet still managed to create original stylistic effects that set them apart from the competition in the mid 1980s. This seems to parallel what Duffy describes as "the gradual transition from 'original' physical effects to the 'next generation' of digital/computer generated models."

The third chapter in this section, Paul Rixon's "*Star Trek*: Popular Discourses—The Role of Broadcasters and Critics," considers the "hook" of the high concept movie and television franchise, namely, the marketing discourses attached to the release and critical reception of the *Star Trek* series in Britain. Rixon specifically examines how Paramount and the BBC, in their attempts to creative a narrative image for the series, presented a particular view of the films and episodes sent from America in order to attract a new audience in the UK. Alongside the image presented in the national press these discourses have helped generate and sustain over thirty years of *Star Trek* in the British consciousness, helping to market the franchise to both an uninitiated public audience and a devoted fan community.

The Fans

The fan community provides the focus for the fourth section of this book. The *Star Trek* effect on millions of fans worldwide has been documented and analyzed in myriad forms for a number of years, so it is not the aim of this section to go over familiar ground. However, it is important to remember that although fans have been the focus of numerous texts, Henry Jenkins's *Textual Poachers* (1992) being the most celebrated, scholarship has tended to concentrate on fans as an extraordinary group, held in a position outside the cultural mainstream in comparison to more conventional television audiences. Writing slash fiction, stories written mainly by female fans (Slashers) that focus on the sexual coupling of male characters such as Kirk and Spock (see Penley, 1997), and making costumes became the focal point for fan research since these activities spoke to certain areas of cultural studies at the time. The study of individual fan behavior which went against predisposed social and gender norms meant that the more "typical" fan who did not "rebel" against the text was ignored; it was as if they did not have anything to say about the text, and even if they did it would not be worth studying. This section redresses the imbalance found in *Star Trek* fan studies since it does not exceptionalize those fans that are more visibly active or are members of distinct fan clubs. Instead, the four chapters level the playing field and concentrate on what all types of fan have to say about the text and how they engage with it on a more personal and emotional level.

In chapter ten, "*Star Trek*: The Franchise!—Poachers, Pirates, and Paramount," Sue Short looks at the concept of the "Trekkie" and to what extent we can now see the fan community as simply those who "will buy virtually anything with a *Star Trek* logo on it." Moving on from Jenkins's notion of the fan as "textual poacher," where they adapted the text rather than take it at face value, Short argues that fans, in an age of increasing audience fragmentation and network pursuit of ratings, have become integral in the show's development by consuming merchandise promoted by Paramount. While trying to sustain the franchise, Paramount has started to alienate fans as it seeks to capitalize on their devotion, bringing out new licensed products and cracking down on those fans who produce and sell their own products to other fans. Continuing on from Short's analysis, Justin Everett's "Fan Culture and the Recentering of *Star Trek*" focuses on the fans' own productions, namely homemade movies, and theorizes that while they continue to watch the fictional narrative on screen fans are starting to create products that conform more closely to their own idea of *Star Trek*. These personal stories, although not official within the canon dictated by Paramount, have become part of the overall fan narrative that builds upon the original; the fans' own personal enjoyment of the series is enhanced by their own fictional and creative worlds. Although the idea of fan creativity is not new, the fact that these "home movies" are becoming more popular than the official text signals a significant change in the *Star Trek* fan community.

While Everett is suggesting fandom has changed, Angelina I. Karpovich, in "Locating the '*Star Trek* Experience,'" suggests that the franchise is also changing in an attempt to keep up with fan demands. Paramount has tried to create fan spaces around the world with both the *Star Trek* Experience in Las Vegas and popular global tours that bring props, relics, and costumes to millions of fans. These spaces act as fixed physical locations, in contrast to the transient social space of the local convention, allowing fans to travel and see artifacts from their favorite series, thus locating their love for a fictional future text in a real and historically accurate present.

The book's final chapter, Karen Anijar's autobiographical critique "A Very *Trek* Christmas: Goodbye," investigates contemporary *Star Trek* fandom through an analysis of recent online fan debates over the fifth and most recent series, *Enterprise*. Tracing fan narratives from the start of the series to its final days, Anijar as both a lifelong fan and cultural critic comments on its recent turn to a more conservative view of the future and posits that the series failed because it did not "make sense for many (young) people since they reside in a postapocalyptic universe whose politics speak to a revolutionary formation in which *Star Trek* is at best an anachronistic story belonging to a world that no longer exists."

If *Star Trek* were to return to the small screen, the financial success of the movie blockbuster not withstanding, the franchise as a whole has to take into account a younger generation of science fiction fans. It has to adapt to incorporate a nation and a world where the political and social ramifications of change have become intertwined with the lack of confidence in the future after the tragic events of 9/11. Since the "*Star Trek* effect" relies on the premise that the future will be better than the present, the series will have to wait until society starts to believe in that very same possibility again before it returns as the definitive vision of a future utopia.

Works Cited

Barrett, Michèle, and Duncan Barrett. "*Star Trek*": *The Human Frontier*. Cambridge: Polity Press, 2001.

Berman, Rick. "Roddenberry's Vision." *Farewell to "Star Trek: The Next Generation."* TV Guide Collector's ed. Edited by Lee Ann Nicholson. Toronto, OT: Telemedia Communications Inc., 1994: 2–3.

Geraghty, Lincoln. "The American Jeremiad and *Star Trek*'s Puritan Legacy." *Journal of the Fantastic in the Arts* 14, no. 2 (2003): 228–245.

Gregory, Chris. *"Star Trek" Parallel Narratives*. London: Macmillan Press, 2000.

Jenkins, Henry. *Textual Poachers: Television Fans and Participatory Culture*. New York: Routledge, 1992.

Penley, Constance. *NASA/TREK: Popular Science and Sex in America*. New York: Verso, 1997.

TV Guide. "25 Top Cult Shows Ever!" 30 May 2004: 26–40.

Wyatt, Justin. *High Concept: Movies and Marketing in Hollywood*. Austin: University of Texas Press, 1994.

PART I
THE FRANCHISE

1

Eight Days That Changed American Television

Kirk's Opening Narration

LINCOLN GERAGHTY

"Just words."
"But good words. That's where ideas begin."
—Kirk and David, *Star Trek II: The Wrath of Khan* (1982).

Many studies have attempted to demonstrate the connections *Star Trek* has with American culture through its representations of society in all five series and ten feature films. What lies at the bottom of all this interest? When the façade of twenty-fourth century gadgetry is peeled back, what is at the root of *Star Trek*'s storytelling? Following on from that, what makes it so long-lasting and popular? These sorts of questions, along with many others, have been asked by academics interested in uncovering the worldwide appeal of the science fiction phenomenon created by Gene Roddenberry in 1966. From readings focusing on *Star Trek*'s representation of social, philosophical, and ethical issues to interpretations of its progressive and humanist representations of race, gender, and class, the plethora of academic studies on the television series continues to grow as the series continues to attract fans.[1] Recognizing its various applications and interpretations, Matt Hills (2004: 197) has said of *Star Trek* that "as one of the longest running and most multifaceted programs in television history, it would indeed be surprising if the *Star Trek* franchise could ever be convincingly reduced to one coherent and comprehensive 'reading.'" As a scholar of *Star Trek* and its fans, I would agree that such an achievement would be astonishing, if only because academic and fan analyses are continually influenced by the critic's own personal investment in the series. Nevertheless, whether Hills is right to predict *Star Trek*'s infinite potential for rereading, I believe that *Star Trek* can be at least better understood by reducing its reading to a few core themes—not one reason perhaps, but a few important reasons for its continued popularity. The themes I want to highlight are utopia and community and, more specifically, how the combination of the two can produce an appropriate rationale for *Star Trek*'s popularity.

Utopia, in *Star Trek*, means the doing away with ethnic conflict, bigotry, cultural power struggles and racial prejudice, and is encapsulated in the phrase "Infinite Diversity in Infinite Combinations." For fans, *Star Trek*'s vision of the future is utopian by the very fact that Roddenberry wanted to show humanity had progressed and people had found a way of living together without killing each other. Hills correctly points out that the utopianism portrayed in the series has limits and these limits detract from its humanitarian ethos (Hills, 2004: 196). However, Hills stops before discussing the *Star Trek* fan community and therefore cannot go on to show how its investment in the franchise obviates these limitations. Daniel Bernardi has described *Star Trek* as a "*mega-text*: a relatively coherent and seemingly unending enterprise of televisual, filmic, auditory, and written texts," and these texts as a shared fan mythology are susceptible to the same flaws as America's own mythology (Bernardi, 1998: 7). While Bernardi believes that *Star Trek* continues to perpetuate an exclusive view of the future, I believe its text provides fans with unlimited freedom for their imaginations, fulfilling their own dreams, desires, and fantasies. The once constrictive and absolute *mega-text* is at the same time a vehicle to release fans' creativity and create a sense of personal identity. The utopian text that has limitations, described by Hills, Bernardi and many other scholars, gives the fan community—including people of all marginalized groups—an inclusive space within which they can imagine themselves. For the fan community *Star Trek* is an open text and this can be identified in one of the most recognized and famous aspects of the original series: the opening narration.

The opening monologue spoken by Captain Kirk in the sixties and Captain Picard in the eighties and nineties underwent some rapid and important changes before it was used on the series. As one can see below, the evolution of the short narrative was closely monitored by Gene Roddenberry and his colleagues Robert Justman and John Black, who had to send their versions to Roddenberry for his approval. The first and subsequent drafts were fashioned over a period of eight days, and in that short time the ideals and ethos of Roddenberry's utopian vision for the program seem to have also evolved to become less constrained by function or law and more open to possibilities such as meeting alien life and going boldly into unknown space. The following texts personify *Star Trek*'s utopian vision but also, as I will point out, they speak to the audience, drawing them into a program where seeking out "new life and new civilizations" is imperative in building a community.

Original Teaser Narration

August 2, 1966[2]

Robert Justman to Gene Roddenberry—Teaser Narration

"This is the story of the Starship Enterprise. Its mission: to advance knowledge, contact alien life and enforce intergalactic law ... to explore the strange new worlds where no man has gone before."

John D. F. Black to Gene Roddenberry—Needs more drama

"Space ... the final frontier ... endless ... silent ... waiting. This is the story of the United Space Ship Enterprise ... its mission ... a five year patrol of the galaxy ... to seek out and contact all alien life ... to explore ... to travel the vast galaxy where no man has gone before ... a Star Trek."

Anonymous

"This is the adventure of the United Space Ship Enterprise. Assigned a five year galaxy patrol, the bold crew of the giant starship explores the excitement of strange new worlds, uncharted civilizations and exotic people. These are its voyages and its adventures...."

John D. F. Black to Gene Roddenberry—Kirk's Voice

"The U.S.S. Enterprise ... starship ... its mission ... a five year patrol to seek out and contact alien life ... to explore the infinite frontier of space ... where no man has gone before ... a Star Trek."

Anonymous—Opening Narration ST

"This is the story of the United Space Ship Enterprise. Assigned a five year patrol of our galaxy, the giant starship visits Earth colonies, regulates commerce, and explores strange new worlds and civilizations. These are its voyages ... and its adventures."

August 10, 1966

Standard Opening Narration

"Space ... the final frontier. These are the voyages of the starship Enterprise, its five year mission
 ...to explore strange new worlds
 ...to seek out new life and new civilizations
 ...to boldly go where no man has gone before."

If one were to take Robert Scholes' and Robert Kellogg's (1966: 4) view that "to be a narrative no more and no less than a teller and a tale are required," then *Star Trek* seemingly does not represent a narrative because there is an absence of a teller. There are many stories played out week after week but who is telling them?

> Narrative focuses our attention on to a story, a sequence of events, through the direct mediation of a "telling" which we both stare at and through, which is at once central and peripheral to the experience of the story, both absent and present in the consciousness of those being told the story [Hawthorn, 1985: vii].

In the above quote Hawthorn also points out that the "telling" focuses our attention on the story so much that it can itself become central to the experience of the story; the telling becomes part of the story and part of the recipient of the story (see also Kozloff, 1992). It is obvious from these analyses of narrative that the narrator is important; this may be true but it does not necessarily rule out *Star Trek* as a narrative. For example, *Star Trek*'s most famous line, "space, the final frontier," comes from the opening narration first used in the episode "The Corbomite Maneuver" (1966). Every episode began with Kirk speaking to the audience, "telling" them that what they were about to see was a true and correct account (or *history*) of the voyages of the crew aboard the *Enterprise*. There was a story about to be told and those immortal words were a harbinger of the wondrous tales about to unfold on-screen. In linguistic terms the opening narration signals a form of social relationship between the teller (Kirk) and the listener (TV audience) marked by the sentence starting "These are the voyages...." The word *these* is a pointing word, or deictic, which works by pointing out to the viewer/listener that the following events or situations being described are pertinent to them (Beaugrande & Dressler, 1981: 167–168). It brings the audience into a personal relationship with both the narrator and the proceeding text. According to Mick Short, deixis are "one of the ways in which writers persuade readers to imagine a fictional world when they read poems, novels and plays" (1996: 100). I believe that the use of deixis was integral to the success of the series as each week Kirk recounted the voyages of the *Enterprise* to the audience, thus drawing them in to believe that the text was a potential utopian reality. As the series went on to become the most popular program in American television history that potential utopian reality continues to be one of the *main* reasons why so many people like and watch *Star Trek*. Furthermore, since the audience has been invited into that fictional world via the opening narration they feel comfortable staying there:

> Space, the final frontier. *These* are the voyages of the Starship Enterprise. Its five-year mission: to explore strange new worlds, to seek out new life and new civilizations, to boldly go where no *man* has gone before [quoted in Sherwin, 1999: 301 (my emphasis)].

The tradition of the opening narration continued on *Star Trek: The Next Generation* (*TNG*) (1987–1994), which highlighted the importance of the "telling" aspect at the beginning of *Star Trek* episodes. How every episode began with this narration was, as Hawthorn suggests about narrative, both "central and peripheral to the experience of the story," and "both absent and present in the consciousness of those being told the story."

Just as *Star Trek* uses a narrative opening to begin its stories on-screen, *Star Wars* (1977) begins with the line "a long time ago in a galaxy far, far away." In fact, where *Star Trek* has taken myth and "clothed [it]," according to William B. Tyrrell (1977: 712), "in the garb of science fiction" in order to present a story about a possible and positive future, *Star Wars* has taken ancient myth and created an "alternate reality" admittedly set in the past. Within this new, and at the same time ancient, reality, stories about technological advancement and the future are set "a long time ago in a galaxy far, far away." Steven Galipeau (2001: 60) identifies it as a "mythic time" created by the "interweaving myths of technology and religion occurring in some other galaxy." For *Star Wars*, mythology is a historically based series of symbols and characters which connect with human society and tell us how things were done in the past; perhaps this is why some fans of *Star Wars* say it is not science fiction but rather science fantasy. However, for *Star Trek*, mythology is a narrative tool with which it can illustrate stories about correcting historical indiscretions, frame many of its episodes and plotlines, and create hope for the future. At the same time this enables fans to believe wholeheartedly that *Star Trek*'s reality has existed, still exists, and will continue to exist far beyond their lifetimes. Examining *Star Trek*'s knack for telling good stories might seem rather easy if one were to take Brent Spiner's explanation of its popularity at face value: "The reason *Star Trek* is so popular is that I honestly think [creator] Gene Roddenberry came up with what is the single greatest formula for a TV show.... It never ends, because traveling the galaxy offers thousands of stories to explore" (Spiner, 2001: 6). This statement is partly true: *Star Trek* does have a great formula which was shared by many other popular television series, such as *The Fugitive* (1963–1967) and *Quantum Leap* (1989–1993) to name just two; but that does not fully explain its popularity. Spiner, who plays the character Data in *The Next Generation*, has got it only half right because he thinks the show's popularity relies on there being thousands of episodes revealing countless things about aliens and the universe. I believe that *Star Trek* is so popular because it is the exact opposite of Spiner's theory; it offers only a handful of stories through which the audience can explore the universe, and, at the same time, explore themselves.

Children have all been read stories that start "once upon a time," and they know that they are about to be told something. With *Star Trek* it is no different. This was Gene Roddenberry's way of telling the audience his story, one which he had battled to get on television, so that they, too, could be enthused and engaged in what he believed was the most important story of all: the human story. Other television series at the time may well have tried to tell important stories, even more important than Roddenberry's, but it was the way *Star Trek* expressed and told them that enabled it to shine out from the rest. For David Carson (2001: 46), if *Star Trek* "dealt with racial tensions and tried to preach to the masses, the masses would not watch." However, placing those issues on a science fiction drama set in the future extinguishes its didacticism and allows "a storyteller, be you a writer or director, the opportunity of telling a story that has something to say."

The opening narration has entered popular culture just like the characters of the shows: It was inevitable that it would be used on *TNG* but only after it had been updated. *Star Trek*'s mission statement was modernized to suit an age that recognized women were not just there to support the men as they explored the galaxy, but were there to do the exploring themselves. However, this egalitarianism was not fully validated until Kate Mulgrew became the first woman to command a starship, assuming the lead role in *Star Trek: Voyager* (1995–2001). *TNG* begins:

> Space. The final frontier. *These* are the voyages of the Starship Enterprise. Its continuing mission, to explore strange new worlds, to seek out new life and new civilizations, to boldly go where no *one* has gone before [quoted in Sherwin, 1999: 312 (my emphasis)].

Both series that followed *TNG*, *Star Trek: Deep Space Nine* (*DS9*) (1993–1999) and *Voyager*, were unique in that they did not adopt the concept of the opening narrative monologue to begin each episode. Instead, their credits were accompanied by orchestral music on a backdrop of the relevant space vehicle: for *DS9* slow motion shots of the space station alongside the Gamma Quadrant wormhole (from the fourth season onwards the station was seen in use with ships docking); for *Voyager* the eponymous starship was pictured gliding through several spectacular space phenomena, including nebulas and starfields, before going into warp speed towards a rising sun. These two opening sequences epitomized the new direction the franchise was taking with the two series; they both distanced themselves somewhat from their famous predecessors (attracting new audiences) by introducing new narrative formats. In *DS9* the ship was literally stationary, if there was any exploring to do then the aliens would have to come to the station. Its premise was suggested by Paramount executives as being: "Rather than a 'Wagon Train to the Stars,' a 'Rifleman' in space" (Dillard, 1996: 152). For the starship *Voyager*, the crew was not exploring the uncharted frontiers of space on purpose; it was trying to find its way home after being lost 70,000 light years from Earth with no conceivable way back. The series' tag line, "charting the new frontier," implied that the old frontier, the frontier of past *Star Trek* incarnations, had been explored.

However, as with the original opening narrative, these visually stunning and acoustically dramatic opening credits did invite the audience to enter their own particular story, whether it was getting "lost in space" with the crew of *Voyager* or experiencing the life of the crew onboard the space station in *DS9*. Although not necessarily concerned about searching for utopia, these two series created similar utopias within the confines of their new formats. The fifth series, *Star Trek: Enterprise* (2001–2005), as well as being named after the famous starship from the original series, proved to be a radical return to the franchise's roots. The story involved a ship and crew from before the time of Kirk; their story was one set in a history that was not yet written for us but was part of the fictional narrative history that formed the basis for the canonical events, aliens, and characters that dotted the time lines of the first four series. Its opening narration, although again not spoken, signaled to the audience that this story was part of *Star Trek* history. The events and actions that took place in the following episodes were not only part of *Star Trek* canon but also part of humanity's exploration of space.

This point is intriguingly underlined in the final episode of the series, "These Are the Voyages..." (2005), when we see that Riker and Troi from *TNG* are actually viewing the captain's logs from the *Enterprise* series' early missions in a holodeck re-creation onboard the USS *Enterprise-D*. The finale literally implies that the previous four seasons were a story being told and listened to by characters with whom we are already familiar in the *Star Trek* universe. Where I have maintained that the original opening narration in the sixties was a signal to the audience that a story was about to be told, the season finale of *Enterprise* affirms that indeed the *Star Trek* story has been told. The episode's title emphasizes this fact even more as it takes its words from the original opening narration written on August 10, 1966, "These are the voyages...," and uses them to introduce the logs that are being viewed as a historical story.

The opening titles on *Enterprise* were a departure for a *Star Trek* series; they were the first to be accompanied by a song: Diane Warren's "Where My Heart Will Take Me" sung by Russell Watson. The scenes from human history depicting the evolution of spaceflight and humanity's passion for exploration locate *Enterprise*, and therefore *Star Trek*, within a very specific American narrative: the history of spaceflight and exploration. The scenes from our own real and future history play out as follows:

Enterprise Title Sequence Visuals[3]*:*

A *Kon-Tiki* crossing the Pacific Ocean;
HMS *Enterprise* and nameplate;
Auguste and Jean Piccard, High Altitude Balloonists;
Charles Lindbergh and the *Spirit of St Louis*, 1927;
Space Shuttle *Enterprise*, unveiled by the *Star Trek* cast in 1976;
Amelia Earhart;
The Wright Brothers at Kitty Hawk, NC, 1903;
NASA *Explorer* Submarine;
The Bell X-1 and Chuck Yeager, 1947;
Alan Shepard and *Apollo 14*, 1971;

John Glenn Aboard Space Shuttle *Discovery*, 1998;
Dr. Robert H. Goddard, Rocket Pioneer;
Apollo 11 Moon Landing, 1969;
Sojourner, The Robotic Mars Rover, 1997;
International Space Station;
Lunar Orbiter, 2039;
The *Phoenix*'s First Test Run, 2063;
NX 01 *Enterprise*, 2151.

It is this tradition that perhaps accounts for *Enterprise*'s turn to the past at a time of American uncertainty; the series aired shortly after 9/11. When the nation feels threatened, deprived, or isolated American society requires an affirmation of its role within the larger global community. This role is depicted in the title sequence as being a leader in the development of spaceflight and a pioneer in the technological advancement of human civilization, but it is not restricted to the fictional history of *Star Trek*. America saw its mission to land on the moon and beat the Soviets in the space race as an extension of its mission to bring freedom to the world, literally to create a utopia.

Star Trek's appropriation of what appears to be an overtly American version of history seen in the opening title sequence indicates that it is trying to ground its vision of the future in a mythic retelling of the past. Celebrating American achievements on the sea, in the air, and in space appears to be part of a process of "reinterpretation" or "revisioning" of history which Sarah Neely (2001: 74) describes as a "retrovision." A "retrovision is a 'vision into or of the past' and implies an act of possessing the ability to read the past, in the way that one would possess a prophetic vision." For Deborah Cartmell and I.Q. Hunter (2001: 7) retrovisions are "makeovers of history," and I apply the term to *Enterprise* here since it is trying to refashion *Star Trek*'s universal historical narrative by making it part of a very specific American mythic history. *Enterprise* offers an American society unsure of the future a possible utopian future through a revisioning of a celebratory past. However, *Enterprise*'s future also appears to be the only one that we as a global community can achieve because it has eliminated all vestiges of humanity's international achievements and replaced them with images of America's attempts at exploring space. *Enterprise*'s "faith of the heart" as described in the title song persuades the audience that *Star Trek*'s future is going to be a reality; the exceptionalism personified by America's aviation achievements in the credits proves that the future will be a bright one. Such optimism, however, can only come if you have faith in the past, celebrate American success, and ultimately rely on America "getting" you "from there to here." The optimism of *Star Trek*'s utopian future, as introduced to us by Kirk and Picard in the opening narration, is still present but in a rather conservative and backward-looking form.

Star Trek is not just any utopia. It is a specific American utopia, which may appear to be a contradiction in terms, for a utopia is not a place. But *Star Trek is* a place and space in the American imagination, and as such it embodies that which is missing, lacking, and absent in America. The future of *Star Trek* is the counterpart to the reality of America, a possibility that has never been realized except in the imagination of its creator, Gene Roddenberry, and the fans who were invited into his world through the opening narration. And, just like the many versions of the narration, it is in constant need of revision, review, and reconstruction because American society keeps changing. *Star Trek* acts as a canonical reference to what makes America American, and what will make Americans more human, a story that invites the viewer to take part in a supportive and inclusive utopian community. In some senses then, perhaps this is what has continued to make it so popular, and what might in the end be considered a valid "coherent and comprehensive 'reading.'"

Acknowledgments

I would like to thank the staff at UCLA's Arts Library Special Collections archive for helping and guiding me with the material housed in the *Star Trek* collection, particularly Lauren Buisson and Julie L. Graham for their knowledge and assistance. I would also like to thank the British Association of American Studies for their financial assistance, as a student travel award allowed me the opportunity to travel to the U.S. and undertake this research in 2003. For providing funds to present a shorter version of this chapter at the *PCA/ACA* 35th and 27th Joint Annual Conference (2005) in San Diego, I would like to thank CEISR at the University of Portsmouth.

Notes

1. See for example Daniel L. Bernardi, *"Star Trek" and History: Race-ing Toward a White Future* (New Brunswick, NJ: Rutgers University Press, 1998); Robin Roberts, *Sexual Generations: "Star Trek: The Next Generation" and Gender* (Urbana: University of Illinois Press, 1999); Michèle Barrett and Duncan Barrett, *"Star Trek": The Human Frontier* (Cambridge: Polity Press, 2001); Karin Blair, *Meaning in "Star Trek"* (Chambersberg, PA: Anima Books, 1977); Jay Goulding, *Empire, Aliens, and Conquest: A Critique of American Ideology in "Star Trek" and Other Science Fiction Adventures* (Toronto, ON: Sisyphus Press, 1985); Chris Gregory, *"Star Trek" Parallel Narratives* (London: Macmillan Press, 2000); Taylor Harrison, Sarah Projansky, Kent A. Ono, and Elyce Rae Helford, eds., *Enterprise Zones: Critical Positions on "Star Trek"* (Boulder, CO: Westview Press, 1996); Mike Hertenstein, *The Double Vision of "Star Trek": Half-Humans, Evil Twins and Science Fiction* (Chicago, IL: Cornerstone Press, 1998); Ross Kraemer, William Cassidy, and Susan Schwartz, *Religions of "Star Trek"* (Boulder, CO: Westview Press, 2000); Jennifer E. Porter and Darcee L. McLaren, eds., *"Star Trek" and Sacred Grounds: Explorations of "Star Trek," Religion, and American Culture* (Albany: State University of New York Press, 1999); Micheal C. Pounds, *Race in Space: The Representation of Ethnicity in "Star Trek" and "Star Trek: The Next Generation"* (Lanham, MD: Scarecrow Press, 1999); Thomas Richards, *The Meaning of "Star Trek"* (New York: Doubleday, 1997); Jon Wagner and Jan Lundeen, *Deep Space and Sacred Time: "Star Trek" in the American Mythos* (Westport, CT: Praeger, 1998); Judith Barad, with Ed Robertson, *The Ethics of*

"*Star Trek*" (New York: HarperCollins Publishers, 2000); Richard Hanley, *The Metaphysics of "Star Trek"* (New York: Basic Books, 1997).

For studies of the *Star Trek* audience see Henry Jenkins, *Textual Poachers: Television Fans and Participatory Culture* (New York: Routledge, 1992); Camille Bacon-Smith, *Enterprising Women: Television Fandom and the Creation of Popular Myth* (Philadelphia: University of Pennsylvania Press, 1992); John Tulloch and Henry Jenkins, *Science Fiction Audiences: Watching "Doctor Who" and "Star Trek"* (London: Routledge, 1995); Constance Penley, *NASA/TREK: Popular Science and Sex in America* (New York: Verso, 1997); Lincoln Geraghty, *Living with "Star Trek": American Culture and the "Star Trek" Universe* (London: I.B. Tauris, 2007).

2. These early drafts and final version come from the Gene Roddenberry *Star Trek* Television Series Collection, 1966–1969, (Collection 62): Box 29, folder 8, Arts Library Special Collections, Young Research Library, University of California, Los Angeles.

3. In the build-up to the third season of *Enterprise* in September 2003 the *Star Trek* Website posted a timeline that charts the history of space exploration. Included in this timeline are key dates in the history of *Star Trek*'s future narrative, many of which are pictured in the opening credits sequence. See "Key Events in Exploration History,"http://www.startrek.com/startrek/view/features/documentaries/article/462.html> (accessed 10 September 2003). Below are a few extracts:

> **1799**—Henry Spencer of Baltimore, Maryland, builds a sailing ship, a schooner named *Enterprise*.
>
> **1903**—The Wright brothers build and fly the first motorized airplane in Kitty Hawk, North Carolina, forever giving mankind "wings."
>
> **1957**—Earth's Space Age, and the so-called space race, begins when the USSR puts an artificial satellite, *Sputnik-I*, into orbit around the planet.
>
> Although unverified, it has been reported that in October of this year a Vulcan scientific party observes Earth and the *Sputnik* launch. After three weeks of surreptitious intelligence gathering, the party is forced to land on the planet. The fate of the four Vulcans remains a mystery.
>
> **1976**—NASA unveils *Enterprise* (Space Shuttle OV-101), the prototype for its new fleet of reusable Earth-orbiting shuttles. Flight testing begins the following year.
>
> **2063**—In the postwar era, Zefram Cochrane converts an intercontinental ballistic missile (ICBM) into the first faster-than-light, or warp, spaceship—the *Phoenix*. On April 5, the *Phoenix*'s test flight attracts the attention of other space travelers [*sic*]and "first contact" is soon made between humans and Vulcans.
>
> c. **2143**—Starfleet pilot Jonathan Archer meets engineer Charles "Trip" Tucker III while the two officers are working together on tests for the warp-capable NX-Alpha and Beta ships. Henry Archer, Jonathan's father, was the main designer of the NX ship engine.
>
> **2151**—With veteran Starfleet pilot Jonathan Archer at the helm, the first Warp 5 capable ship, the *Enterprise* NX-01, is sent on its first mission. The actual launch is pushed forward to April 15 when a diplomatic crisis escalates. The ship's assignment: to return a mysterious Klingon who landed on Earth at Broken Bow, Oklahoma, back to his homeworld.

Works Cited

Beaugrande, Robert-Alain de, and Wolfgang Dressler, *Introduction to Text Linguistics*. Harlow: Longman, 1981.

Bernardi, Daniel L. *"Star Trek" and History: Race-ing Toward a White Future*. New Brunswick, NJ: Rutgers University Press, 1998.

Carson, David. "Generation Games." *"Star Trek" Monthly Magazine* (September 2001): 44–47.

Cartmell, Deborah, and I.Q. Hunter. "Introduction: Retrovisions: Historical Makeovers in Film and Literature." *Retrovisions: Reinventing the Past in Film and Fiction.* Edited by Deborah Cartmell, I.Q. Hunter, and Imelda Whelehan. London: Pluto Press, 2001: 1–7.

Dillard, J.M. *"Star Trek": "Where No One Has Gone Before": A History in Pictures.* New York: Pocket Books, 1996.

Galipeau, Steven A. *The Journey of Luke Skywalker: An Analysis of Modern Myth and Symbol.* Chicago and La Salle, IL: Open Court, 2001.

Hawthorn, J., ed. *Narrative: From Malory to Motion Pictures.* London: Edward Arnold, 1985.

Hills, Matt. *"Star Trek": Fifty Key Television Programs.* Edited by Glen Creeber. London: Arnold, 2004: 193–197.

Kozloff, Sarah. "Narrative Theory and Television." *Channels of Discourse, Reassembled: Television and Contemporary Criticism.* 2nd ed. Edited by Robert C. Allen. Chapel Hill: University of North Carolina Press, 1992: 76–100.

Neely, Sarah. "Cool Intentions: The Literary Classic, the Teenpic and the 'Chick Flick.'" *Retrovisions: Reinventing the Past in Film and Fiction.* Edited by Deborah Cartmell, I.Q. Hunter, and Imelda Whelehan. London: Pluto Press, 2001: 74–86.

Scholes, Robert, and Robert Kellogg. *The Nature of Narrative.* New York: Oxford University Press, 1966.

Sherwin, Jill. *Quotable "Star Trek."* New York: Pocket Books, 1999.

Short, Mick. *Exploring the Language of Poems, Plays and Prose.* Harlow: Longman, 1996.

Spiner, Brent. "Data Retrieval." *"Star Trek" Monthly Magazine* (March 2001): 6.

Tyrrell, William Blake. *"Star Trek* as Myth and Television as Mythmaker." *Journal of Popular Culture* 10, no.4 (1977): 711–719.

2

The Accidental Apotheosis of Gene Roddenberry, or, "I Had to Get Some Money from *Somewhere*"

DAVE HIPPLE

Star Trek collapsed as a TV production in 1969, but by 20 years later had become a monolithic cultural presence. Its story is inseparable from that of Gene Roddenberry, but not entirely for the positive, synergistic reasons that routinely accompany popular assessment of the franchise.[1]

Some hold the following "truths" to be self-evident....

Star Trek, the preeminent science fiction show originally created at Paramount by executive producer Gene Roddenberry, premiered on the NBC network and ran from 1966 to 1969. Finding no sustainable audience, it was cancelled. It was *almost* cancelled twice before that, but each time was kept in production when what fans it had spontaneously mobilized to send staggering amounts of mail to NBC. In worldwide repeats thereafter, however, *Star Trek* slowly but surely accrued a huge following receptive to its quality and positive message. Audience commitment was confirmed by the sales of printed adaptations, and, unprecedented for a single TV show, the appearance of regular, dedicated fan conventions. Paramount responded by resuscitating *Star Trek* in the form of a film a decade after cancellation of the TV show. More films followed, their success triggering a new series (*The Next Generation*). Yet more films and series proliferated, until *Enterprise* was cancelled in 2005; but a new film seems due in 2008, the *Star Trek* essence still being strong. At this point, some (such as "MadGraceOakum," posting on 27 April 2006 to the imdb.com message board) worry that such a film may not reach the standards that it rightly should: "Yeah, I'm afraid all the good writers went to write for

SG-1 and *Atlantis. Star Trek* needs something fresh. It needs a visionary type like Gene Roddenber[r]y to revamp it."[2] What we have there is not actually the history of *Star Trek*, but its legend. As with many good legends it contains elements of truth, but, while superficially coherent to the point of seeming obvious, this story really is too good to be true. The subject at hand is, after all, a commercial product aimed in various guises by innumerable contributors at the popular cultures of five different decades. The simple legend also conflates popularity with quality, avoiding critics' widespread doubt as to *Star Trek*'s effectiveness or even significance as science fiction (SF) and instead celebrating a façade of inexorable achievement.

To be sure, many of the countless books about *Star Trek* purport to reveal indications that all was not as smoothly preordained as popular assumption might have it. Most, however, tend nevertheless to reinforce the notion of *Star Trek*'s underlying quality, adopting its popular prominence not as a phenomenon to be interrogated but as a secure starting point. Market success is taken to be merely the grubby, commercial tip of an iceberg otherwise composed of serene vision, artistic nuance and buoyant philosophy. The recent TV documentary *How William Shatner Changed the World* (Jones, 2005) insists that this optimism was *Star Trek*'s central business, and that the franchise's subsequent accommodation of more matter-of-fact issues caused its downfall. We shall see, however, that interested constituencies have constantly striven to perpetuate association with the original's iconic naiveté.

One problem here is the very identity of *Star Trek*: there is the commercial material launched into a cutthroat market by employees whose job it is to enrich their management; and there are conventional perceptions of *Star Trek* as the quintessence and ongoing statement of something more abstract. At one extreme, enthusiasts celebrate an irreproachable, humanistic vision; other observers apprehend *Star Trek* as conclusively demonstrating science fiction's self-evident tackiness. Yet others lament it spearheading television's betrayal of the genre. As a favor to Roddenberry, Isaac Asimov disingenuously reversed his 1966 *TV Guide* disparagement of *Star Trek* (Solow and Justman, 1996: 300–303). Elsewhere, Asimov (1983b: 129) values at least its "attempt" to tell credible and interesting stories, but concludes that the essential appeal of visual SF is mere spectacle. Discussing visual SF in general he opines (without mentioning *Star Trek* at all) that *some* can be tolerable, "if it contains humour and has the grace not to take itself too seriously" (Asimov 1983a: 134).

Star Trek's ubiquity can provoke the unexamined assumption that it is (for good or ill) admirable *as science fiction*, as well as simply popular viewing. This was never really so, the following being typical even of commentary written before the franchise's longevity appeared to imply excellence in the original. Paul Carter (1977: 221) sees *Star Trek* as shackling itself to the old-fashioned, one-dimensional style of pulp magazines: "Television, in this case and as usual, waters down everything it touches." Sam Lundwall (1977: 191) likewise contrasts the "growing sophistication of [SF] books and magazines" with *Star Trek*'s retreat to an approach consolidated in 1920s pulps. Norman Spinrad (1985: 79) generously values the public embrace of SF in the form of *Star Trek*, "whatever the show's artistic shortcomings," admiring its commercial *concept* "as opposed to the wildly uneven quality and level of intent of the episodes." I.F. Clarke (1979: 10) finds it simplistically comforting by SF standards: "the never-failing powers of the sky-god [Kirk] and the never-ending successes of the U.S.S. *Enterprise*." For J.A. Sutherland (1979: 163), SF's most infectious "cult" fixations (including *Star Trek*) "have propagated an extravagantly traditional SF," altogether reactionary in comparison to progressive efforts but so prevalent that "The manufacturing system, dazzled by the market revealed in the *Star Trek* cult, put a premium on 'ray gun and monster' SF" (173–4). J. Michael Straczynski (1995) found *Star Trek*'s sprawling presence a serious obstacle when pitching an ambitious SF show to TV executives; and some viewers avoided his *Babylon 5* (1993–1998) on the assumption that it would resemble *Star Trek*, while others rebuked it precisely for being different. This marketplace has interpreted *Star Trek*'s popularity as indicating both distinction and unassailability as TV SF, and has located its merit in the name most vividly connected with it.

The influence and relevance of an identifiable "creator" can be problematic for any artistic endeavor, but never more pointedly than here, where Gene Roddenberry's name has always (although he died in 1991) figured as the most prominent screen credit for new material, suggesting an umbilical link to a glorious essence first promulgated 40 years ago. Indeed, this effect reaches beyond *Star Trek*: Jan Johnson-Smith (2005: 62–3) has noted that *Star Trek* will be forever associated with Gene Roddenberry, and the posthumous *Earth: Final Conflict* is seldom known just as that, but rather as *Gene Roddenberry's Earth: Final Conflict*. Similarly titled is *Gene Roddenberry's Andromeda*. The cult marketing power of the Roddenberry name as a signal of production values, ideology, and association overrides the name of the series.

The notion of *Star Trek*'s "glorious 40-year lineage" so consistently goes unchallenged that Tara DiLullo need not explain that phrase before continuing (2005: 53): "*Enterprise* is finally finding its creative groove this year by digging deeper into [the] mythology of the previous series and films, creating episodes that are seducing the fans again with their deep respect for, and liberal references to, the franchise's history." DiLullo reports joining a tour of the *Enterprise* studio, the group suddenly "looking incredulously at the spitting image of the classic *Star Trek* bridge in all its drool-worthy retro glory." The turbo-lift doors are deemed convincing ("swish!"); one regular actor sports makeup reminiscent of "the classic two-parter, 'The Menagerie' (1966)"; one wears "the Nurse Chapel-style blue miniskirt uniform," her unaccustomed wig evoking the earliest episodes; another wears "a velour wrap-around uniform shirt, much like the one Captain Kirk used to strut his stuff back in the day." A crew member "whistles an uncannily good version of the original *Trek* theme song," these flashbacks being blamed on "some kick-ass Romulan Ale." It emerges that the *Enterprise* episode being filmed ("In a Mirror, Darkly, Part 2," 2005) is a prequel to "Mirror, Mirror" (1967) and a direct sequel to "The Tholian Web" (1968). *Star Trek* does not typically present long-running stories but since 1979 has persistently rehearsed and reinforced its own narrative history; and it is typical of fans to articulate a sense of community by celebrating such minutiae. DiLullo's article demonstrates this, even with its hollowly ironic structure of joyfully recounting the above experiences before dolefully reporting *Enterprise*'s cancellation five days after the visit.

Fixation on *Star Trek*'s narrative history has extended beyond its individual fictions to become a lifestyle suggestion for any existing or potential audience. At the time of this writing, the British channel Sky One (which shows *Star Trek* endlessly) is repeating a set of brief "documentaries" that teach "history" to a viewer positioned as a deferential year-2400 student. After brief attention to real history, these recount Federation exploits from events presented in *Star Trek: First Contact* (1996) to the decommissioning of the *Enterprise*, periodically dwelling on prominent characters from the franchise. The breezy tone suggests that this is only a bit of fun, but these pieces' simple presence indicates considerable business-related thought: Sky One is a commercial channel, and the longest of these interludes is precisely timed to occupy an entire five-minute break at the expense of advertising revenue.

Such encouragement to invest in *Star Trek* "continuity" (actually patchy accretion over decades), alongside the franchise's relentless invocation of Gene Roddenberry's name, demands consideration of exactly what Roddenberry's significance is. In 1978, we are told, Paramount "put aside its aversion to Gene Roddenberry (taking into account the importance of his name) and contracted for him to produce *Star Trek: The Motion Picture*," an arrangement that, as we shall see, ultimately crippled Roddenberry's already slender credit with the studio (Solow and Justman, 1996: 423). In 1994, nonetheless, Paramount's announcement of *Star Trek: Voyager* celebrated the franchise's progress through *The Next Generation, Deep Space Nine* and the first six films, with this conclusion:

> Viewers, fans and television experts agree that the *Star Trek* phenomenon has grown out of Gene Roddenberry's futuristic optimism, and his beliefs in human life and the human race's ability to triumph over greed, aggression and prejudice.[3]

In 1996 the BBC's listings weekly, *Radio Times*, published (small print: licensed from Paramount) a *Star Trek* 30th anniversary volume. A four-page article on Roddenberry (Logan, 1996) was entitled "The Great Bird of the Galaxy," the title itself interesting beyond its apparent triviality. Wikipedia[4] tells us that "Fans bestowed upon [Roddenberry] the affectionate nickname 'The Great Bird of the Galaxy," after a mythical creature referenced in '[The] Man Trap," the first aired episode of *Star Trek*."[5]

This seems simple enough: a report of communal admiration spontaneously expressed in a quirky moniker. Bob Justman, however (Solow and Justman, 1996: 219–20),[6] explains that he first borrowed the term from "The Man Trap" when writing to the owner of their mimeo service, in a first-season memo copied to Roddenberry. He used it again in an internal memo, addressing perceived slackness in production:

> I jokingly threatened that the Great Bird of the Galaxy, Gene Roddenberry, would fly over and deposit cosmic doo-doo on them if they didn't shape up.
> After that, Gene was 'The Bird.' It became my personal nickname for him...
> Gene liked his new name and used it in a second season memo....
> The name stuck to him for the rest of his life.

An evolving in-house joke is one thing, but the notion of fans' unprompted creation of a playful epithet makes for much better press, so Logan (1996: 12) simply tells us that "As one of the entertainment world's few true visionaries, *Star Trek* creator Gene Roddenberry soared so high that he was affectionately known as The Great Bird of the Galaxy." Logan allows the legend to stand that this usage arose from fans' esteem, even though on reflection it seems certain that Roddenberry (on his conspicuous round of promotional appearances) must have encouraged its use.

"I am *Star Trek*," intones Roddenberry repeatedly, towards the end of his life (Fern, 1995), in one volume of the University of California Press "Portraits of American Genius" series. In truth the book offers little illumination of "genius" but much opinion. Reviewing it for the journal *Science Fiction Studies*, Gary K. Wolfe (1994) remarks that "The main point of the book seems to be to chronicle the developing spiritual bond between Fern and Roddenberry—she seems to want to portray herself as Joy Davidman to Roddenberry's C.S. Lewis," referring to the meeting of minds and subsequent religious conversion/awakening famously dramatized in the film *Shadowlands* (1993). Wolfe also observes:

> What this book reveals is that, whether or not Roddenberry had a thoroughly thought-out *Star Trek* philosophy when he began, he certainly developed one once he realized how many people were listening to him.

Melinda Snodgrass (1991: 52), a writer on *The Next Generation*, had already elaborated this problem in *Omni* (in print, presumably coincidentally, mere weeks after Roddenberry's death).[7] Incidentally promulgating some elements of the popular legend, Snodgrass fretted:

> *Star Trek*'s creator and executive producer, Gene Roddenberry, has joined the august group of men with an agenda. Beware of men concerned with their place in history. With politicians this obsession usually ends up costing you in either money or blood. In the case of *Star Trek: The Next Generation*, it ends up wasting your time.
>
> In 1966, when *Star Trek* first beamed into millions of homes, Roddenberry's agenda was getting a TV show on the air so he could make some money—a sensible and laudable goal. Although the show limped through three seasons, receiving only marginal ratings, it delighted those of us who read science fiction and were starved for a visual presentation of our favorite genre....
>
> But all things pass, including Classic *Trek*. It faded away to that limbo where old television shows go to die, until it rose from the dead in the form of *Star Trek* conventions.
>
> And the conventions begat movies, and the movies begat the new series. Amen. The dreadful effect of all the hype was that Roddenberry decided he could no longer just do a television show so he could make some money. Now he had to speak to the ages because this was serious shit, this was *philosophy*.

Snodgrass describes Roddenberry accepting messianic status, perhaps because of "his inability to deny good things said about him" (Solow and Justman, 1996: 324), and perhaps also because none of his post–*Star Trek* projects came to fruition. Roddenberry's identification with the show seems to have ossified the position signified by Brian Ash's 1976 guide to SF personalities (167–8), which tells us of *Roddenberry* only that he was born in Texas in 1921, was a TV producer and was "the begetter of *Star Trek*." The remaining 92 percent of Ash's article relays *Star Trek* trivia. Even 15 years later, Roddenberry may as well have been telling Fern, "I am still only *Star Trek*."

This is tragic and ironic, since for many years Roddenberry had had minimal creative influence upon *Star Trek*'s continuations: he was maintained as a figurehead. Following *The Motion Picture* (Solow and Justman, 1996: 423), the studio "felt that Roddenberry was ill-equipped as a motion picture producer and removed him from consideration as the producer of any future *Star Trek* movies." Roddenberry's *name* was retained for subsequent films, Paramount recognizing that "The Roddenberry myth and the *Star Trek* legend had taken such a hold on the millions of *Star Trek* fans," but his position was purely consultative: "He could read the scripts and make suggestions, but the studio was under no obligation to accept or implement his input." Paramount was convinced that Roddenberry's active involvement in a project was counterproductive, an attitude rooted in the early years of production and the questionable activities of Lincoln Enterprises, established in 1968.[8]

Lincoln Enterprises first appears in the literature in Whitfield and Roddenberry (1968). Stephen Whitfield first encountered *Star Trek* (Whitfield and Roddenberry, 1968: 11) as a hobby kit company representative, and asked permission to chronicle production. Roddenberry agreed, in exchange for coauthorship credit and hence half the royalties, saying, "I had to get some money from somewhere. I'm sure not going to get it from the profits of *Star Trek*" (Solow and Justman, 1996: 401–2). This is the same line Roddenberry offered when bestowing upon himself half the royalties otherwise due composer Sandy Courage (Solow and Justman, 1996: 178–85), by writing some reputedly unperformable lyrics for the *Star Trek* theme tune—lyrics that appear in the front matter of Whitfield's book as if to declare legitimacy. That book reports in a footnote (1968: 379n) Roddenberry's supposed response to fans' devotion:

> Roddenberry was finally forced to form a company, Lincoln Enterprises ... in order to handle the continuous flood of fan mail and requests for actor photos and for other Star Trek souvenirs.

Lincoln is often presented as a philanthropic organization reciprocating fan commitment. Majel Barrett[9] claims (Davidsmeyer, 1993) that Isaac Asimov once wrote to Roddenberry with "a very intelligent question," but received in return only an autographed cast photo. According to Barrett, "Isaac called Gene and Gene in a fit of rage and everything said, 'We're gonna handle this fan mail ourselves, darn it!' So he asked me if I'd take it over and that's basically how it started."

Barrett explains further that, when the studio perceived the show as failing, support evaporated for sending out (presumably free) mementoes to fans—"so the thought was now that 'Gee, we don't have the money for this, but maybe if they want it enough, they'd be willing to pay for it.'" Barrett carefully characterizes a shoestring operation designed solely to support fans. William Shatner (1993: 383), conversely, introduces Lincoln alongside Roddenberry's retreat from creative input on the show in 1968:

> Most disheartening of all, however, were Roddenberry's blatant attempts to milk every possible cent from his dying cash cow known as *Star Trek*, even at the expense of our scripts.
>
> For example, a Roddenberry-approved mail-order house called Lincoln Enterprises (which was actually owned by Gene's lawyer [Leonard Maizlish]) had recently begun selling a small line of *Star Trek* merchandise.

Bjo[10] Trimble set up Lincoln (with husband John)[11] and contradicts Barrett's characterization (1982: 77–9). She contrasts an earlier, free-and-easy atmosphere allowing fans to collect film frames unused in finished episodes, for swaps among themselves and sale for charity. Then, however,

"When we set up the *Star Trek* souvenir sales company, Lincoln Enterprises ... that was the end of free give-aways from the studio. It is not logical to give away something you can sell." Roddenberry exploited the Trimbles' experience in setting up mail-order operations, and their direct access to a market of large, energetic fan networks.

They established Lincoln as a stable operation but, "After less than nine months, the Trimbles were summarily fired" (Joel Engel, 1994: 116) and replaced by none other than Stephen Whitfield.[12] Trimble reports (1982: 79) setting Lincoln up "for Gene Roddenberry and his wife," which must be technically inaccurate: Roddenberry was married to Eileen, but among many other liaisons was becoming increasingly attached to Barrett and later said that he set up Lincoln "to give Majel something to do" (Solow and Justman, 1996: 400). Harlan Ellison suggests that the plan boiled down to profiting from *Star Trek* as quickly as possible and hiding any proceeds from potential divorce proceedings, given the likelihood of Roddenberry leaving his wife for Barrett (1996: 25). With Lincoln evidently under Roddenberry's control, but distanced from him by Barrett's nominal leadership and Maizlish's ownership, this certainly seems plausible.

To support his complaint that production was subordinate to Roddenberry's financial preoccupations, Shatner discusses the third-season episode "Is There in Truth No Beauty?" (1968). Senior officers welcome Dr. Miranda Jones (assistant to the Medusan ambassador), their dialogue conventionally setting up plot elements. Jones suddenly breaks off and turns to Spock:

> JONES: I was just noticing your Vulcan *iddick*, Mr. Spock. Is it a reminder that, as a Vulcan, you can mind-link with the Medusans far better than I could?
>
> [The camera lingers briefly on a hitherto unnoticed ornament pinned to Spock's uniform.]
>
> KIRK: Well, I doubt that Mr. Spock would don the most revered of all Vulcan symbols merely to *annoy* you, Doctor Jones.
>
> SPOCK: As a matter of fact, I wear it this evening to honor you, Doctor.

Nothing here progresses the story or elucidates what the "*iddick*" actually is: it's an awkward *non sequitur* that Kirk must interrupt, and it disappears until the closing sequence. Spock, now wearing it as a medallion, bids farewell to Jones, who seems to glance at it.

> JONES: I understand, Mr. Spock: the glory of creation is in its infinite diversity.
>
> SPOCK: And the ways our differences combine, to create meaning and beauty.

Even here the bauble is not explained, but another Whitfield and Roddenberry footnote (1968: 226n) is telling:

> Star Trek's third season will emphasize the Vulcan philosophy of universal brotherhood via an unusually shaped medallion Mr. Spock will receive from "home" and begin to wear. Its design reflects the Vulcan belief that the greatest joy in all creation is in the infinite ways that infinitely diverse things can join together to create meaning and beauty.

No such philosophical emphasis really occurs, but Shatner (1993: 383–7) elucidates. Long absent from input to the series, Roddenberry suddenly tried to insert into this episode a sequence where Kirk would bestow upon a delighted recipient a distinctive medallion symbolizing mastery of the fundamental *Federation* (not Vulcan) notion of "Infinite Diversity in Infinite Combination": IDIC. Kirk's panegyric was not incompatible with the story, but added nothing to it.

Shatner claims to have rejected this irrelevant and wordy interlude, which then mutated to center on Spock. Nimoy in turn balked at the "meandering and pointless" scene, but traces remain in the episode (Nimoy, 1995: 122). Simply, Roddenberry wanted to market a distinctive *Star Trek* souvenir, so invented a pretext for its appearance on TV, apparently contemptuous of NBC's policy against product placement (Solow and Justman, 1996: 191–200). Whitfield's footnote is a blatant advertisement.

Solow and Justman recount other Lincoln activities, including the sale of scripts—abuse of Paramount property and "an apparent violation of the studio's basic bargaining agreement with the Writers Guild of America" (1996: 400–401). They also report a film editor, seeking a stock shot, asking a studio guard to unlock the *Star Trek* film vault and finding it bare. The guard explains that "Mr. Roddenberry and his friend, that girl from *Star Trek*, Mabel something," had emptied the vault into a truck. Lincoln was selling film frames soon afterwards. It was a sensitive matter for the Paramount executives, as the film was owned by the studio and not Gene Roddenberry. The upshot was that everyone pretended not to know what had happened. So it continued to happen.

Lincoln Enterprises also figures in some reports of the "Save *Star Trek*" campaigns. Engel (1994: 119–20) and Ellison (1996: 36–8) outline the first: at Roddenberry's request Ellison (although still resenting his own episode script's treatment)[13] formed the so-called Committee of SF writers, putting their names to a letter suggesting that fans beseech NBC not to cancel the show. Even by the letter's date (1 December 1966) only 12 episodes had been aired, but Ellison (1996: 37) "believed (what is generally now acknowledged to be utterly untrue) that there were idiot monsters at NBC who were [already] trying to scuttle *Star Trek*." David Alexander (1994: 265) quotes the *Chicago Tribune* (May 1967) explaining this false alarm, and one "well-placed individual" assuming that the hoped-for support would simply increase the studio's leverage in negotiations with the network. As it was, the modest but unnecessary response annoyed and embarrassed NBC (Solow and Justman, 1996: 305), so at best the campaign was a stunt that backfired.

The 1968 campaign was more elaborate, although again apparently gratuitous. Trimble constantly insists (e.g., Stephen Wolcott, 2004; David Gerrold, 1996: 137) that she and John both initiated this campaign and ran it, distancing Roddenberry from unprofessional involvement. Solow, on the other hand (1996: 378), reports Roddenberry explaining that he had hired Trimble to run it. Barrett (Davidsmeyer, 1993) characterizes both campaigns as Lincoln operations (despite its 1968 inauguration), the Trimbles being merely "very instrumental" for the second. There is no doubt that the Trimbles sent out thousands of letters and that NBC consequently received much mail protesting the supposed cancellation.

It remains likely that Roddenberry coordinated the whole affair. For comparison, Roddenberry hosted some students from the California Institute of Technology on the set and allowed them to believe that renewal seemed doubtful (Alexander, 1994: 302). When *they* suggested a protest march on NBC, he encouraged them. A local radio announcer (who was a fan) was contacted by the *Star Trek* office, and began making announcements supporting the planned march. The Caltech (all-male college) students also wanted to meet girls, the best local supply of those being the University of Southern California, so the third radio announcement gave the "information" that many colleges were now committed to participation—except USC. As a result, of the hundreds of students on the march—secretly observed by Roddenberry (Engel, 1994: 118; Solow and Justman, 1996: 382)—USC provided the second-largest contingent. Students from other colleges marched on NBC, New York (Solow and Justman, 1996: 382).

In the mean time Roddenberry was (with permission) using Asimov's name on 250 telegrams protesting the show's imminent demise, and was employing acquaintances to decorate NBC executives' cars with "Mr. Spock for President" bumper stickers that he had had printed, all at studio expense (Solow and Justman, 1996: 385–6). Roddenberry's 19 February letter to the *Miami Herald* (Solow and Justman, 1996: 379) brags that, after a special committee of NBC vice presidents failed to conclude that the campaign was organized in-house, NBC *reversed* its premature decision to cancel *Star Trek*.

Grant Tinker[14] (then NBC head of West Coast programming) tells Engel (1994: 121) that *Star Trek* could have been in no danger at the time: both renewals would have been business decisions unaffected by mail campaigns. Shatner (Wolcott, 2004) and Solow (1996: 305–7) concur. Tinker also doubts the existence of the "committee of vice-presidents," since he would undoubtedly have been *on* it. Herb Schlosser (then NBC vice president) confirms (Solow and Justman, 1996: 379) that *Star Trek*'s renewal was already likely (and no cancellation had occurred). Rodden- berry's involvement in the annoying campaigns was strongly suspected. The likelihood is that Lincoln's activities and the mail campaigns (that saved the show, folklore adamantly proclaims) were essentially self- centered antics attracting the antipathy of *Star Trek*'s home studio *and* host network towards the show in general and its executive producer in par- ticular (Solow and Justman, 1996: 378).

Star Trek was finally cancelled after its third season, and no notice- able campaign took place to save it. It is widely agreed that the third sea- son dipped sharply in quality, Justman suggesting (e.g., Wolcott, 2004) that new staff tried unsuccessfully to reinvent the show. The third season's graveyard slot of 10:00 P.M. on Fridays could not have helped attract view- ers, but Engel (1994: 126) notes that that arose from initially low ratings having already declined further. He further speculates as to what *would* have been saved, had the effort been made. If it were more shows like "Turnabout Intruder" (1969), the series swan song, then, in the opinion of many fans who kept waiting for the consistent week-to-week quality of the first and second seasons, *Star Trek* wasn't worth saving. Nimoy (Shat- ner, 1993: 396) amplifies this point:

> I thought, "I'm sorry to see this go, but on the other hand, I'm glad to see it going away before we have a chance to find ourselves totally in the toi- let." ... I have to say I felt a sense of relief, in that we wouldn't have to worry about the fourth season being even worse than the third.

This assessment is not entirely universal: Wikipedia explains that the superior third season included "much of the best material of the series" but appeared too late to repair the damage caused by the first two.[15]

Perhaps for having avoided further decline *Star Trek* was indeed remembered as having been more good than bad, its most conspicuous merchandising manifestation being the print adaptations of existing episodes by James Blish. Their popularity (alongside the well-received but later disowned 1973–74 animated series) helped to sustain the *Star Trek* brand through the 1970s. The 1970s also saw *Star Trek* gathering new viewers through syndicated repeats (this fact and book sales presumably reinforcing each other). We are conventionally invited to assume that this naturally followed from the quality of the series but, as so often in this story, external accident intervened.

Trimble draws a direct causal line from the second campaign to third- season renewal, to the existence of enough episodes for syndication to be viable (and, by implication, to the franchise's subsequent develop- ment).[16] On the "Director's Edition" DVD of *The Motion Picture*, Barrett states that at least 100 episodes would normally be required for a series to be picked up for syndication, but that *Star Trek*'s total of 79 was *just* enough, which appears to be not *exactly* false but entirely misleading. A meeting occurred in 1967 between Dick Block, president of Kaiser Broadcasting (five small local stations), and Bob Newgard, head of Paramount Domestic Syndication (Solow and Justman, 1996: 417–8). Block enjoyed SF and, against all industry convention, was offering to buy syndication rights to *Star Trek* there and then, at a reduced advance price for however many episodes might ultimately be made. An informal agreement was reached. Come cancellation 79 *Star Trek* episodes existed, and Block got his syndication rights.

Guessing that *Star Trek*'s appeal might not be to avid observers of current affairs, Kaiser carefully scheduled *Star Trek* against competitors' news programs at 6:00 P.M., airing the entire run over 16 weeks and immediately beginning a cycle of repeats. Its ratings for that slot improved startlingly. Other small independent stations followed this lead, and *Star Trek* began its now-legendary climb to worldwide popularity in repeats after dying on its feet in its first run. The legend tends not to mention that 79 episodes of a failed series would have had virtually no chance of reaching syndication at all without Block's extremely eccentric approach, or that *Star Trek*, whose makers have always praised their viewers' informed wisdom (e.g., Whitfield and Roddenberry, 1968: 396), eventually found its breakthrough audience among viewers uninterested in the news.

Snodgrass (1991) implies that *Star Trek* conventions arose directly from this new audience, confirming the viability of a film, but again there is more to this. Alexander (1994: 393) quotes Lichtenberg, Marshak and Winston (1975) to the effect that *Star Trek* fans were at best "tolerated" at serious science fiction conventions, and that, "We thought if a couple of hundred of us got together we could talk about *Star Trek* as much as we liked, with no one to sneer."[17] The first film's genesis, moreover, was much more convoluted than a simple response to conventions. This period has been thoroughly documented by Judith and Garfield Reeves-Stevens (1997) and is too complex to allow more than a summary here.

Paramount was aware of *Star Trek*'s popularity, spin-off books having sold well since 1967 and conventions now proliferating. Serious discussions of a film spin-off began in 1973. A new TV series was initiated: *Star Trek: Phase II* was to be the flagship show for a Paramount network. When the network plan was shelved, so was *Phase II*. Plans also veered wildly between a major feature film and a TV movie. All were complicated by Roddenberry's insistence on control over any new project. Test scenes had already been shot for a *Phase II* pilot with a new cast, and a film had been in preproduction to the tune of $500,000 and then cancelled, when in 1977 *Star Wars* (closely followed by *Close Encounters of the Third Kind*) saved *Star Trek* by proving that science fiction film could be enormously profitable. Paramount immediately announced a new series, soon afterwards committing to a major film instead and fixing a premier date.

Star Trek: The Motion Picture (1979) was expensively cancelled or paused several times. Its script was initially cobbled together from existing material for *Phase II*, itself based on earlier episodes.[18] Production was fraught with delays and budgetary troubles, and effects houses failed to complete their contracted tasks. The director, Robert Wise, had no time to complete the film properly once all available shots were in, so the best cut achievable on the spot was rushed out *just* in time for the premiere. The lumbering film's reviews were generally poor and even fans dubbed it "The Motionless Picture," but that was irrelevant. Trading purely on nostalgia its box office receipts were impressive, verifying the huge audience available for new *Star Trek* material.

Wise is affable about *The Motion Picture* during his contributions to its "Director's Edition" DVD release. During DVD commentary for *The Day the Earth Stood Still* (1951), however, Wise emphatically reports his disheartening experience; explaining his preference for filming from a finalized script, shots planned and interlocking as designed, Wise notes two exceptions in his career. After briefly mentioning *Run Silent, Run Deep*, he continues:

> The worst example was *Star Trek: The Motion Picture*.... We were rewriting the script all the way through that film, all the way to the very end. In the last few days I was getting two or three sets of changes a day for the next day's work. Terrible, terrible way to work....
>
> Minor changes of dialogue on the set happens all the time, but I'm talking about *major rewriting* going on all the time, and that's a terrible way to work.

The editor of *Citizen Kane* (1941) and director of the intricate *The Sound of Music* (1965) and *West Side Story* (1961), who had demonstrated an assured, grounded style in science fiction directing *The Day the Earth Stood Still* and *The Andromeda Strain* (1971), was shocked by this constant fiddling until the last minute with the basic material. Roddenberry was again in the thick of this.

Alan Dean Foster, an established SF writer, generated the initial *Phase II* pilot script, which Harold Livingston took over rewriting when Foster left. Roddenberry persistently rewrote Livingston's rewrites. This situation was worsening when Wise was engaged to direct a film version. Roddenberry continued secretly to intercept scripts and rewrite them as they were sent out for director's approval, causing Livingston to quit several times. As has been shown, Paramount resolved (albeit temporarily) not to involve Roddenberry in any future productions, and even when further films became inevitable his role was minimized.

One reason for *The Motion Picture* being wildly over budget was that it had carried the financial deficit of the abortive *Phase II* and film developments. The much smaller budget provided for *Star Trek II: The Wrath of Khan* (1982) forced production strategies that worked to the franchise's benefit, principally the adoption of a comparatively inexpensive visual style more reminiscent (along with abandoning the muted palette of *The Motion Picture*) of the original series (see Michael Duffy's chapter in this volume). Such affinity was firmly established by *The Wrath of Khan* being a direct sequel to "Space Seed" (1967), crucially reprising Ricardo Montalban's commanding performance as the villain, and instantly made the film more accessible to viewers. Peter Nicholls (Nicholls, 1984: 131) is unusual among critics for using the same evidence to praise the first film instead. As the first film confirmed, *Star Trek*'s two crucial icons were Spock and the *Enterprise*. When the sequel sacrificed Spock, and when *Star Trek III: The Search for Spock* (1984) located his husk but destroyed the ship, the scene was set for *Star Trek IV: The Voyage Home* (1986), which fully reinstated both emblems while also telling an unusually entertaining story with pointedly contemporary resonance.

    Star Trek IV completed a trilogy that rehabilitated *Star Trek* as more than a failed series of affectionate memory: the films now *were* a new *Star Trek* series, and suddenly it also seemed current and relevant. As usual Roddenberry claimed considerable credit, especially for having guided *Star Trek IV* to its great success, although "Bennett and Nimoy both say that Roddenberry was, if anything, [even] less involved on *IV* than on the previous two films" (Engel, 1994: 203).

    Prior to *Star Trek IV*'s release Paramount announced an imminent new *Star Trek* television series for 1987, with Roddenberry grudgingly assigned to create and produce it (Engel, 1994: 209):

> Roddenberry did not, in fact, enjoy the contractual right either to control *Star Trek*'s destiny or to demand the job of executive producer. [But] studio executives believed—and Roddenberry knew they believed—that a discouraging word would travel at warp speed through fandom and doom the series before its birth.

This chapter's scope does not include full production of *Star Trek: The Next Generation*, beyond recognizing that its triumphal launch marked a crucial juncture in the legend of this franchise: second time round, live-action television *Star Trek* seemingly demonstrated its essential robustness (see chapter 3). Engel's final chapter to his book ("The Clothes Have No Emperor") details the extraordinary problems imposed by Roddenberry upon other staff, from preproduction onwards, as he frequently mistreated people or took credit for their ideas, apparently insecurely needing to affirm control. Solow and Justman (1996: 432–433) say little about Roddenberry's role there, as if to suggest that his personal input into what the series became was minimal. Both books report that by 1986–87

Roddenberry was showing signs of what would become his final illness, including erratic tendencies that cast doubt upon any *chance* of rational contribution. Engel notes (1994: 245) that, like its original, *The Next Generation* inspired generally lukewarm reviews. Its target audience was also unimpressed, apparently continuing to watch "only because of pent-up demand."

We will never know for sure how *The Next Generation* might have fared if confronted by normal market conditions. Roddenberry's name, for those who valued it, naturally implied authenticity. Commentators also commonly mention its unusual launch directly into syndication (rather than premiering on a network) and its instant success there: notwithstanding its cool reception, it somehow became quickly and widely established. The fans described by Engel could, then, continue to give it the benefit of the doubt until it naturally became something of a fixture in its own right. Máire Messenger Davies and Roberta Pearson (2003) highlight two main reasons for this—the first being that by 1987 the original series had, partly thanks to the films, become a valuable commodity in the syndication market. Paramount now offered stations (not networks) *The Next Generation* as well, and offered it *free of charge* in exchange for advertising time within each episode. There was an even more creative wrinkle, however:

> The clincher was that the stations couldn't have [the original series] (highly profitable for them) unless they took the new series too.

Here, then, the idealistic story of *Star Trek* demonstrating the purity and power of its creative core continues to be considerably more tortuous than it might first appear. Wikipedia is correct, as far as it goes, in reporting that:

> [*The Next Generation*] gained a considerable following during its run, and like its predecessor, is widely syndicated. Its popularity led to a line of spin-off television series that would continue without interruption until 2005. The series also formed the basis of the seventh through tenth movies of the *Star Trek* theatrical film series.[19]

The important missing fact here is that, in a reversal of normal circumstances, the market was maneuvered to serve the show. No station could refuse to air it without also giving up the lucrative original series. Neither poor reviews nor fan apathy could affect *The Next Generation*'s continuance in broadcast schedules, and consequently the superficial but potent appearance of widespread success from the outset. It could, in effect, become famous by *seeming* famous; and it would inevitably generate comment as it entwined itself with the original's narrative history, which it did immediately by adopting the "Space, the final frontier..."

formulation (see chapter 1). Also, its first standard episode (after the two-part "Encounter at Farpoint") was "The Naked Now" (1987), a "naked" remake of the fourth episode ever broadcast, "The Naked Time" (1966).

Jonathan Frakes states (Jones, 2005) that *The Next Generation* took a year to gather a viable audience. No TV show can normally expect such leeway in the face of audience indifference—but here, uniquely, the market itself could be manipulated. From that point the franchise's further survival was assured, not necessarily on any particular grounds of quality, but through the *appearance* of having succeeded in the face of all doubt and criticism. Such apparent durability also encouraged the view that this was in some way testament to Gene Roddenberry's golden touch, despite his virtual absence from development (Engel, 1994: 247–8). Henry Jenkins's research (1991: 191) indicates that:

> The fans respect the original texts yet fear that their conceptions of the characters and concepts may be jeopardized by those who wish to exploit them for easy profits, a category that typically includes Paramount and the network but excludes Roddenberry and many of the show's writers.

As stated at the beginning of this discussion, the *Star Trek* mega-text is widely perceived as articulating an ongoing, positive philosophy with Roddenberry as its fountainhead, when indications are overwhelming that he was as corruptible and hard-nosed as the next scrambling television producer. Despite that, the legends of man and franchise feed each other to support a mythology of irresistible progression through slow-burn popularity to books, conventions, films, a triumphant return to TV and the spawning of further series that (until 2005) seemed destined to continue indefinitely.

The evidence, conversely, suggests a sequence of accidents and catastrophes whose careful reinterpretation has been presented as manifest destiny. An adequate show, seldom interesting as SF, was cancelled (probably at least partly due to its figurehead's self-enrichment and self-promotion activities) before it could become entirely awful. It gained an improbable chance to attract nonmainstream viewers in syndication. The science fiction community's (and the wider public's) disdain for TV SF created a defensive fan group that, far from finally receiving their demands, coincidentally provided a critical (in both senses) safety net when the post–*Star Wars* SF film boom provided Paramount with a use for its disastrous work towards launching its own network. The resulting fiasco of a movie benefited sufficiently from nostalgia not to disappear as a failed experiment but to serve as a dry run for further films, which developed a sustainable returning audience. This audience didn't care for the subsequent new series, which might well have failed immediately without purely commercial arrangements applying a stranglehold to broadcasters. Throughout this period Paramount reluctantly retained the increasingly unreliable and distrusted Roddenberry, to imply and symbolize a continuity of vision that actually had little relevance to the material produced—but which ironically remains a component, however illusory, of the audience's image of *Star Trek* even today.

For various reasons, *Star Trek* attained an omnipresence that dominated public perception of SF for 40 years. It becomes easy to understand why some SF critics, and television producers with other ambitions for the genre, could despair of how *Star Trek* affected public and industry expectations of science fiction's potential scope. On the other hand, *Star Trek* provides a landmark stereotype against which some shows have productively struggled. It may, despite itself, instigate a flowering of science fiction.

Notes

1. Some of this material was included in the author's paper "The Accidental Rise of *Star Trek*" at the Journeys Across Media conference, University of Reading, 23 April 2004.
2. Available at http://www.imdb.com/title/tt0796366/board/nest/41986960 (accessed 12 May 2006).
3. *Star Trek—A Short History*: http://www.ee.surrey.ac.uk/Contrib/SciFi/StarTrek/history.html (accessed 5 May 2006). Paramount's methodology for both distinguishing and surveying "viewers," "fans" and "television experts" is not explained.
4. Wikipedia is an interesting online resource, offering myriad essays available for correction by anyone, evidently in the hope that each will gradually become a complete, authoritative account. With some material, however, this produces merely *consensus*. Wikipedia can therefore provide a useful view of what many authors *assume* to be the case: democratic and dynamic as it is, its processes are automatically prone to popular misconceptions, so its content's accuracy is never guaranteed. Here, Wikipedia demonstrates the persistence of some pervasive beliefs that are at best conjectural.
5. Available at http://www.en.wikipedia.org/wiki/Gene_Roddenberry (accessed 5 May 2006).
6. Herb Solow was *Star Trek*'s executive in charge of production; Bob Justman was coproducer.
7. Roddenberry's October 1991 death was not noted in *Omni* until a short encomium by Arthur C. Clarke appeared in the February 1992 issue (40). Snodgrass's article appeared in the December issue, which would have circulated in November, its text surely finalized earlier. Snodgrass's remarks might constitute the final open, public comment while Roddenberry was still alive.
8. Majel Barrett gives (Davidsmeyer, 1993) claims that Lincoln Publishing originally belonged to "another gentleman," whose attorney was Leonard Maizlish, also Roddenberry's attorney and business manager: "For some reason or another he gave the incorporation to Leonard. I don't know how it basically happened, but it really belonged to Leonard Mai[z]lish until he gave it to me in the early eighties." This is consistent with speculation that Lincoln Enterprises represented a scheme to accumulate money not directly traceable to Roddenberry.
9. Appearing in the original *Star Trek* pilot, with a different role in the series and a recurring part in *The Next Generation*, Barrett became a significant presence in the franchise generally. Popular accounts frequently romanticize her role. Wikipedia (http://www.en.wikipedia.org/wiki/Gene_Roddenberry) straightforwardly notes that Barrett was Roddenberry's second wife: "They were married in Japan in a traditional Buddhist-Shinto ceremony on August 6, 1969," which sounds rather touching and spiritual. In fact,

Roddenberry and Barrett had had a long affair since before *Star Trek* began production, the Japanese "marriage" being at most a gesture since Roddenberry was still married to Eileen (Alexander, 1994: 372). Roddenberry and Barrett married legally following his divorce.

10. Bjo (pronounced "Bee-Jo"): not a misprint, but a name bestowed on Betty Joann Trimble by prominent SF fan Forrest J Ackerman, who was much given to such contracted neologisms. Trimble first met Roddenberry (Trimble, 1982: 13–16) at the 1966 World Science Fiction Convention (Worldcon) while organizing its "Futuristic Fashion Show 2" in which Roddenberry persuaded her to include *Star Trek* costumes to help promote his forthcoming show.

11. Reproducing Eugene Roddenberry's announcement of Lincoln Enterprises returning as The Roddenberry Store (including the statements "Majel & Gene Roddenberry started Lincoln Enterprises in 1968. Majel has always been the driving force behind the company"), Bjo felt moved to elucidate:

> Actually, John & Bjo Trimble set up the original Lincoln Enterprises. Neither Gene nor Majel had any idea how to set up a mail-order business, while the Trimbles have put together several such businesses. At Creation Grand Slam, Eugene Roddenberry acknowledged our efforts with a big hug & thanks.

This was available at http://www.bjotrimble.com/talktrek_files/talk_trek.htm (accessed 24 November 2004). (Mysteriously, bjotrimble.com now seems to be a commercial source for kitchen gadgets.)

12. This may explain Bjo's unelaborated mention of a period when she and John parted company with Roddenberry for a while (Trimble, 1982: 102), and why she describes Roddenberry as a "conniver" (http://www.trektoday.com/news/070503_04.shtml).

13. Of all the original *Star Trek* scripts, Ellison's "The City on the Edge of Forever" in particular represents an extended saga of rewrites and vituperation. Ellison's 1996 book unpicks the writing of "City" and later infighting over its provenance. His fury succumbs to the occasional lapse of detail, so while the book is vastly informative it must be treated carefully.

14. Solow describes Tinker (Solow and Justman, 1996: 426–7) as "the most thoroughly trustworthy, decent, thoughtful and talented executive I have ever dealt with in the television industry."

15. Available at http://www.en.wikipedia.org/wiki/Star_Trek_Curse (accessed 14 May 2006).

16. Available at http://www.trektoday.com/news/070503_04.shtml.

17. Even before *Star Trek*'s growing fan movement retreated from other gatherings, serious science fiction conventions justifiably greeted TV science fiction with suspicion. Some *film* attempts to tackle SF were respected, but TV SF was generally regarded as vapid "sci-fi." Roddenberry was treated gruffly at the 1966 Worldcon, and even though his screenings there of the two *Star Trek* pilots were warmly received he was given short shrift during his contorted (but successful) campaign to win a Hugo award at 1967's Worldcon (Engel, 1994: 109–113).

18. In *Star Trek: The Motion Picture*, a Voyager probe returns to Earth in search of its creator, having acquired phenomenal levels of "machine consciousness" and destructive power, indiscriminately annihilating anything that interferes with it, including any "carbon units" attempting communication. This recycles the basic scenarios of "The Changeling" and "The Doomsday Machine" (both 1967).

19. Available at http://www.en.wikipedia.org/wiki/Star_Trek:_The_Next_Generation (accessed 14 May 2006).

Works Cited

Alexander, David. *"Star Trek" Creator: The Authorized Biography of Gene Roddenberry*. New York: ROC, 1994.
Ash, Brian. *Who's Who in Science Fiction*. London: Sphere, 1976.

Asimov, Isaac. "The Boom in Science Fiction." *Asimov on Science Fiction.* St. Albans: Granada, 1983a.
_____. "How Science Fiction Came to Be Big Business." *Asimov on Science Fiction.* St. Albans: Granada, 1983b.
Carter, Paul A. *The Creation of Tomorrow: Fifty Years of Magazine Science Fiction.* New York: Columbia University Press, 1977.
Clarke, I.F. *The Pattern of Expectation, 1644–2001.* London: Jonathan Cape, 1979.
Davidsmeyer, Jo. "Lincoln Enterprises: A Little Piece of *Star Trek*—An interview with the 'First Lady of Star Trek,' Majel Barrett Roddenberry." *Strange New Worlds Science Fiction Collectors Magazine* 10 (October/November 1993), available online at http://www.strangenewworlds.com/issues/feature-10.html.
DiLullo, Tara. "The Mirror Cracked." *SFX* 129 (April 2005): 52–56.
Ellison, Harlan. *The City on the Edge of Forever: The Original Teleplay that Became the Classic "Star Trek" Episode.* Clarkston: White Wolf, 1996.
Engel, Joel. *Gene Roddenberry: The Myth and the Man Behind "Star Trek."* London: Virgin, 1994.
Fern, Yvonne. *Inside the Mind of Gene Roddenberry, the Creator of "Star Trek."* London: HarperCollins, 1995.
Fulton, Roger. *The Encyclopedia of TV Science Fiction.* 3rd ed. London: Boxtree, 1997.
Gerrold, David. *The World of "Star Trek."* London: Virgin, 1996.
Jenkins, Henry. "*Star Trek* Rerun, Reread, Rewritten: Fan Writing as Textual Poaching." *Close Encounters: Film, Feminism and Science Fiction.* Edited by C. Penley, E. Lyon, L. Spigel, and J. Bergstrom. Minneapolis: University of Minnesota Press, 1991.
Johnson-Smith, Jan. *American Science Fiction TV: "Star Trek," "Stargate" and Beyond.* London: I.B. Tauris, 2005.
Jones, Julian. *How William Shatner Changed the World.* Handel Productions, 2005.
Logan, Michael. "The Great Bird of the Galaxy." *"Star Trek," 30 Years.* Radio Times Official Collector's Edition. Edited by Lee Ann Nicholson. Paramount Publications, 1996.
Lundwall, Sam J. *Science Fiction: An Illustrated History.* New York: Grosset & Dunlap, 1977.
Messenger, Davies, Máire Pearson and Roberta E. Pearson (2003), "'NO NETWORK!': *Star Trek* and the American Television Industry's Changing Modes of Organization." Presentation to MiT3: Television in Transition, MIT, Cambridge, MA (May 2003): 2–4.
Nicholls, Peter. *Fantastic Cinema: An Illustrated Survey.* London: Ebury Press, 1984.
Nimoy, Leonard. *I Am Spock.* London: Century, 1995.
Reeves-Stevens, Judith, and Garfield Reeves-Stevens. *"Star Trek Phase II": The Lost Series.* New York: Pocket Books, 1997.
Shatner, William. *"Star Trek" Memories.* With Chris Kreski. London: HarperCollins, 1993.
Snodgrass, Melinda. "Boldly Going Nowhere." *Omni* 14, no. 3 (December 1991): 52.
Solow, Herbert F., and Robert H. Justman. *Inside "Star Trek": The Real Story.* New York: Pocket Books, 1996.
Spinrad, Norman. "Books into Movies." *Isaac Asimov's Science Fiction Magazine* 9, no. 11 (November 1985). Reprinted in Norman Spinrad. *Science Fiction in the Real World.* Carbondale: Southern Illinois University Press, 1990.
Straczynski, J. Michael. "The Profession of Science Fiction, 48: Approaching Babylon." *Foundation: The Review of Science Fiction* 64 (Summer 1995).
Sutherland, J.A. "American Science Fiction since 1960." *Science Fiction: A Critical Guide.* Edited by Patrick Parrinder. London: Longman, 1979.
Trimble, Bjo. *On the Good Ship "Enterprise": My 15 Years with "Star Trek."* Norfolk, VA: Donning, 1982.
Whitfield, Stephen E., and Gene Roddenberry. *The Making of "Star Trek."* New York: Ballantine Books, 1968.
Wolcott, Stephen R. "'To Boldly Go...' Season Three." *Star Trek* Season Three DVD, 2004.
Wolfe, Gary K. "On Some Recent Scholarship." *Science Fiction Studies* 21, no.3 (1994), available online at http://www.depauw.edu/sfs/review_essays/wolfe64.htm#Star%20Trek.

3

Franchise Fatigue?

The Marginalization of the Television Series after The Next Generation

INA RAE HARK

In May of 1994 *Star Trek: The Next Generation* aired its series finale. After seven seasons, Paramount executives and executive producer Rick Berman chose to free up its cast to continue the feature film franchise, even though the show's ratings in first-run syndication remained high and it had just been nominated for an Emmy as Best Dramatic Series. Although the third spin-off series, *Star Trek: Deep Space Nine,* had not been the syndicated ratings juggernaut that *The Next Generation* was, there was enough confidence in the viability of the franchise for Paramount owner Viacom to launch its own "weblet" UPN in January 1995 with the fourth Trek series, *Star Trek: Voyager,* as anchor.[1]

What looked like a surefire, industry-tested franchise strategy in 1994, however, led in another decade to the fifth Trek series, *Enterprise,* staving off cancellation at the conclusion of its third season only by cutting in half the license fee it was charging UPN and moving to a dead-end Friday time slot. The next year it was canceled, ending eighteen consecutive seasons of at least one first-run *Star Trek* series being on the air. Berman attributed the failure of *Enterprise* to achieve the seven-season run granted to the other three "modern" Treks to "franchise fatigue":

> "There are a lot of people who criticized us for saying what I'm about to say, but I do believe that there was some degree of fatigue with the franchise," [executive producer Rick] Berman said in a conference call interview. "I think that we found ourselves in competition with ourselves. *Enterprise* in many markets was running against repeats—whether it be cable or syndication—of the original series, *Next Generation, Voyager* [or] *Deep Space Nine.* And I think that after 18 years and 624 hours of *Star Trek* the

41

audience began to have a little bit of overkill with *Star Trek*, and I think that had a lot to do with it. And I think if you take a look at the last feature film we did, *Nemesis*, which I still believe was a fine movie, it did two-thirds the business that the previous films had done. So I think it's, again, another example of the franchise getting a little bit tired" ["Berman"].

Berman's explanation eschews any blame that might fall upon the heads of himself and his creative team. They merely turned out so much of a good thing that it became too much.

Any sort of in-depth consideration of the history of science fiction on television during the past decade, however, can suggest more concrete reasons for the specific failure of *Enterprise* and the general decline of the fortunes of the Trek franchise. This essay will explore how Berman and the Paramount executives mishandled the post–*TNG* series by not responding to radical changes in the way science fiction television was produced and marketed; it will also explore how the very long history and exceptional status of the Trek franchise may have made it impossible to do so. Having discovered the perfect formula for making a cult, space-based science fiction show into a lucrative commercial property in the late 1980s, Trek's creators got stuck in the spatial anomaly of their own success. By the time *Enterprise* ended it had failed to keep up either the cult or the commerce.

Going to Warp Again

Before analyzing how the franchise faltered, let's consider how it succeeded in reinventing itself for a new generation. Paramount, which had bought all rights to the franchise from Roddenberry, had intended to make a second series, *Star Trek: Phase II,* with a mixture of original and new cast members, as the foundation of a weblet in 1977. The idea proved to be ahead of its time, however, and UPN would be the last of the three movie-studio based networks to launch rather than the first. The material created for *Phase II* ended up being folded into the first Trek feature film in 1979 (as described in chapter 2).

By 1986 the franchise was humming along profitably on the back of syndicated reruns of the original and four profitable feature films starring the original cast. Yet it had to be apparent also to Paramount that continuing an action-adventure franchise on the backs of performers rapidly approaching social security eligibility was not a recipe for long-term success. Therefore, the studio once more decided to return *Star Trek* to television, this time with an all new crew of a new *Enterprise* pursuing its mission 75 years later than the original. Paramount also had a new business model for the series, seeking neither to place it on an existing network nor to use it to create a new one. It would be an original, scripted dramatic hour offered directly to local stations via syndication. As Joel Engel points out:

> The studio was having difficulty selling product to the major networks, but its programs like *Entertainment Tonight* and *Solid Gold* were performing spectacularly in first-run syndication. Unlike dramatic shows sold to networks, which studios or production companies generally finance at a deficit to the network's license fee in the hope of scoring on the come, first-run syndicated hits can bring vast riches from the first—the way *Star Trek: The Next Generation* would [Engel, 1994: 220].

All the elements came together to make this a brilliant business decision. Not only would Paramount profit immediately, but each local station could schedule *TNG* in a time slot most conducive to the maximum viewership in their area. The show would not be subject to the whims of its own network's schedulers or the competition other networks decided to throw against it, decisions that would affect every market nationwide. This was how the original series had moved from mainstream flop to cult phenomenon, and the pattern repeated itself. The fame of Trek brought in a large number of viewers to sample the show, and many of them stayed. In fact, the numbers watching *TNG* actually grew once early problems with uneven script quality and rapid staff turnover were solved in its third season by the installation of Berman as executive producer, Gene Roddenberry's retreat from hands-on participation as show-runner, and the hiring of Michael Piller to head the writing staff. Average yearly household ratings climbed from the 10s to the 12s,[2] with a slight decline occurring only during the seventh and last season. In absolute numbers of households, the third and the last seasons reached just under ten million, while seasons four through six averaged nearly eleven million (Fuller, 1999).

Having no competitors in the first-run syndication market at the outset, *TNG* also had the outer space science fiction television landscape pretty much to itself as well in 1987. The original series got on the air because of excitement in the 1960s about the U.S. space program, excitement that also put *Lost in Space* on a network schedule. In the wake of *Star Wars*, short-lived space-based shows such as the original *Battlestar Galactica* and *Buck Rogers in the 25th Century* appeared. But most American "genre"[3] shows of the '70s took place on present day Earth, with just a few technological miracles factored in, as with the *Six Million Dollar Man* and *Bionic Woman*. Extraterrestrials had last had a regular network slot from 1983 to 1985 in the alien invasion miniseries and spin-off *V.* When *TNG* debuted, it was the only science fiction show on U.S. television, a welcome arrival for cultists who had been subsisting on reruns or off-the-air tapes of the original *Star Trek* or of British stalwarts *Doctor Who, Space: 1999* and *Blake's 7.*

So great was the iconic status of the original *Star Trek* and the ratings success of *TNG*, that its paradigm went essentially unduplicated for 25 years. Let's look at the components of that paradigm:

1. The action is set in the future on a spaceship. No one is a twentieth century human who goes into suspended animation only to revive in the future.

2. The protagonists belong to the military branch of an interstellar federation presented as benevolent in its aims, despite the occasional corrupt officer or bureaucrat. The captain is a human, but the crew contains at least one alien and/or artificial life form.

3. A liberal humanist ideology underpins the action. Embodying the "Roddenberry vision," the *Star Trek* series posit a one-world human government that has created a peaceful and prosperous utopia on Earth and has then spread it to the stars. Although not all aliens embrace the Federation's philosophy, no species is seen as irredeemably evil.

When others did venture into the future-spaceships-aliens genre in the wake of *TNG*'s success (significantly only after Roddenberry's death in 1991), they were careful to distance themselves from this Trek paradigm. Some portrayed any Earth-centric interstellar or intergalactic alliance as corrupt and totalitarian, as had precursor *Blake's 7*, with its villainous Federation, whose name was clearly no accident. Some focused on ragtag crews of small ships just trying to survive. Some eliminated aliens from the future. Some were set on contemporary Earth and brought the aliens and spaceships to us from elsewhere. Some chronicled the fall of great alliances like Trek's Federation. None, except *Babylon 5*, advanced the concept of a benevolent, multi-species alliance of the future, which deserved the loyalty of the protagonists. And that alliance formed in *Babylon 5* only after the human protagonists staged a mutiny against a corrupt and totalitarian "EarthGov."

While these moves may have been inspired by a desire to get out of the way of the Trek franchise's might, their cumulative effect was to make the franchise look like the outlier. Getting stuck in a paradigm that had worked so well up through 1994 would doom *Enterprise* a decade later. This was one way in which the franchise's former status as innovator in science fiction television was lost, and it began to look anachronistic and out of step with what a still later generation of science fiction television viewers would come to expect. However, we cannot discount extratextual factors. Before looking at changes in the expected themes, characters and narrative structures treasured by genre fans, I want to examine how the franchise became unable to respond to rapid changes in the economic models for producing science fiction television and how its creative personnel lost sight of how to function as a cult phenomenon in the new world of Internet fandom.

The Colonization of Uninhabited Broadcast Space

Paramount should have panicked about the franchise's durability much earlier. Every season after 1992–93 saw the yearly average household rating of the highest rated Trek series decline from that of the year before. *DS9*'s first season averaged an 11.5, its seventh 4.4. *Voyager* began at 8 and ended at 3.4. Yet so many major changes were going on in broadcast television "space" that it is hard to determine whether these changes, rather than a falling off in the core audience for Trek, are to blame for the ratings decline.

Shortly after *TNG* debuted, the new FOX broadcast network premiered its first prime time shows on a series of affiliates put together from owner Rupert Murdoch's purchase of six Metromedia stations in major U.S. markets and a coalition of 90 independent stations. Although air time booked on formerly independent stations reduced potential slots for airing first-run syndicated programs, *TNG* did not lose markets. However, in 1993, Murdoch's News Corp. acquired many more groups of affiliates and in 1994 won broadcast rights to NFL football. At the beginning of 1995 rival studios Warner Bros. and Paramount launched their two networks. With programming from three new networks crowding the broadcast airways, overall viewership for original syndicated programs began sinking rapidly as they were either dropped by independents now become affiliates of the emerging networks or pushed into time slots when few viewers were watching.

The 1993–94 season also saw the premiere on FOX of *The X-Files,* which would run for nine seasons, often in the top 20 of the Nielsen ratings, demonstrating that a cult program about the existence of extraterrestrial life (among other monstrous and supernatural phenomena) could attain mainstream broadcast success. Sara Gwenllian-Jones and Roberta Pearson (2004: xv–xvi) observe that this success "ensured that from the early 1990s onward cult television has become an industry in and of itself," with producers seeking "to win not just large audiences but large *avid* audiences—audiences that will not only treat the series as 'appointment viewing' but also become consumers of a full range of officially produced merchandise."

That Viacom and Paramount wanted the Trek franchise, based on "the ur-cult television show" (Gwenllian-Jones and Pearson, 2004: xiv), to anchor the new UPN network made perfect sense, and the success of *The X-Files* proved that an upstart network could gain a niche audience through the use of cult programming. Leaving *DS9* to its own devices in syndication, the studio concentrated on the newest spin-off, *Star Trek: Voyager,* to achieve the status of broadcast network hit that had eluded all previous entries in the franchise. *Voyager* did regularly top the UPN ratings, but that wasn't saying too much. The network struggled to acquire and retain primary affiliates and by the time *Voyager* concluded still did not reach 15 percent of households. As a result, *Voyager* lagged behind *DS9* every season the two were on the air simultaneously (1994–1995 through 1998–99). *Voyager*'s yearly average was slightly ahead of that of its sister show during its premiere season, but even then its lowest rated first-run episodes fell to levels below those of *DS9* (see Henderson, 2005). Indeed, first-run syndication proved just as viable as UPN or the WB network well into the nineties.

Furthermore, the *X-Files* phenomenon did not prove replicable for any network. FOX itself launched countless genre shows without coming close to the combination of cult devotion and ratings-induced longevity. The other network cult sensation of the 1990s, *Buffy the Vampire Slayer*, which debuted in the spring of 1997, rarely rose above a 4.0 rating or beyond four million viewers for most of its run on the WB and then UPN, although it is the only other network genre show to run the seven or more seasons achieved by *X-Files* and *Voyager*. Nevertheless, genre shows multiplied in the decade following *X-Files*' debut, including other "space operas" like Trek; their producers simply accepted that "genre" was usually a niche market and so sought out venues and budget-cutting schemes that would make a small but devoted cult following sufficient to keep their shows profitable.

Throughout the rest of the 1990s, first-run syndication remained a viable venue, but not for programs filmed at the big Hollywood studios. While StudiosUSA chose New Zealand as the location for the popular *Hercules: The Legendary Journeys* and its feminist-chic spin-off *Xena: Warrior Princess*, other shows like *Relic Hunter, Earth: Final Conflict, Beastmaster, Andromeda*, and *Mutant X* followed *Highlander* and the early seasons of *X-Files* to film in Canada. Vancouver especially became the location headquarters for genre programming and continues to be, with many network and cable channels filming shows there. By going offshore, production companies generally received subsidies from the local governments, escaped high union labor costs, and cast all but their starring roles with lower-salaried indigenous performers.

When the bottom started to drop out of first-run syndication in the 2000s, niche market shows also found a place on many basic cable channels, which began to supplement their reruns and movies with a limited amount of original programming. The launch of the Sci-Fi Channel in 1992 was especially propitious, although it did not originate any breakthrough cult hits until it coproduced *Farscape* in 1999. A cable channel would sometimes pick up the last year of new episodes for a series in financial straits in return for broadcast rights to the other seasons. TNT did this for *Babylon 5* in 1998 and Sci-Fi made a similar arrangement with *Andromeda* in 2004.

The canniest creators and marketers of a science fiction series in the last decade are the creative team behind *Stargate SG-1,* produced by MGM and first aired on premium cable channel Showtime beginning in 1997. While it didn't have the franchise recognition of a new Trek series, there was a pre-sold identity for science fiction aficionados, since it was based on a 1994 film that introduced the broad parameters of its universe. To maximize an audience for the show and its universe, MGM syndicated it to broadcast affiliates on a one-season delay. When Showtime canceled the series after five seasons, the Sci-Fi Channel picked up a sixth (and supposedly final) season. *Stargate* began earning some of the highest ratings of any Sci-Fi series and more seasons were ordered, as well as a spin-off, *Stargate: Atlantis.* Currently in its tenth season, *Stargate SG-1* has surpassed *The X-Files* as the longest-running science fiction series on U.S. television.

The paradox of doing space-based science fiction for the last several decades is that it has bigger budget requirements than the standard cop or lawyer show and yet appeals to a much smaller segment of the audience. *Stargate*'s producers were able to control the costs inherent in doing a science fiction show in several ways. They chose to film in Vancouver and used a predominantly Canadian cast except for 1980s U.S. television icon Richard Dean Anderson in the lead role of Jack O'Neill. Although CGI (computer-generated imagery) aliens and spaceships and space battles were used when desired, the series' mythology allowed for human actors without prosthetics to play the parts of the chief enemy, the Goa'uld (who parasitically control human hosts from inside), and the inhabitants of most of the planets visited by the SG-1 team, since the "Ancients" who created the stargate system were human ancestors indistinguishable in appearance from their distant progeny and the populations of the gated worlds were comprised of human laborers sent to them millennia later by the Goa'uld.

By July 26, 2003, with *Enterprise* faltering, a *TV Guide* cover was ready to proclaim "Forget Trek! *Stargate SG-1* is now sci-fi's biggest hit!" The article it headlined asserted that "*Star Trek* is so five minutes ago," attributing *Stargate*'s wider appeal to the fact that "people don't feel like they have to be an ubergeek to enjoy *Stargate*" and the show "isn't about some futuristic society. It's about people who are pretty similar to the people watching. It's really just about a bunch of schmoes" (21). The article omits to mention that *Enterprise* had concluded its current season with a 2.89 household rating while *Stargate*'s was about 1.7.

Yet that absolute comparison doesn't negate the thrust of the *TV Guide* piece. *Stargate* had found a formula for success and profitability on a niche cable channel that the current installment in the Trek franchise could not replicate in the network broadcast television market. Realistically, there was no way that the Trek franchise was going to pull up stakes and go to Vancouver. Various forms of televised and feature film Trek had been ensconced on several soundstages of the Paramount lot for nearly two decades. Skilled Hollywood technicians had given the franchise its sleek look, many of them onboard for several five-year missions. It inhabited a large galaxy full of advanced civilizations, space battles, and aliens wearing prosthetic makeup. A certain economy of scale accrued with the collections of costumes, wigs, models, library effects, and set pieces that could be recycled from one Trek manifestation to the other, but this in no way allowed for a series to come in on the kind of budget necessary for the license fees and advertising revenues a cable station could reasonably afford. As Rick Berman remarked when the cancellation of *Enterprise* was announced, "One of the greatest things that Paramount has offered us over the last 18 years has been the kinds of budgets that have allowed us to produce the show at the quality that it's been done.... The budget that all of our Star Trek series have demanded are the kinds of budgets that would be prohibitive on cable" ("Enterprise").

Trying to Escape a Decaying Orbit

The dilemma facing the creative team as it developed the fifth series, then, was to come up with a premise that could halt the yearly erosion of ratings so as to keep them at the minimum expected of a UPN show receiving renewal. An added pressure had materialized in 1999, when Viacom and CBS television merged. By the time the restructuring of the new company was complete, CBS's Les Moonves had final say on programming for both CBS and UPN, and he was looking to make UPN competitive, with no particular inclination to give Berman a pass on an underperforming series simply because of Paramount's vested interest in the Trek franchise. In looking for the audience to assure a turnaround, Berman and show-runner Brannon Braga needed to court three separate if sometimes overlapping constituencies, which the above discourse of the *Stargate* producers articulated.

The first category would include the "regular schmoes." These would be frequent television viewers not averse to watching a science fiction show, without being the types of dedicated SF buffs who pore over DVDs, post on the internet, attend fan conventions, or generate creative products such as costumes, fan fiction, models and blueprints, role-playing games or encyclopedias and guides based on a series' texts and characters. However, "space operas" like Trek have always proven a hard sell to these more general audiences, because they take place in a universe completely divorced from present day reality.

Gwenllian-Jones' (2004: 90) concept of the "portal format" illustrates the way in which many genre shows create a general audience appeal because they manage to "maintain a stable, contained setting at one level of reality but furnish within it some mechanism that opens the localized world onto an alternate reality." She cites *The X-Files* and *Buffy* as horror prototypes, *Beauty and the Beast* as fantasy, and *Stargate* as science fiction, with its wormholes providing a literal portal to alien worlds. While the alternate realities may differ, all these series position the localized world as a present or near-future Earth, inhabited by human beings. Logic would dictate that the success with the "regular" viewer of these series, and others like USA Network's *The 4400* or the current surprise ABC hit *Lost*, has to do with providing a known and realistic base into which the alien and fantastic enter, to interact with people very much like ourselves.

If we eliminate the Trek series, the number of multi-season genre shows that did not bring the extraterrestrials or alien technology or demons or creatures of myth into the viewer's present day world are very few. On network broadcast television, there have been none in the last twenty years, and even on cable and in syndication, where much smaller viewership is required; the few Trek-like space operas have in fact strong Trek pedigrees. *Gene Roddenberry's Andromeda* was based on ideas from the Trek creator and developed by former *DS9* writer Robert Hewitt Wolfe. The new version of *Battlestar Galactica* has former *TNG* and *DS9* writer Ron Moore as cocreator and show-runner. And J. Michael Straczynski, the singular vision behind *Babylon 5*, is a strong admirer of the original *Star Trek*.[4]

The Trek series' exceptionalism in this regard no doubt had to do with the franchise itself. Elements of the Roddenberry universe and precepts saturate popular culture to the extent that a person who has never seen one episode has a vague idea of what a phaser, warp drive, and Klingons are. Although often not flattering, the Trek name brands a kind of science fiction television and a type of cult television fan in the same way that "kleenex" has come to signify all facial tissues and "xerox" all photocopies.

After the end of *TNG*, each new Trek series could draw an impressive number of initial viewers. *DS9*'s premiere reached 19 percent of households, *Voyager*'s 13 percent *Enterprise*'s numbers were down to 7 percent, but even those 13 million viewers would certainly have kept UPN happy if they had stayed with the show. However, in its latter seasons *Enterprise* attracted only two million viewers. Increasingly the Trek brand name could beam the general audience to the Trek universe for a visit, but could not prevail upon them to remain in orbit.

Thus the franchise post–*TNG* depended increasingly on two other categories of viewers: devoted Trekkers who had followed *Star Trek* and/or *TNG* obsessively and the "ubergeeks" who made up the core cult SF audience and populated the growing Internet fan culture. To the nonfan, it might appear that the "ubergeek" and the Trekker were synonymous with one another, or a subset of one another, but by the mid–1990s this was not really the case. Cult bona fides proceed from attachment to a text that only the discerning aficionado can appreciate. As Mark Jancovich and Nathan Hunt (2004: 28) observe: "The exclusivity that gives value to a cult text may not be sustainable. As others come to appreciate the text, fans must either find new forms of exclusive appreciation or reject or relegate the text to the passé." Simply by being the "franchise" and the "ur-cult," its catchphrases a part of common parlance, Trek was likely to be disdained by the true cultist.

Moreover, unlike the cult writer-producer always conceived of as the fans' hero going up against the "suits," Rick Berman and Brannon Braga were increasingly demonized by Trekkers, who blamed them for the franchise's decline. Even the mainstream press had picked up on the hostility by the time *Enterprise* ended. Dave Itzkoff's (2005) *New York Times* article reports that "Mr. Berman remained remarkably sanguine for a man so frequently threatened with bodily harm on Internet message boards," and Rob Salem's piece in the *Toronto Star* quoted Berman laughing about "Brannon flying out of town ... the fans are chasing him with scythes."

Another difficulty for the post–*TNG* series had to do with a mismatch between the Roddenberry vision and narrative paradigm of the earlier shows and the attributes that attached to cult favorites of the 1990s. Using *X-Files* to exemplify the ur-cult of the digital age, Gwenllian-Jones and Pearson (2004: xv) cite as one "of the strategies that make a television series 'cult'" an "ongoing story arc or mythology." Another is the incorporation of a "dark subject matter [that] resonated with the wider zeitgeist of paranoia that followed the end of the Cold War and the countdown to the new millennium." Trek's self-contained episodes and utopian vision didn't track with this zeitgeist. Neither did its unwavering faith in a huge and benevolent galactic government. As an Internet poster recently remarked on the way to praising the libertarian philosophy of the cult favorite *Firefly*: "At its best, science fiction advocates liberty. While *Star Trek* lamentably supported a 'Federation knows best' mentality, other works like *Star Wars* and Robert Heinlein's novels have promoted the dissolution of central rule and the triumph of the individual. For the science fiction writer, space means one thing: freedom" (Hinson, 2005).

The reception of *Deep Space Nine* illustrates the tension between appeal to 1990s cult audiences and to the veteran Trek faithful. Created by Rick Berman and Michael Piller after Roddenberry's death, it abandoned the boldly going starship for a precariously sitting postcolonial space station on which the Federation detachment served like NATO or UN peacekeepers, the minority among a large cast of non-Federation aliens. Ira Steven Behr, who was the show-runner after the second season and the only writer-producer to work on the series from beginning to end, made no bones about trying to debunk certain aspects of the Trek universe:

What I resented a lot of the time in both series, *TOS* [The Original Series] (which I was a huge fan of) and *TNG*, was their "having their cake and eat it too" attitude. When they needed to blow up ships, they blew up ships. But there was no repercussions to it, usually, not really. No one sweated, it was like a tea party in the Hamptons. People were getting killed, there was no sweat, there was no fear, there were no repercussions, and I don't care whether they're people on a ship and you don't see them and you don't care—bad, bad, bad, no good, bad, bad, image!—[and] bad storytelling. We wanted to say, "hey, people in this world that we live in can't get along in this little tiny planet and we have more in common than Cardassians and humans and *we* can't get along." So why do we believe in our absolute arrogance that in the future we can have these disparate races and they will all find ways to avoid war, and we will find ways to avoid war especially with our Federation way of sucking people into our Federation [Krutzler, 2004].

Yet, to remain a part of the franchise, *DS9* could not destroy the Federation or show its darker impulses winning out over its more enlightened ones. David Weddle, who got his first job writing for television on that show, notes: "'Deep Space Nine' was the best of the modern 'Star Treks.' Ira and Ron [Moore] and the rest of the staff pushed the envelope and fought against the aesthetic constrictions that slowly strangled the franchise, and came up with a truly remarkable and unique show" (Ryan, 2005a). He enumerates some of those "moribund aesthetics" when he describes how the new *Battlestar Galactica*, for which he currently writes, "shed the antiseptic freeze-dried dialogue of 'Star Trek,' the hokey rubber-headed aliens and juvenile melodrama of space anomalies and time warps and made it a show about people grappling with the very real problems of survival, faith, or the loss of faith, love or the inability to sustain love" (Ryan, 2005a).

Yet it didn't help *DS9*'s appeal to the cult audience that *the* cult space opera of the 1990s was airing simultaneously with its second through sixth seasons. *Babylon 5*, also set on a space station, was a serialized "novel for television." Small, apparently insignificant details planted in early episodes would come to have monumental significance years later.[5] As Petra Kuppers (2004: 47) explains, "accounts of the birth of *B5* cast the small guy with the big vision against the giant corporations, their cynical vision of fandom, and the evils of modern television. Eventually *B5* emerges from the struggle between [creator] JM[ichael]S[traczynski] and the industry, seemingly subverting 'normal' science fiction television with its original and demanding narrative structure, the five-year arc."

Kuppers acknowledges that the first creator of a cult television show to narrativize himself in this fashion was Trek's own visionary, Gene Roddenberry. But the series Berman and Piller created (*DS9*, *Voyager*) had no way to exploit such a "David and Goliath" myth. Despite declining ratings, these shows each ran seven seasons without any apparent danger of cancellation and had lavish budgets that the famously frugal *B5* producers could only dream of. Moreover, JMS had pitched the *B5* concept to Paramount before selling it to Warner Bros. and he implied in numerous Internet postings that *DS9* was a rip-off of his ideas. Thus the efforts of Behr and his writers to create a radical departure from the previous Trek model got little credit among much of fandom, who instead (erroneously) saw the franchise as incapable of doing anything original unless it stole the work of others.

Unable to achieve status by cult standards, *DS9* also had its difficulties with the dedicated Trek fans, who felt that its emphasis on war, terrorism, and genocide betrayed the optimistic Roddenberry vision. Rick Berman shared these concerns, and the *DS9* writers in interviews consistently speak of being advised to pull back, not take risks, and play it safe. The only Trek series never to air for a full season without new episodes of another franchise show in competition, its actors and writers referred to it as the "bastard stepchild of the franchise" and "the neurotic's *Star Trek*." "Niners," the minority of Trekkers who prefer the series over the other "modern Treks," view themselves as an authentic cult within Trek fandom, showing just how decisively the series fell between the two stools of general cult fans and Trek fans.

As different as *DS9* might have been from *TNG*, both of them, as well as the original series, had a consistency of approach and vision. A viewer knew what principles the characters operated on and what their missions were, both as dictated by Starfleet and as impacted by external events. *Voyager*'s premise provided the long-term arc of an odyssey to return home, while in the short term it dictated an uneasy alliance between Maquis and Starfleet crew members, terrifying isolation from all support customarily provided by the Federation, and a continual battle against scarcity, whether of power, food or spare parts. And yet, beginning with the Maquis crew donning Starfleet uniforms by the end of the pilot episode, *Voyager* soon stopped being about any of these things. Murmurings about these inconsistencies erupted among fan groups when *TNG* and *DS9* writer Ron Moore joined the *Voyager* staff in 1999, then quit a month later, after locking horns with his former friend and writing partner, Brannon Braga, *Voyager*'s show-runner since the fourth season. Bitter and angry, Moore gave a lengthy interview/diatribe to an online journalist, detailing everything that was, in his opinion, wrong with the series: "*Voyager* had a great premise and a great pilot, and promptly fell back on the familiar and went in a direction that didn't really say, 'wow, look at this, this is not like *Next Generation* at all, this is something completely different.' I think ultimately it became *Next Generation* by another name" (Kosh, 2003). Moore's anger against Braga has moderated somewhat during the intervening years, and like other former Trek writers and actors he now points the finger at Berman: "I think [Brannon] got conservative and safe in what he thought the show could be as a result of what Rick kept saying the show was" (Ken P., 2003).

As *Voyager* ended its run and plans for the fifth series were being developed, the creative team was at a crisis point. Michael Piller had served as a consultant for *Voyager* only in its later seasons, and he had no part in creating or writing for *Enterprise*. During his time running the *TNG* writing staff, he had developed young talent and recruited more experienced writers who had spent many years working for the Trek franchise. *DS9* and *Voyager* had the advantage of several experienced *TNG* staff coming over to their shows. Ira Behr on *DS9* had also given breaks to freelancers such as Michael Taylor and Bryan Fuller, who later joined the *Voyager* staff. But when *Voyager* ended, only Brannon Braga of the *TNG* veterans remained with the franchise. This is hardly surprising, given Moore's assessment of the "writers' room" on *Voyager:* "The politics of the show were such that the egos of the people in charge of the series were threatened by the people who worked for them. To be blunt, Bryan Fuller and Mike Taylor were treated very shabbily, and it pissed me off. They took a lot of crap, and the only reason it was done was to keep the guys on the top of the pyramid feeling good about themselves" (Kosh, 2003).

Berman had not served primarily as a writer on any of the four Trek series he executive produced. He had received teleplay credit for only two Trek scripts other than the pilot episodes for *DS9* and *Voyager*, cowritten, respectively, with Piller and with Piller and Jeri Taylor, but he now became show-runner Braga's writing partner. During the first season, as they tried to introduce new staff to the conventions of writing for Trek, Berman and Braga had teleplay or story credits on the first seven episodes and wrote stories and teleplays for 18 of 26 season one *Enterprise* episodes. In these episodes, as in the overall concept for *Enterprise*, internal contradictions were painfully evident.

Creating a Brand Old Enterprise

The fifth Trek series abandoned the twenty-fourth century, the time period of all the spin-offs, to turn back the clock: set in the mid–twenty-second century, it took place aboard the first Starfleet (but not Federation) deep-space-faring vessel, named, like those in *Star Trek* and *TNG*, *Enterprise*. Although there was some shuffling of genders and job descriptions, its ensemble duplicated that of the original series. In casting *Quantum Leap*'s Scott Bakula as Captain Jonathan Archer, Berman and Braga were emulating the more buzz-producing space operas of the previous decade. All their commanders had been white American males, and several (Bruce Boxleitner, Richard Dean Anderson, Kevin Sorbo) had previously starred in U.S. television series. William Shatner's Kirk had also fit this paradigm, but the previous Trek spin-offs had (commendably) put an Englishman (playing a Frenchman), an African American and a woman in the captain's chair.

By doing a prequel series, Berman and Braga would seem to have been appealing to the core Trekker fanbase. Only these viewers, one imagines, would want to connect the dots between Zefram Cochrane's first contact with the Vulcans after his invention of warp drive and the full-fledged Federation fleet to which all the crews of the first four Trek series belonged. For the more casual viewer, knowing what happened subsequently in the Trek universe would cut down on any suspense as to whether Archer at the end of *Enterprise*'s plot arc would succeed in bringing about the creation of the Federation in the face of Romulan aggression.

Other elements present in the two-hour pilot, "Broken Bow," seemed to indicate, however, that the appeal was specifically to non-Trekkers. The opening credits revealed that the series had eliminated *Star Trek* from its title. It was merely called *Enterprise*. As fan Haasim Mahanaim noted, "The show premiered sans-prefix due to the unhip and uncool connotations of those two words, only to then later be added to attract loyal fangeeks in an effort to bolster flagging ratings—that is after premiering with 13 million viewers that eroded to around 2 million within a year." In place of the standard orchestral score as the ship whooshed through a starfield, there was a montage of exploration, from the *Kon-Tiki* rafters to Cochrane's first vessel, as the lyrics to the pop song "Where My Heart Will Take Me" played over the images (see chapter 1).

There were also elements of the premise that went against Trekkers' perceptions, even if they could technically be reconciled with the other series. For one thing, the primary antagonists were the Vulcans, responsible for holding back humans' drive to explore space because they believed them too immature and emotional to be let loose on the galaxy. It is true that all Trek's Vulcans displayed a certain disdain for human emotionalism and an arrogance about their own culture, but the species was also portrayed as honorable, truthful, pacifist and forward-looking. *Enterprise*'s Vulcan hierarchy, on the other hand, engaged in deception, covert operations, state prejudice against minorities and other quasi-totalitarian practices. They expressed outright bigotry toward humans, complaining especially of their foul body odors. Apparent revisionist history about first human contact with the Klingons, Ferengi, and Borg also disturbed the fanbase. Even one of the cast, Jolene Blalock (T'Pol) "a lifelong 'Star Trek' fan ... said she was dismayed by early 'Enterprise' scripts that seemed to ignore basic tenets of the franchise's chronology, and that offered revealing costumes instead of character development. 'The audience isn't stupid,' she said" (Itzkoff, 2005). Such complaints prompted Braga angrily to label such fans as "continuity pornographers."

Moreover, if the premise of a starship whose primary mission was exploration, boldly going once more to places no human had ever been, seemed a return to the narrative mode that *Voyager* eventually adopted despite its conflict with that show's original premise, continued conflicts of this sort were also inherent with *Enterprise*. The vessel began its maiden voyage ahead of schedule because of events that were part of a "temporal cold war," a continuous battle among a number of powers from the thirty-first century who possessed the technology to travel through time. This was in itself an intriguing concept, but the epistemology of a universe constantly under revision by combatants from the future would have destabilized everything known about the Trek mythology and led to a fictional reality in perpetual flux, like the constant quantum slippages portrayed in Braga's *TNG* episode "Parallels" (1993). As with the desperate isolation of *Voyager*, this situation seemed unlikely to spawn the leisurely encounters with various aliens and stellar phenomena that both *Voyager* and *Enterprise* spent most of their time attending to.

When this mixed-bag approach led to the steep ratings decline in the second season, the producers stuck first to one half of the premise, and then turned back to the other. *Enterprise*'s third season was an attempt to emulate the paranoid, serialized format of 1990s cult hits. For the whole season, the crew raced to discover and prevent the utilization of a super-weapon to be deployed by the Xindi in order to obliterate Earth before, they mistakenly believed, Earth would launch a preemptive strike against them. The 9/11-influenced plot had promise, but it spent too much time dealing with the dreaded spatial anomalies in an area called the Delphic Expanse. When it turned out that time-traveling aliens from another dimension were manipulating the Xindi to get rid of Archer and the potential Federation so that they could turn the entire galaxy into this sort of environment in order to invade, the temporal cold war finally had some usefulness, but the fact that such a near-cataclysmic event had never been mentioned in any of the previous series distanced viewers from the conflict. At the very least the Suliban, Archer's chief temporal cold war antagonists in his own time frame, should have been the source of the threat, rather than the unknown Xindi.

Having nearly been cancelled after trying this approach, *Enterprise* for its fourth season became the sort of "inside baseball" prequel fans had expected at the outset: "When it was time to start the writing for Season 4, we were mostly gearing episodes towards people who knew the 'Star Trek' universe. We were not worried so much about people who didn't. They were gone anyway," said Manny Coto, a self-described Trekkie who was brought in to run the writing staff (Itzkoff, 2005). It was too late for the series to find its footing, however. New management at Viacom and UPN had reenvisioned the network's desired demographic as young women; it no longer made sense to anchor it with an older, male-skewing space opera. Having presided over a failing enterprise for more than a decade, Berman and Braga wrote a series finale for *Enterprise* that revealed the failures of imagination and frustrations that had informed the entire series. Throughout the run of *Enterprise*, many episodes dealt with members of the crew trapped, marooned, imprisoned, held hostage, and often beaten or otherwise brutalized. This narrative pattern suggests that Berman and Braga may have themselves felt constrained by all the expectations inherent in doing a Trek show, especially those of the dedicated fans. In that final episode, "These Are the Voyages..." (2005), the fulfillment of the *Enterprise* crew's series-long plot arc, the signing of the Federation Charter, is depicted in the form of an interactive holodeck program used by *TNG*'s Will Riker to help him resolve a dilemma presented in that series' seventh season episode, "The Pegasus" (1994). Jonathan Frakes and Marina Sirtis guest starred and had the episode's final scene, cutting off Jonathan Archer's important, Federation-founding speech. It was as if Berman and Braga could not accept having created the only Trek spin-off to be cancelled and thus relegated it to the status of a holodeck fantasy in the franchise's one unequivocal success, *TNG*.[6] If anyone was suffering from franchise fatigue, it was perhaps not so much the audience as the last of the *TNG* producers left on board.

Franchise Obsolescence?

The history of the post–*TNG* Trek series outlined above suggests that *Enterprise* failed not because of franchise fatigue—something that can be cured by taking a few years off before launching another series—but by franchise obsolescence. Jan Johnson-Smith in her book *American Science Fiction TV* entitles the chapter on modern Trek "Yesterday's Enterprise," with the emphasis on yesterday. She concludes her analysis of *Enterprise*: "*Enterprise* shows space as the final frontier, but it relies upon anachronistic 'old frontier' ideologies in much of its approach, a sad comment upon *Star Trek*'s overall ideological direction" (2005: 117). Most of the punditry about the failure of the franchise has also stressed the need for Trek to drop those elements that don't coincide with the current indicators of cult SF television success. When *Enterprise*'s ratings took their precipitous slide during the second season, *TV Guide* offered a number of suggestions on "How to Fix Trek." These included "Make it Ominous"; "Make it More Real"; "Open Fire and Close Those Pie Holes"; and "Get Us on the Edge of Our Seats" (Nollinger, 2003: 19). None of these prescriptions calls for the stylized and cerebral utopianism of the *Enterprise* under Jean-Luc Picard. At the July 2005 San Diego Comic Con, a giant and influential meeting of media producers and fans, "A panel of supposed *Star Trek* experts concluded on Thursday that *Star Trek: Enterprise* failed because it wasn't enough like the new *Battlestar Galactica*, which was labeled more realistic and relevant than the newest *Star Trek* series." As has become standard with critics of the franchise, the term "spatial anomalies" was used to sum up all that is wrong with Trek's storytelling, and there was no lack of those in *TNG* either (Michelle, 2005). Future viability for the franchise, according to such thinking, is for *Star Trek* to stop being *Star Trek*.

The only way to tell for certain whether the Trek paradigm has become irrevocably obsolete is for someone with fresh ideas and enthusiasm for that universe to create the best possible new series that hews to the major principles of the franchise and is realistic about matching budget and audience projections to the expectations of the network on which it is broadcast. If such a series cannot succeed, it is time to end the franchise once and for all. No brand name lasts if the products that carry its label are of inferior quality, are not profitable to manufacture, or are no longer of use to potential consumers.

But it is also premature to declare the franchise dead on the basis of the eleven seasons of Trek on UPN, during which Berman appeared willing to churn out mediocre product upon which to slap the Trek brand for the sake of profit. Mahanaim (2005) writes, "I find it interesting how the word franchise is often used to describe *Star Trek*; it conjures up images of fast food—bland, barely palletable [*sic*] and often consumed due to a lack of options." That's not what Trek started out to be, and it is worth the attempt to revive Trek for the twenty-first century with a conviction that its essential components are neither obsolescent nor fatiguing, but timeless. As Maggie Ryan (2005b) of the *Chicago Tribune* wrote in her valedictory:

> Most modern televised sci-fi is edgier, sexier, more angst-ridden than "Trek" ever was. Which is only appropriate, considering the edgy, sex-obsessed, angst-ridden age we live in. Still, though fans were often frustrated with the various series' stodginess—not to mention their dependence on "holodeck malfunction" plots and aliens with bumpy foreheads—"Trek" stood for something. Perhaps the idea of taking a mixed group of humans, androids and aliens, putting them on a ship and having them attempt to spread the concepts of fair play and justice across the galaxy is hopelessly square, but so what? If that's square, that's fine with us. To the "Trek"-ian mandate—to "boldly go" into new realms of human endeavor while holding on to compassion, ideals and a commitment to freedom—we say, live long and prosper.

Notes

1. There are various short-form conventions for the titles of the five *Star Trek* series. I have chosen to use *Star Trek* only for the original series and to refer hereafter to *Star Trek: The Next Generation* as *TNG*, *Star Trek: Deep Space Nine* as *DS9*, *Star Trek: Voyager* as *Voyager* and *Star Trek: Enterprise* as *Enterprise*. I use the nonitalicized "Trek" to refer to the fictional universe which comprises the franchise and its many manifestations.

2. Comparing ratings from different years or among different distribution formats

can be misleading. As the audience grows, one Nielsen household ratings point can represent very different numbers of actual viewers. A syndicated show earning a 5.0 in 1990 could actually have fewer people watching than a big three network show earning a 3.5 in 2005. But the household rating number is consistent in one respect: it measures the percentage of households that tune into a show from among all the households that can receive it. Over the long history of the Trek franchise, the household rating provides a stable index of the *proportion* of the audience that watched the various series.

My ratings figures come from a variety of Internet articles and Websites: Fuller, 1999; Henderson, 2005; *Voyagerview* and Enterprise Nielsen Ratings.

3. *Genre* has become a term common in fan discourse to denote any printed or media text that falls into the category of science fiction/fantasy/horror.

4. Two exceptions to this paradigm are *Firefly* and *Farscape*. Both are space operas, but neither wholly follows the Trek model. *Firefly*, though set on terraformed planets and moons five hundred years in the future, with Earth abandoned, posits a universe devoid of aliens. *Farscape* is set in a far corner of the galaxy inhabited by some of the most exotic species Jim Henson's Creature Shop could create, but its protagonist is a contemporary American scientist who was transported there via a wormhole. This is the portal formula, except that the lone figure of audience identification drops in on the alien landscape, rather than the reverse.

5. The emergence of complete season sets of new and old television series on DVD, and their high sales figures, was another factor that led to the calculated creation of cult television series during the last decade.

6. Berman eventually imported *TNG* characters into every one of the succeeding series in hopes of regaining that show's lost viewers. The Klingon Worf was added to the regular cast of *DS9* in its fourth season, and Deanna Troi and Reg Barclay both became recurring characters during the final seasons of *Voyager*.

Works Cited

"Berman: Trek Needs a Rest." *SCI-FI Wire* (April 29 2005), available at http://www.scifi.com/sfw/issue419/news.html.

Engel, Joel. *Gene Roddenberry: The Myth and the Man Behind "Star Trek."* New York: Hyperion, 1994.

Enterprise Nielsen Ratings. available at http://www.ece.ucdavis.edu/~mvrojo/entratings.htm (accessed on July 15, 2005).

Fuller, Greg. "*Star Trek* Ratings History." *Trek Nation* (July 7, 1999), available at http://www.treknation.com/articles/ratings_history.shtml.

Gwenllian-Jones, Sara, and Roberta E. Pearson, eds. "Introduction." *Cult Television*. Minneapolis: University of Minnesota Press, 2004: ix–xx.

Gwenllian-Jones, Sara. "Virtual Reality and Cult Television." *Cult Television*. Edited by Sara Gwenllian-Jones and Roberta E. Pearson. Minneapolis: University of Minnesota Press, 2004: 83–98.

Henderson, David. "Re: [9-anon] Hey Jackie Bundy," and "Re: [9-anon] OT: further question re: Trek ratings [was: Re: Hey Jackie Bundy]" posted to listserv 9-anon@yahoogroups.com, March 5, 2005.

Hinson, Sarah T. "Freedom and *Firefly*." *Brainwash* (August 7, 2005), available at http://www.affbrainwash.com/archives/020132.php.

Itzkoff, Dave. "Its Long Trek Over, the Enterprise Pulls into Dry Dock." *New York Times*, May 1, 2005, section 2, p. 13.

Jancovich, Mark, and Nathan Hunt. "The Mainstream, Distinction, and Cult TV." *Cult Television*. Edited by Sara Gwenllian-Jones and Roberta E. Pearson. Minneapolis: University of Minnesota Press, 2004: 27–44.

Johnson-Smith, Jan. *American Science Fiction TV*. Middletown, CT: Wesleyan UP, 2005.

Kosh, Hypatia. "The Ron Moore Interview." Hypatia Kosh Web page, September 2003, available at http://hypatia.slashcity.org/trekshack/moore.html.

Krutzler, Steve. "Ira Steven Behr Reflects on the Legacy of *Deep Space Nine*." *TrekWeb Fea-*

tures (July 14, 2004), available at http://www.trekweb.com/stories.php?aid=
40f49602300c0.

Kuppers, Petra. "Quality Science Fiction: *Babylon 5*'s Metatextual Universe." *Cult Television.* Edited by Sara Gwenllian-Jones and Roberta E. Pearson. Minneapolis: University of Minnesota Press, 2004: 445–60.

Mahanaim, Hassim. "*Star Trek*: Failed Enterprise." *Kuro5hin* (May 9, 2005), available at
http://www.kuro5hin.org/story/2005/5/9/0045/76043.

Michelle. "Trek needs to be more like Galactica, Panel Says." *Trek Today* (July 15, 2005),
available at http://www.trektoday.com/news/150705_02.shtml.

Nollinger, Mark. "The Future of *Star Trek*." *TV Guide* (March 3, 2003): 17–20.

P., Ken. "An Interview with Ron Moore." IGNFilmForce (December 4, 2003), available at
http://www.filmforce.ign.com/articles/444/444306p1.html.

Rhodes, Joe. "Ace in the Wormhole." *TV Guide* (July 26-August 1, 2003): 18–21.

Ryan, Maureen. "'Battlestar Galactica' Exclusive !" *Chicago Tribune,* April 1, 2005a, available at http://www.chicagotribune.com/entertainment/chi-aprilblog,1,565884.
htmlstory?coll=chi-entertainment-hed.

_____. "Captain! We're losing power!: Saying goodbye (for now) to 'Star Trek.'" *Chicago
Tribune,* May 11, 2005b, available at http://www.chicagotribune.com/entertainment
/chi-mayblog,0,1931723.htmlstory?coll=chi-ed_opinion_bloggers-utl.

Salem, Rob. "Enterprise Limps Off to Oblivion." *Toronto Star,* May 9, 2005: 23.

SCI-FI Wire. "Enterprise Won't Be Shopped." February 5, 2005, available at http://www.
scifi.com/scifiwire2005/index.php?category=0&id=30331.

Voyagerview. "Voyager Ratings." available at http://www.sandiegometro.com/2001/mar/
career.html, as accessed on July 13, 2005.

PART II

THEMES

4

Crossing the Racial Frontier

Star Trek *and Mixed Heritage Identities*

WEI MING DARIOTIS

In this chapter, racial identity and imperialism in *Star Trek* will be explored from a perspective informed by Ethnic Studies, and more specifically by Mixed Heritage Studies.[1] Although one film, *Star Trek III: The Search for Spock* (1984), will be considered substantially, the main focus will be on three of the five *Star Trek* television series: The Original Series, *Voyager*, and *Deep Space Nine*. This analysis is concerned with mixed heritage[2] identity as a recurring and central trope in *Star Trek*, in particular as it is manifested in Spock, the mixed heritage character[3] without whom *Star Trek* would not have had the impact it has had; in Seven of Nine, the human woman who was trans-"racially" adopted by the Borg,[4] or the Borg who is transracially[5] adopted by humans; and in Odo, the shape-shifter who was "adopted"/assimilated into Bajoran culture. Finally, I briefly examine the dialogue around empire in *Star Trek*, for it is through imperialism and colonialism that people of mixed heritage are created in large numbers, and it is also in this context that the dialogue about mixed heritage identity becomes fraught with meaning about race and identity in the context of racial hierarchies. In *Star Trek*, these mixed heritage characters, set in the context of an intense debate over the nature of imperialism, allow us to address the central question of all science fictions: What is human?

Part I: Spock as the Embodiment of Infinite Diversity in Infinite Combinations (IDIC)

Created by Gene Roddenberry in 1964, *Star Trek* has from the beginning focused on issues of race and identity—and racial identity boundary transgression in the form of mixed heritage characters. The first pilot created by Roddenberry featured the mixed heritage Vulcan-human science officer, Mr. Spock, and the actress Majel Barrett (later Majel Barrett Roddenberry) as the brunette and highly intellectual first officer, Number One ("The Cage," 1964). Although NBC executives liked the basic premise of the show, they hated all of the details, particularly the "demonic" Mr. Spock and the too strong, too intellectual female Number One. The network demanded that the cast be changed and the pilot redone. Roddenberry, in order to keep the show alive, agreed to the network's demands, but, forced to choose between promoting something akin to a feminist agenda and promoting racial tolerance, insisted on keeping the character of Mr. Spock, whom he felt was integral to the meaning of the show. Gene Roddenberry remembers that "they particularly asked that Spock be dropped.... But I said I would not do a second pilot without Spock because I felt we had to have him" ("Great Birds of the Galaxy," 13). Spock is the ultimate symbol of Roddenberry's vision of racial harmony precisely because he is both human and alien; thus it is because of his mixed heritage that Spock functions as the moral heart of the series.

In her autobiography, *Beyond Uhura*, Nichelle Nichols (who played Communication Officer Uhura) explains Roddenberry's devotion to the idea of racial harmony when she quotes an interview that appeared in *The Humanist*. Roddenberry says, "*Star Trek* is more than just my political philosophy. It is my social philosophy, my racial philosophy, my overview on life and the human condition" (1994: 14). During Roddenberry's time as a Los Angeles police officer in the 1960s he saw firsthand the tensions that led to the Watts Riots of 1965. This racial strife inspired him to create a narrative vehicle for exploring racial harmony. In *Star Trek*, this idea of "racial harmony" was literally embodied by the racial diversity of the cast. However, in order to realize his message fully, Roddenberry could not simply rely on this racial diversity (which often functioned as tokenism at best and racial and ethnic stereotyping at worst). Roddenberry had to have an alien-human mixed heritage character as part of the crew to challenge audiences' perceptions of what it means to be "human" (like us) and to be "alien" (different). Spock's quest to discover his true identity in the transgressive space between being human and Vulcan is what makes *Star Trek* an important piece of the public dialogue about race, both in the United States and internationally.

Infinite Diversity within a Finite Space

Nichelle Nichols attributes her comfort with Roddenberry's intensity of vision to the fact that she grew up "in a racially integrated family that was shaped over three generations by the same so-called 'futuristic' concepts of racial equality and reason that Gene put forth in *Star Trek*." Even more to the point, Nichols says that, "[w]hen I first told Gene my family's story, he listened with rapt attention. I know he felt they were his kindred spirits, too" (1994: 14–15). Her grandparents had risked everything to be together, and their story provides a meaningful context for Nichols' interpretation of Roddenberry's vision. Nichols explains the rationale for the antimiscegenation laws that prevented her grandparents from legally marrying:

> Slavery had been abolished—at least legally—for over a decade, yet the power of that unsavory institution endured on both sides of the Mason-Dixon Line. The notion of a white man proclaiming his love for a Black woman was unthinkable.
>
> One reason why is that any child born to parents of the different races was automatically regarded as Black. To acknowledge the offspring of such a union in those days—which was usually by rape—would be to grant equality to a child considered Black. The white mother of a Black child lost her social "value," and a Black woman had none to begin with. To elevate either woman by marrying her and therefore recognizing her children as anything other than Black, and thereby inferior, threatened the very foundation of American society, North or South [21].

Thus Nichols targets the rule of hypodescent[6] and antimiscegenation[7] laws as the forces used to "stabilize" American society by prescribing racial boundaries. Nichelle Nichols and William Shatner transgressed these boundaries in their groundbreaking, first-ever televised kiss between a black woman and a white man seen in "Plato's Stepchildren" (1968). The threat of this kiss to the social establishment of the time is not to be underestimated. That the kiss had to be staged as an unwilling act—forced upon Captain Kirk and Lt. Uhura by their alien captors—demonstrates the transgressive power of that kiss. It is through interracial sexual transgression, more than through any other interracial relationship, that the boundaries of race in the U.S. are most challenged because of the potential for the boundaries of racialized groupings to be blurred by children of mixed heritage. It was fear of the transgressive power of interracial sexuality that kept African American children in the South and Asian American children in California in segregated schools. If the children played together, it was feared, they might become too familiarized with each other and not remember to maintain the boundaries.

The Starship *Enterprise*, and by extension, the Federation, are meant to suggest a utopic society free of warfare and strife, with all of the members of the society leading fulfilling lives without the onus of racial discrimination. However, every incarnation of *Star Trek* has reproduced racial stereotypes (a notable example is the anti-Semitism apparent in the representation of the Ferengi). And, in reality, the original *Star Trek* exhibited clear-cut racism and sexism: the three lead actors were European American men and people of color and women were relegated to subordinate roles.[8] Furthermore, the racial strife that was banned from the bridge of the *Enterprise* (not always successfully), often reemerged embodied as "aliens" who were cast in the mold of the racial "Other."

This is particularly true of the Vulcans, who were clearly constructed from Orientalist stereotypes, outfitted with mysterious mental powers and mystical philosophies and rituals, encased in stylized Orientalia.[9] Because the Vulcan we know is the half-human, half Vulcan Mr. Spock, a template is created whereby aliens are represented by mixed heritage characters whose human side represents whiteness and whose alien side represents the ethnic Other. Spock's mixed human-alien heritage provides Roddenberry an opportunity to express the Vulcan philosophy that embodies the appeal of *Star Trek*: "Infinite Diversity in Infinite Combinations," or IDIC. In this sense, Mr. Spock is crucial because, in our (or Nurse Chapel's) unrequited "love" for him, we welcome the alien within us, and thus, hopefully, the "aliens" within the nation. Nichelle Nichols proposes that Roddenberry may have felt that science fiction was perhaps the only genre in which social issues such as diversity and prejudice could be explored on television with relative impunity. Nichols writes:

> As a setting for the thought-provoking and idealistic series Gene had in mind, the future had everything. By virtue of its being unknown and unknowable it offered infinite possibilities for character and plot development. Through Mr. Spock, for instance, *Star Trek* explored story lines concerning his mixed heritage (half human, half Vulcan), the challenges of his parents' mixed marriage (which the network abhorred), and his father's rejecting Spock for his "human" attributes. Speciesism, racism—call it what you will—the point is that Gene created in *Star Trek* a multidimensional, multiracial, multipurpose metaphor through which he could express his personal, progressive ideals. *He might have made exactly the same points writing the same stories with Spock being the mulatto human child of a Black parent and a white parent living in the sixties. The problem is that it never would have gotten on the air* [my emphasis, 138].

In the forty years since *Star Trek* first aired, a major network has yet to air a prime time lead character that is of mixed heritage. Richard Hanley writes: "In each of the [*Star Trek*] television series, the most interesting characters frequently are those who are like us but also not quite like us" (1997: 4). In the crossing of boundaries the limits around identity are challenged and the line between "us" and "them" is blurred. Interracial relationships—and mixed heritage people—entail a challenge to notions of who belongs and who does not, a question which science fiction generally raises in terms of who is human, or who is seen in full round rather than in shallow stereotype.

Sexing Spock

The angst surrounding Spock's racial identity is both matched by and causative of his sexual identity crisis. When we first see the otherwise impassive Mr. Spock exhibit sexuality in an overt way, it is explosive and completely uncontrolled. In the episode "Amok Time" (1967), Spock's inability to come to terms with his alien (Vulcan) sexuality literally threatens his life. By succumbing to *pon farr*, the Vulcan equivalent of an intense sexual "heat" that requires that one mate or die, Spock is deeply embarrassed to the point of profound shame. Whereas Spock usually revels in being Vulcan, to the exclusion and even the repudiation of his human heritage, in this case his relationship to his multiple heritages is much more complex. When he is struck by the seven-year cycle of *pon farr*, Spock is living between worlds, literally on the starship, and figuratively in his absence from his home planet. Instead of insisting on a return to Vulcan, where he could exercise his physical need to mate either by joining his Vulcan wife[10] or fighting his (sexual) rival in a contest to the death, Spock refuses to be forthcoming about his condition. Is he exhibiting shame for his Vulcan heritage within the context of his human surroundings? Is he attempting to be as Vulcan as he can by refusing to have any kind of emotional need? This would appear to be a most illogical course of action. As Spock spasms in physical pain he also seems to be doubled up in shame for something that is both culturally and biologically demanded. Spock's assimilation into dominant Federation culture, which we can read as dominant "white" culture, causes him to overcompensate in a way that makes others recognize him as "inauthentic"—both inauthentically human and inauthentically alien. In fact, by trying to hide his alien biology, Spock succeeds only in making it much more obvious to the entire crew. Spock is illogical in his refusal to return to Vulcan while he is experiencing pon farr. In his extreme attempts to repress his emotions, Spock actually misinterprets the emotion-control philosophy of his father. It was, after all, Sarek, Spock's father, who chose a human wife, Amanda, because it seemed the most logical thing to do at the time ("Journey to Babel," 1967). Sarek, as an ambassador, may in fact have made his choice of mate as a movement towards cultural assimilation. His son Spock's attempts to assert a monoracial (i.e., fully Vulcan) identity in the context of his choice to live as a Starfleet officer is reminiscent of the immigrant who clings most fiercely to the culture she has left behind, only to find that, like all culture, it has changed in her absence. Ironically, the original sexual transgression of Spock's parents becomes converted into a motivation for Spock to attempt to subsume the sexual transgression that his Vulcan sexuality (pon farr) represents.

Vulcan sexuality, as presented in "Amok Time," appears terrifying. The violence that marks Spock's interactions with Nurse Chapel, his adoring, human supplicant, is reminiscent of the implied or actual violence directed by "Oriental" men towards "white" women in films such as *The Bitter Tea of General Yen* (1933) and *Flash Gordon*. (The three original films were released in 1936, 1938 and 1940, and the remake was released in 1980.) Unlike General Yen or Ming the Merciless, however, Spock's violence—specifically, throwing against the wall the soup brought to him by Nurse Chapel—is consciously meant to reject her sexual advances towards him rather than to compel her to him. Yet the implied threat of his "Oriental" sexuality remains the same: it is not "normal" or healthy. In fact, his sexuality is coded as a health problem, as Dr. McCoy informs the captain that if something is not done about Spock's state, Spock will die. Thus, it seems clear that there is no chance Spock can resolve his sexuality by engaging in the same kind of transgressive reproduction that produced him in the first place; he is not allowed by the logic of this narrative to choose Nurse Chapel, or, ultimately, any woman. Instead, he must engage in a homoeroticized battle with his dear friend, Captain Kirk, in order to release his sexual tension while subsuming the threat of miscegenation (no matter which female—human or Vulcan—he chooses, it will be miscegenation) under the veil of homoeroticism. Constance Penley, in her analysis of the "slash" fiction written in fanzines around the homoeroticism of Kirk/Spock, raises this issue of "interracial" homosexuality:

> To make the slash fiction do the "cultural work" the fans want it to do, the slashers have ingeniously rewritten and recast the American mythos of interethnic male bonding by making that relationship homoerotic rather than homosocial. Ensuring the democratic equality of the pair, the slashers have eliminated its racism by celebrating miscegenation.... (Penley, 1997: 145).

Furthermore, in "Amok Time," Captain Kirk resolves the deliberately arcane social intricacies of Spock's situation by injecting himself with a substance that makes him appear dead. This resolution of sexual tension by death is familiar in English literary tradition from at least the Middle Ages in which an orgasm is known as a "little death." In this we see the emergence of a trope connecting transgressive sexuality and alterations of identity with the transformative powers of death[11] that will be picked up again in *The Search for Spock*.

In "Amok Time" the death of the beloved, Captain Kirk, changes Spock from the demonic uncontrolled alien back into Kirk's gentle friend. When Spock himself dies, in *Star Trek II: The Wrath of Khan* (1982), his death and subsequent resurrection serve to raise questions about how imperialism, colonialism and immigration might alter personal and communal identities. The location where someone is born is commonly regarded as a clear indicator of identity-meaning; where you are from is equivalent to who you are—"nationality" to most people means the same thing as "ethnic identity." People of mixed heritage are often asked, "Where are your parents from?" as a way to discern their ethnic heritages and thus their identities (because heritage and identity are often conflated). The place where someone dies, however, is rarely considered to carry as much significance in determining identity. However, *The Search for Spock* recognizes the way in which people—for example, colonists or immigrants—come to belong to the land in which they are buried.[12]

At the end of *The Wrath of Khan*, Spock sacrifices himself to save the *Enterprise*. Having exposed himself to deadly radiation, he dies in front of his horrified friends, but not before he is able to transfer his essence into the mind of Dr. McCoy. At the end of the film, Spock's casket is laid to rest on the Genesis planet, which has just undergone a radical new terraforming process. With the Genesis device, an inhospitable, "dead" world is made to come to life. In the following movie, it becomes clear that the Genesis effect is not everything its developers had hoped it would be: the planet is highly unstable, and begins to rip apart under the stress of developing too quickly. Spock has become inextricably tied to the land where he had been laid to rest. Just as he is marked by the planet, so, too, is the planet forever marked by being Spock's burial site; as his body matures it undergoes pon farr, and it seems as though his pon farr triggers the seismic instability of the planet. Finally, the only way to save him is to remove his new body from this now cataclysmic planet, and reunite his body with his spirit, which has been stored in the mind of his human friend, Dr. McCoy. This literalization of the Cartesian mind/body split is also a reverse of the typical Hollywood trope of the white hero and buddy "of color." In this case, Spock, the alien/man of color, is the mind while McCoy, the white man, is only the body acting as a vessel for the mind. However, the Orientalization of Spock, which suggests that he is mostly mind and has little emotion—or humanity—disallows an easy reading of this situation. Suffice it to say the two men are joined in an intimate fashion, and, as in an interracial union, the child (in this case the reborn Spock) takes on a little of both "parents." The reborn Spock thus exhibits both aspects of his Vulcan heritage as well as a new found sense of humor attributed to the often wry personality of Dr. McCoy.

That an entire movie could be built around "the search for Spock" emphasizes the extent to which Spock symbolizes the philosophy behind *Star Trek*. Nichelle Nichols, in her memoir, says, "To what degree Leonard really believed he would be killing off Spock with that [death] scene, only he can say. But from the moment I heard about it, I thought it was a bad idea and a betrayal of *Star Trek*'s ideals. Some would argue that without Spock there could be no more *Star Trek*, theoretically or in reality" (1994: 246–7). Spock and his identity crises represent, in many ways, the foundation of the *Star Trek* phenomenon as he himself continually articulates the question: Who am I? which translates into the larger question: What is human?

Part II: Transracial Adoption and Empire

In several iterations of *Star Trek*, "ultimate enemies" from past series have been "adopted" into the Federation, in particular by humans. *Star Trek*'s Klingons became humanized in *The Next Generation*'s Worf; *The Next Generation*'s Borg were assimilated by humans in the body of Seven of Nine. *Deep Space Nine* reversed this trend by first introducing an apparently harmless alien, Odo, and only later revealing that he was a member of the most terrifying enemy yet—the Founders whose empire, the Dominion, threatened to overrun the quadrant occupied by the Federation. When the contemporary transracial/transnational adoption industry was founded in the middle of the twentieth century following U.S. wars in Asia, a significant portion of adoptees were children of mixed heritage who were seen as a product of the war and a sign of the defeated countries' shame. In other words, it is no mistake that *Star Trek* narratives emphasize the power relationship between the hegemony of the "adopting" culture and the conflicted positionality of the adopted individual.[13] This dynamic is as central to the meaning of *Star Trek* as is Spock's quest to locate his identity.

Prime Directive: The Right of Self-Determination

In *The Meaning of "Star Trek,"* Thomas Richards (1997) argues that in *Star Trek* "the ultimate nightmare the series has to offer is not the breakdown of political instability in the quadrant but the breakdown of the inner stability of the individual" (32). Unlike Richards, I do not see these two threats as opposites. On the contrary, the fear of the breakdown of political stability *is* the fear of a breakdown of borders, because of how those political borders are constructed to define individual identities. Thus the most frightening thing the Borg could do was not destroy worlds but assimilate an individual, most devastatingly the individual who was the hero of *Star Trek: The Next Generation*: Captain Jean-Luc Picard. Likewise, the way to defeat the Borg (and make them much less frightening as enemies) is to individualize them—as in the fourth season of *Star Trek: Voyager*, which introduces a new Borg "individual": Seven of Nine. The Borg are arguably the most effective enemies introduced in *Star Trek*, and thus the integration of a Borg into a Federation crew symbolizes the integration of the most feared alien "Other" into the community. To understand the significance of this, we must first understand how the Borg are unique in what makes them fearful enemies.

The Borg are a collective; they travel the universe searching, seeking information, new technology, and new civilizations, much like the starships of Federation. Like the Federation, the Borg search out new life. Unlike the captains of Federation starships, however, the Borg do not claim to be merely explorers (as though explorers are not always agents of empire). Nor do the Borg cling to a Prime Directive of noninterference. Rather, if one were to write a Borg Prime Directive, it might read, "Conquer and assimilate all others who are worthy." They cull the weak and assimilate only those of use to the collective.

Star Trek is a hyper-allegory of our world, of empires, collectives, dominions and federations that all function through a vast exploration of space guaranteed to result, *a la* Manifest Destiny, in border-changing and identity-challenging convergences and clashes. Richards notes that, "Historically there is no such thing as exploration for exploration's sake. Exploration usually leads to empire, and empire leads to war" (Richards, 1997:13). The logic of the show requires a mechanism to both prevent this logical outcome and critique it. Thus the function of the Prime Directive becomes clear; it is meant to prevent the Federation "from establishing an empire in outer space" (Richards, 1997: 13). In many ways, this tension is the dramatic core of the original and subsequent series. Interesting moral conflicts for the characters are inevitable as the Prime Directive of noninterference directly contradicts the goal of exploring new lands and meeting new life forms. As Richards notes, "All anthropology is by definition a violation of the Prime Directive" (19). The Prime Directive, in Ethnic Studies terms, might be called the "rights of self-determination and sovereignty," a right that is clearly violated by the exigencies of empire, even when they come in the guise of exploration.

(Inner) Space Invaders

Richards argues, and I would agree, that "the Borg are the classic space invaders of science fiction" (41). Moreover, I see the classic invading aliens of science fiction as reflections of social anxieties about race and immigration in the mid-twentieth century, a time when the U.S. was threatened by the results of its own imperialist actions in Latin America, Asia and the Pacific. As in vampire fictions, the more threatening aliens are not those who want to conquer in a merely military way, but those who want to become us, at least superficially—like pod people—or like immigrants from former or current colonies or places where our military has recently been. As Stephen Arata notes in his article, "The Occidental Tourist: Dracula and the Anxiety of Reverse Colonization," this is the fear of reverse colonization that seems to spur much of the narrative tension of Bram Stoker's *Dracula*. Imperialist excess at the end of nineteenth century Britain resulted in the colonized moving in towards the center of the Empire, which was merely the vanguard of immigration into Europe and the United States that continues to accelerate at the beginning of the twenty-first century. Richards notes that the Borg "do not pose a political or military threat the way the Klingons, Romulans, or Cardassians sometimes do" (41). So what kind of a threat do they pose? The threat of the Borg is the total assimilation of the individual into the collective. Of course, assimilation is also the threat "minority"[14] groups face within composite societies such as the United States. Even though the Borg add the culture and biology of conquered races to their collective in a way that sounds very like corporate additive multiculturalism—the updated "melting pot"—the Borg are viewed by others as genocidal in their intent and effect, and thus as "evil."

Assimilation or Adoption?

When *Voyager*'s Captain Janeway has the opportunity to "repatriate" a human girl who was assimilated by the Borg collective at a young age, the narrative takes on overtones familiar from transracial adoptees memoirs. Janeway functions as the Borg Seven of Nine's adoptive mother figure. Seven tells Janeway, "Your attempts to assimilate this drone will fail. You may alter our physiology, but you cannot change our nature. We will betray you. We are Borg" ("Scorpion, Part I," 1997). This statement is in many ways a reverse mirror[15] of the actions of the Borg. Their attempts to assimilate individual humans, like Picard, could be interpreted as having failed because they "may alter our physiology, but cannot change our nature. We are human." Seven of Nine's underlying "nature," understood in terms of physiology, is human, yet what she seems to mean here is that her culture is Borg, because that is the only culture she really knows, having been assimilated at a very young age. Her reassimilation back into human culture, then, is fraught with questions not only of acculturation but also of identity. Captain Janeway makes a lot of assumptions about Seven's true and original identity. Janeway seems to feel she has saved Seven of Nine by removing her from the collective, and removing the collective from her by encouraging her human immune system to reject her Borg implants (which is never fully successful). Yet Seven of Nine wishes to remain Borg. Janeway overrides the holographic doctor's protocol to honor cultural differences by determining that Seven of Nine has no free will because she was assimilated by the Borg—and assuming that Borg, because of their collective nature, have no free will. Transracial and transnational adoptions have a history embedded in the clashing of communities and nations over land and resources. American Indians and Australian Aborigines, particularly those of mixed European heritage, were often adopted by white families as part of a larger effort to solve the "race problem" they represented to authorities. This history of hurt around transracial adoption is so powerful that in 1972 the

National Association of Black Social Workers called for an end to the placement of Black children into white homes on the basis that this practice amounted to a kind of cultural genocide.[16] Contemporary Asian American and Latin American communities struggle with the continuing legacy of transnational transracial adoptions of children from these regions, especially in the U.S. from Korea, the Philippines, China and Nicaragua.[17] Racism is clearly a significant factor in the dynamics whereby middle class white Americans have the means to adopt children of color. In this context, Janeway's determination that Seven of Nine should be forcibly assimilated into the human-dominated culture of the Federation is highly problematic.

What is particularly fascinating about the position of Seven of Nine is that her situation can be seen as an attempt to address questions of colonization and assimilation from the "other" side. When members of the Federation, the characters with whom the audience identifies, are assimilated into alien cultures, that assimilation has been coded as horrific. On the other hand, Seven of Nine's assimilation by the *Voyager* crew is constructed as being in her best interest. The discussion around this issue is very revealing. When Seven of Nine asks the captain why she cannot be free to make the decision to return to the collective, Janeway tells her, "You lost the capacity to make a rational choice the moment you were assimilated.... I'm making that decision for you." Seven of Nine replies that this action would make Janeway no different from the Borg ("Scorpion, Part I"). This statement seems very odd, considering that Seven of Nine sees the Borg collective as her home, yet it seems here as though she is also capable of discerning that their colonialist/assimilationist impulses deprive other cultures and individuals of their free will. The logic of the narrative thus constructs the loss of free will as being necessary in order to develop a collective benefit. While some viewers might read this as a commentary on communism, I interpret the Borg as being much closer to U.S. colonialist/consumer culture. According to Thomas Richards in *The Meaning of "Star Trek"*:

> The Borg are the ultimate culture of self-improvement. They show that every improvement to a culture comes at a cost. To increase and multiply, any culture must consume things and dominate people. Imperial expansion creates subject peoples. New technologies require raw materials and create waste. Even culture itself is generally developed for the few rather than for the many ... each time the Borg improve themselves, it is at the direct expense of another culture whose life and technology they have consumed in their continuing quest for betterment [49].

Thus the Borg, being the ultimate colonizers, are also the ultimate consumers of culture. This realization provides a direct commentary on our own contemporary consumer society, the colonialist roots of which

are too often conveniently forgotten. Richards continues, "The implication here is that the Borg might not be able to survive without cultures
to consume. Cultures are like food to them, and they stalk them like a
predator seeking prey.... They actually need other societies, if only to consume them" (49). This discussion of the Borg as the ultimate consumer
culture reveals that what is most frightening about them is their similar-
ity to the worst aspects of U.S. culture: the consumerism that is inextricably liked to neocolonialism and imperialism. *Star Trek* has indeed
created in the Borg the "ideal" space invader—i.e., the ultimate "Other"—
by projecting on them the worst aspects of our culture, which have led
to aggressive literal and cultural colonialism.

Against the ultimate invader the ultimate defense is justified: genocide. Genocide is the opposite of the ideal of noninterference. The Federation argument, familiar in this era of the U.S. war in Iraq, seems to
be that the horrible solution of genocide is justified in self-defense against
an ill-defined "evil." In "Scorpion, Part I" the Borg are explicitly called
"pure evil"; however, it is never made clear exactly what is evil about them
except their will to "assimilate." They are not sadists or torturers, they
selflessly put the collective before all else, and they are motivated by the
desire to improve that collective towards perfection. It seems that it is
this selflessness which is what is truly horrible. Is this the greatest fear in
fear of the Other, that they will cause you to lose yourself? The Borg thus
represent the fear of "immigrant hordes" who will cause you to lose your
(implicitly superior) identity through miscegenation as well as through
cultural and physical invasion.

Ensign Kim the Merciless

On *Star Trek*, Asian men have faired poorly when it comes to interracial relationships, particularly with white women. In the *Voyager* episode
that features sexual tension between Ensign Kim and Seven of Nine, there
is clearly no danger of any kind of sexual union ("Revulsion," 1997). In
fact, the writers and directors carefully remove any such "threat" by making Seven the sexual aggressor, and emphasizing Harry Kim's sexual inep-
titude, fully in line with current media stereotypes of Asian men.
Furthermore, Seven of Nine's construction as a kind of hybrid—part
human, part machine—also allows her to fumble through the social awk-
wardness engendered by Kim's attraction to her. Because she is "mixed,"
she does not understand the social niceties of the situation and her dom-
inance over him can be explained as clumsiness.

Ensign Harry Kim's romantic attraction to Seven is only slightly
allayed by her frank talk and direct action. "Shall we copulate?" she asks
him, when she perceives Kim's sexual attraction to her. This scene, while

intentionally comic in its effect, as we can see Kim figuratively "shrivel," additionally conveys the threat of the sexual Other embodied by Seven of Nine, who is neither human nor not-human (and who thus represents the "monster" of antimiscegenation fears). Kelly Hurley, writing about the genre of horror films she calls "body horror," argues:

> Body horror seeks to inspire revulsion—and in its own way, pleasure—through representations of quasi-human figures whose effect/affect is produced by their own abjection, their ambiguation, their impossible embodiment of multiple, incompatible forms. Such posthuman embodiments are liminal entities, occupying both terms (or rather the slash between them) of the opposition human/not-human [Hurley, 1995: 203].

Seven of Nine, though partially "returned" to humanity, retains signs—both physical and cultural—of her mechanistic interface with the Borg collective. Her desire to assimilate into the crew through sexual activity is a parody of the Borg desire to assimilate asexually (through the invasion of the body, beginning with blood). Seven's occupation of a liminal space is not unique in *Star Trek*; rather, liminality in the sense of transgressive identity is the *Star Trek* norm. This fascination with "ambiguation" demonstrates anxiety over questions of identity: how do we determine the boundaries of the self without taking an oppositional stance against the "Other"? This question becomes particularly difficult to answer when the "Other" is within the self or has been taken into the family, as in the case of the transracially adopted Borg or the mixed heritage human-alien.

In *The Next Generation* episode "The Chase" (1993) we discover that all the humanoid species in the universe are related, and though the episode gives us some cause for hope, in the end "identity" or common ancestry may itself be the cause of conflict. It is this common ancestry that the occupants of the *Star Trek* universe seem so often intent on denying thorough their feuds with one another. As Richards writes:

> [In] *Star Trek*, an astonishingly high percentage of conflict in the galaxy is blood feud.... The blood feud is first of all a model of political parity in which conflict is permanent but neither side is able to prevail.... But most of all the blood feud is a model of likeness in a universe of seemingly dissimilar species [Richards, 1997: 39–40].

From the seventeenth century until World War II, the "science" of race was largely focused on differentiating racialized groupings of human beings. Their difference from one another was the main focus of research. The idea of a common origin for all human beings contradicted these pseudoscientists. Early eugenicists and others postulated that because the different racialized groups that they delineated had different origins, they could not interbreed, that the result of interbreeding between a Northern

European and an African would be like a mule—weak and perhaps even sterile. They argued that the offspring would retain only the worst characteristics of each parent race, in other words, the worst of both worlds. They argued that the offspring would lower both parent races. Later sociologists, unable to prove that people of mixed heritage were impossible, and faced with the acknowledgment of the common origin of humanity, argued that people of mixed heritage would be physically weak or "mismatched" and faced with identity crises.[18] *Star Trek*, like other cultural productions, shows us that if there is an identity crisis for people of mixed heritage, it is caused by the deliberate campaign to categorize such people as "marginal men" whose impulses to critique racism and empire reflect only their own "pathological" desire to attain the status of the dominant race.[19]

100 "Transracial Adoptees"

The idea of the un-individuated collective empire representing the ultimate evil is explored further though a race known as the Founders, also known pejoratively as Changelings,[20] and first seen in *Deep Space Nine* in the character of Constable Odo. Like Seven of Nine, Odo is a transracial adoptee; he is one of one hundred "Changelings" that had been left as unformed children scattered around the galaxy in the hope that they would adapt to their "solid" environment and bring useful information back to the Founder collective, known as the Great Link. Odo assimilated into Bajoran culture, and rose to the rank of "Constable" in the Bajoran security force. One episode is focused on Odo's effort to come to terms with his status as an assimilated, or "adopted," member of the Bajoran community. Odo purchases a "Changeling" infant—suggesting overtones of the international transracial adoption "market"—and he tries to bond with it. As he tries to nurture the infant he is reminded of his own days in the laboratory of Dr. Mora Pol, who returns to the station as the leading expert in coaxing unformed "Changelings" into a form that can interact with solids ("The Begotten," 1997). However, his methods were often cruel, even after he was certain that Odo was sentient, and Odo resents him for this past mistreatment. In contrast, Dr. Mora is extremely proud of his work with Odo and treats him paternalistically. Ultimately, the "Changeling" infant dies, and Odo both confronts and then comes to resolution with his "adoptive father," Dr. Mora. This episode raises issues that are often seen in transracial adoption narratives, particularly in the power dynamic that is amplified between parent and child when the parent is a member of the hegemonic group/nation and the child is both racially other and from a subjugated nation (as in the case of Japanese, Korean, and Vietnamese adoptees following U.S. wars in those countries).[21]

It is necessary for this story line that we not know what we learn in later seasons—that Odo's people are not just unknown shape-shifting "Changelings"; rather they are the secretive leaders of the Dominion, known as the Founders by their vassal races.

Because of their ability to transform their very essence through a process of metamorphosis, the Founders are the opposite of the Borg: the Founders are threatening because they can appear to be anyone or anything else, while the Borg attempt to turn everyone else into beings just like them. Both Founders and Borg participate in a collective identity that appears to devalue the individual. And the Founders represent a threat of similar proportions precisely because their ability to shape-shift means they are undetectable. Significantly, the only way to detect a Founder is to draw blood, as in the racist ideology of "good" versus "bad" blood, blood will always "tell." When withdrawn from the body of a Founder, the "blood" will revert back to a viscous fluid, which is the form of Founders at rest or regeneration. In contrast to this invisible, insidious threat,[22] the Borg are highly visible. Whereas, with the Borg blood is the first site of battle, as it is where they begin the assimilation process, with the Founders blood is their weakness, the marker through which they can be identified as inauthentic.

Like the Borg, the Founders seem to represent the fear of being simultaneously self and Other in a way that emphasizes a loss of self, a loss of knowing where the boundaries of self are. Yet this duality is precisely what *Star Trek* instructs us to value: Infinite Diversity in Infinite Combinations (IDIC) and the recognition of the self in Others, in other words, a mixed heritage recognition of the other as kin.[23] The Borg and the Founders threaten that the self will become Other, which is the other side of IDIC and of U.S. "melting-pot multiculturalism." And is this not the basis of xenophobia? Xenophobia can be read as a projection of the worst qualities we find in ourselves onto an "Other" that we then repudiate. We define ourselves, who and what we are, by what we are not. Our inability to identify (in the sense of discovering a spy) the Founders, hidden as "us," is what makes them so frightening. We are not those "Others," but how can we tell? In order to reaffirm our difference from the "Other," we must constantly examine them—particularly their blood— and simultaneously reject them. Likewise, the Federation fears the Borg and the Founders while the narratives of *Star Trek* invite the Borg and Founders as well-loved adopted individuals (Seven of Nine and Odo) into our midst, that is, as long as they prove their loyalty to "us" over the enemies of the Federation.

Odo's struggle to fit into the world of the "solids"—the term the Founders pejoratively use to describe those who cannot morph at will— mirrors that of other transracially adopted and fostered or culturally displaced *Star Trek* characters. Like Worf (the Klingon who was raised by

Russian foster parents) and Seven of Nine before him, Odo has a
conflicted relationship with his human parent figure. And, like Worf and
Seven, romance forms a significant boundary of Odo's identity. When
Odo finally pursues his long unrevealed love for the Bajoran Major Kira
Nerys, it is set up in the narrative as an aspect of his choice to live among
the "solids" rather than link with one of his people ("Chimera," 1999).
Maria P.P. Root, in her "Bill of Rights for People of Mixed Heritage"
(1995), proclaims the right of people of mixed heritage to freely choose
whom to "befriend and love."[24] This proclamation is spurred by the frequent experience of people of mixed heritage and of transracial adoptees
of being questioned about their romantic proclivities. This personal invasion is often justified in terms of the questioner using the answers to
determine the "true" identity of the mixed heritage/transracially adopted
person. Unfortunately lost on most people are the subtle differences
between ethnic heritage, personal identity, communities of affiliation,
and romantic choices. Odo, as a Founder who has been transracially
adopted by a Bajoran, could be seen as choosing his Bajoran identity over
his Founder heritage by choosing a Bajoran mate.

In the first season of *Deep Space Nine*, Odo is tantalized with the evidence that he might not be alone in the universe ("Vortex," 1993). His
search for his place in the universe becomes a recurring theme in the
series that gains urgency during the last three seasons, when his people
are revealed as the leaders of the Dominion. This rival empire seeks to
conquer the quadrant of space occupied by the Federation by using fierce
genetically enhanced warriors in addition to the ability of the Founders
themselves to shape-shift. They cite as the reason for their preemptive
war against the Federation and their allies their experiences of extreme
prejudice at the hands of the "solids"; they had been hunted down almost
to the point of extinction because the "solids" feared their morphing ability. The military threat the Founders present is extensive. At one point
the Founders use the Federation's own defensiveness against them. In
"Homefront" (1996), heightened security measures after sabotage on
Earth include blood screenings of Starfleet personnel and their families.
People begin to distrust their loved ones. The following episode, "Paradise Lost" (1996), reveals that the act of sabotage was staged by a military faction bent on mandating extreme security measures—in effect, a
military coup. Later, we discover that again Starfleet or members of it feel
justified to use genocide in "self-defense" as they unleash a biogenetic
weapon—a fatal disease—on the Founders. Section 31, a rogue "unofficial"
extremist Starfleet organization, has used the Founders' own nature
against them; the disease is passed quickly from Founder to Founder
when they link together in their natural state. Odo remains unaffected
by the disease because of his long separation from his people, but he is
eventually infected and will soon die. In heroic action, two of his "solid"

friends risk their lives to retrieve a cure for him which he then communicates to his people ("Extreme Measures," 1999). At the end of the final season, Odo leaves his beloved, the Bajoran Nerys, to return to the Founder home world and give them the cure. Through his communication of his positive experiences with "solids," he is able to convince his people to end their fear-based war (see "What You Leave Behind," 1999).

Difference Beyond Hierarchy

The U.S. has consumed other cultures through colonization[25] into the myth of the melting pot while relegating the people who create those cultures to second class status. Mixed heritage and transracial adoption result from these processes of colonization as evidenced by even a cursory examination of the demographics of U.S. colonies and of immigrants to the U.S. from places where the U.S. has engaged in military actions. The lines by which we delimit identities are not the boundaries that create hierarchy and thus inequality. We can have identities and community loyalties without having to rely on a repudiation of the Other via racial hierarchy. Mixed heritage identities have the potential to reframe racial hierarchies by challenging the accepted boundaries of categories. For example, when people of mixed heritage and transracially adopted people claim full membership in all of the ethnic groups to which they belong, they emphasize the notion of ethnicity, which is difference without hierarchy, rather than the notion of race, which is a hierarchy of difference.

Will *Star Trek* or any other science fiction provide a tool to dismantle the oppressive nature of racial hierarchy? All they can do is provide a "safe space" for narratives that begin the dialogue: What is human?

Notes

1. A classic anthology in this quickly developing field is *The Multiracial Experience: Racial Borders as the New Frontier,* edited by Maria P.P. Root (1995). A plethora of texts have since been published, many in the United Kingdom.

2. I use the term "mixed heritage" rather than "mixed race" to deemphasize biological race, however, there are ongoing debates about the appropriate terminology to use in the field of Mixed Heritage Studies in an antiracist context (for a strong overview of this debate, please see Jayne Ifekwunige's "Introduction: rethinking 'mixed race'" in her *"Mixed Race" Studies: A Reader* (2004). I am also, perhaps problematically, sometimes using mixed heritage as a more general term that encompasses transracial adoption.

3. Formerly this essay was focused on all *Star Trek* characters that cross various boundaries. However, I found this earlier draft getting overly lengthy as ever more characters became readable as transgressive or as mixed heritage. For a detailed treatment of many of these characters and the subject of "race" in *Star Trek* generally, please refer to Daniel Bernardi (1998) and Taylor Harrison et al. (1996).

4. This vampiric "race" of cyborgs assimilates others into its mechanical/biological

matrix. For a detailed reading of the Borg, please refer to Russell and Wolski (2001), Collado-Rodríguez (2002), and Short (2004).

5. Transracial adoption is a complex social and even political issue; by using the phrase "transracial adoption" in reference to humans and aliens I mean only to illustrate one aspect of how popular culture interprets these issues.

6. This is commonly known as the one-drop rule, which dictates the "blackness" of anyone with "one drop" of "Black blood."

7. Antimiscegenation laws were structured to protect whiteness, thus they prohibited marriages between those categorized as white and those labeled nonwhite. States had their own versions of antimiscegenation laws, and they were not abolished until the Supreme Court case of *Loving v. Virginia,* in 1967.

8. Sadly, the series *Star Trek: Enterprise* reproduces this same dynamic. The African-American helmsman and Asian-American woman translator simply reverse the gender and racial roles of the Asian helmsman and African communications officer of the original series. The three senior officers are white men, distinguished only by their accents, while the second in command position is held by the sexy Vulcan T'Pol, more or less to generate sexual tension with the white male characters.

9. Constance Penley documents the struggle to locate Spock's racial identity in contemporary social terms. She queries:

> But what is Spock's race? ... The history and prehistory of Vulcan is almost invariably written by the fans as an exoticized Asian martial arts culture or a romanticized Native American culture. Never, except for rare efforts to Egyptianize Vulcan history, do the fans touch on anything even remotely African.... They prefer to orientalize or romanticize the color divide in a strategic yet unconscious evasion of what has historically in the U.S. been the most bitterly contentious racial division (Penley, 1997: 137–138).

10. An arranged marriage, clearly invoking European American distaste for marriage customs stereotyped as Asian.

11. My thanks to Julie Schrader-Villegas for suggesting that anxieties about emasculation/castration, as in situations of slavery, might also be at play here.

12. My mother, an immigrant from Hong Kong, surprised me the first time she identified herself as a Chinese American rather than as Chinese. When I asked her why, she said she planned on being buried here so she figured it was time to identify herself as an American.

13. For excellent personal narratives on this issue, please see Deann Borshay Liem's autobiographical documentary video, *First Person Plural* (2000), and Jane Jeong Trenka's autobiography, *The Language of Blood* (2005).

14. In sociological terms, *minority* does not refer to percentage of the population, but rather to those who lack access to institutional power.

15. And we know from the many uses of the "Mirror Universe" that the creators of *Star Trek* are conscious of the idea of revelatory mirroring.

16. For an interesting discussion of the nuances of this argument, please see Barbara Ballis Lal's "Learning to Do Ethnic Identity: The Transracial/Transethnic Adoptive Family as Site and Context" in David Parker and Miri Song (2001).

17. For more information of the complex history and contemporary implications of transracial and transnational adoptions, please see Ruth McCoy and Christine Hall's "Transracial Adoption: In Whose Best Interest?" in Maria P.P. Root (1995). For more on transracial/transnational adoption specifically referencing adoptees of mixed heritage, please see Gina Miranda's "Domestic Transracial Adoption and Multiraciality" and Susan Cox's "International Adoption of Mixed Race Children," both in Maria P.P. Root and Matt Kelley (2003).

18. For the history of eugenics in the U.S., please see Edwin Black (2003).

19. For an analysis of the history of sociological constructions of mixed heritage, especially in the context of colonialism, please see Frank Furedi's "How Sociology Imagined 'Mixed Race'" in David Parker and Miri Song (2001).

20. This name references the European myth of fairy children left in place of stolen human infants. Inevitably, these fairy children would bring "bad luck" upon their adopted

human parents; their "true nature" as supernatural beings would be untamed by their nurturing in a human home. Odo was initially identified as an "unknown sample" by the Bajoran scientist who discovered him and was later jokingly named Odo'ital, meaning "nothing" in Cardassian ("The Alternate," 1994).

21. Please see Deann Borshay Liem (2000) and Jane Jeong Trenka (2005).

22. This threat is like the "threat" of people of mixed heritage who "pass" for members of the dominant culture or homosexuals who "pass" for straight.

23. What I call the "kin-aesthetic" in my article, "Developing a Kin-aesthetic: Mixed Heritage in Asian and Native North American Literature," in *Mixed Race Literature*, edited by Jonathan Brennan (2002).

24. In Root and Kelly (2003): 32.

25. Puerto Rico, the Philippines, Guam, Samoa, and Hawaii to name but a few.

Works Cited

Arata, Stephen. "The Occidental Tourist: Dracula and the Anxiety of Reverse Colonization." *Dracula: Authoritative Text, Contexts, Reviews and Reactions*. Edited by Nina Auerbach and David J. Skal. New York: Norton, 1997.

Black, Edwin. *War Against the Weak: Eugenics and America's Campaign to Create a Master Race*. New York: Four Wall Eight Windows Press, 2003.

Bernardi, Daniel Leonard. *"Star Trek" and History: Race-ing Toward a White Future*. New Brunswick: Rutgers University Press, 1998.

Collado-Rodríguez, Francisco. "Fear of the Flesh, Fear of the Borg: Narratives of Bodily Transgression in Contemporary U.S. Culture." *Beyond Borders: Re-Defining Generic and Ontological Boundaries*. Edited by Ramón Plo-Alastrué and María Jesús Martínez-Alfaro. Heidelberg, Germany: Universitätsverlag C.: Winter, 2002.

Dariotis, Wei Ming. "Developing a Kin-Aesthetic: Multiraciality and Kinship in Asian and Native North American Literature." *Mixed Race Literature*. Edited by Jonathan Brennan. Stanford, CA: Stanford University Press, 2002.

Hanley, Richard. *The Metaphysics of "Star Trek."* New York: HarperCollins, 1997.

Harrison, Taylor, et al. Enterprise *Zones: Critical Positions on "Star Trek."* Boulder, CO: Westview Press, 1996.

Hurley, Kelly. "Reading Like an Alien: Posthuman Identity in Ridley Scott's *Alien* and David Cronenberg's *Rabid*." *Posthuman Bodies*. Edited by Judith Halberstam and Ira Livingston. Bloomington: Indiana University Press, 1995.

Ifekwunige, Jayne, ed. *"Mixed Race" Studies: A Reader*. New York: Routledge, 2004.

Liem, Deann Borshay. *First Person Plural*. Video, 2000.

Nichols, Nichelle. *Beyond Uhura: "Star Trek" and Other Memories*. New York: GP Putnam's Sons, 1994.

Parker, David, and Miri Song, eds. *Rethinking "Mixed Race."* London: Pluto Press, 2001.

Penley, Constance. *NASA/Trek: Popular Science and Sex in America*. London: Verso, 1997.

Richards, Thomas. *The Meaning of "Star Trek."* New York: Doubleday, 1997.

Root, Maria P.P., ed. *The Multiracial Experience: Racial Borders as the New Frontier*. Thousand Oaks: Sage Publications, 1995.

Root, Maria P.P., and Matt Kelley, eds. *Multiracial Child Resource Book: Living Complex Identities*. Seattle: Mavin Foundation, 2003.

Russell, Lynette, and Nathan Wolski. "Beyond the Final Frontier: *Star Trek*, the Borg, and the Post-Colonial." *Intensities: The Journal of Cult Media* 1 (Spring/Summer 2001).

Short, Sue. "The Federation and Borg Value Systems in *Star Trek*." *Foundation: The International Review of Science Fiction* 92 (Autumn 2004): 31–50.

Trenka, Jane Jeong. *The Language of Blood*. Minneapolis: Graywolf Press, 2005.

5

Save the Whales and Beware Wilderness

Star Trek *and American Environmental Views*

Elizabeth D. Blum

In 1865, Jules Verne penned the remarkable *From the Earth to the Moon*, a novel which depicted three men, shot from a cannon, traveling to the moon and returning to Earth via an ocean landing. Remarkably similar to the actual moon excursions of the United States over 100 years later, *From the Earth to the Moon* began a new literary genre, that of science fiction. Since Verne's novel, writers have seen science fiction as a field without boundaries, where people can escape modern conventions and consider the possibilities for the future.

With the American space program in full bloom during the 1960s, Gene Roddenberry developed *Star Trek*, a new television series that would become one of the most popular in American history. *Star Trek* certainly provided an avenue for Roddenberry to comment on his times and foresee a different history than the tumultuous 1960s provided. The series was, as science fiction tends to be, technologically forward looking, with spaceships traveling at warp speed, and transporters efficiently moving people around. *Star Trek* also attempted to be forward-looking in social issues. Produced during the midst of the Civil Rights Movement, racial issues played a prominent role in *Star Trek*. The *Enterprise* crew consisted of a variety of ethnic backgrounds, and an African-American woman sat on the deck of the ship as communications officer. *Star Trek* directly addressed the issues of racial equality and pushed the bounds of television with the first interracial kiss.[1]

In addition to the Civil Rights Movement, the 1960s also saw other social movements rise to national prominence. Native Americans, homosexuals, and other minority groups fed from the energy of African-American successes to demand their own rights. Angered by the Vietnam War, the antiwar movement jockeyed for accountability in government and peaceful resolution of conflict. The women's movement pressed for the goals of equality in citizenship, economic rights, and in private affairs like childcare and housework.[2]

With all these other campaigns, the environmental movement also took on new significance and prominence in the 1960s and continued to be relevant into the twenty-first century. Historians and activists have argued that the environmental movement fundamentally changed how people thought about a variety of problems, including toxins, waste management, scarce resources, energy, other life, and views of landscapes. Since the *Star Trek* series and movies span the period in question, and became such a prominent mode of popular culture, they serve as a relevant vehicle to examine the impact of environmental views. However, unlike the forward-looking racial equality in the series which preceded American views, *Star Trek* fails to escape the bonds of its time in environmental views, instead reflecting the outlook of its writers and creators. In fact, in many cases, rather than functioning as a method to examine the future for the environment, *Star Trek* apes much older, established views, with story lines and concepts often lagging behind major environmental changes by more than a decade.

Ideas about Wilderness: Historical Trends and the Original Star Trek *Series*

In the 1964 pornography case of *Jacobellis v. Ohio*, Supreme Court justice Potter Stewart noted that "I shall not today attempt further to define the kinds of material I understand to be embraced [by the word pornography] ... [b]ut I know it when I see it" (197). Environmental historians have had the same type of difficulties with conceptions of wilderness. "Wilderness" as a culturally constructed concept has changed over time to include areas populated by dangerous animals and absent of humans at one point to the tangle of city streets at another. In his seminal work entitled *Wilderness and the American Mind*, Roderick Nash (1982) traces the origins of the word *wilderness* to the "place of wild beasts," in "forested land." Yet, as seen in the Bible, the word also encompasses, and has since the 1300s, "the uninhabited, arid land of the Near East in which so much of the action of the Testaments occurred ... [encompassing] the concept of a treeless wasteland" (2–3).

Early British colonists to America brought with them standard Judeo-Christian views which portrayed wilderness as both a place of evil and a testing ground for spiritual faith. As Nash makes clear, God cursed regions by drying up sources of water. For their evil ways, Sodom and Gomorrah "became parched wastes of salt pits and thorny brush" (Nash, 1982: 14). Yet, the Bible also portrays desert wastelands as areas for spiritual testing. Jesus spends forty days and nights fasting in the desert to be tested by the Devil. Roger Williams, who founded Rhode Island, reflected this negative view of wilderness when he stated, "The Wildernesse is a cleer resemblance of the world, where greedie and furious men persecute and devoure the harmlesse and innocent as the wilde beasts pursue and devoure the Hinds and Roes" (quoted in Nash, 1982: 34). These views continued with the early British settlers, who had a tendency to see the New World as a dangerous, wild place to be conquered and "civilized" into a pastoral environment (9–14, 17, 24–31).

The original *Star Trek* series expresses some of these very longstanding views of wilderness. The less hospitable a planet for human occupation, the more likely the characters are to be sorely tested or placed in danger in some way. On M113, in "The Man Trap" (1966), Kirk, McCoy, and the rest of the landing party beam down to a dusty, sandy planet with rocks, sparse vegetation and an orange, yellow, and red sky. Kirk describes the planet as "hot and arid." In the ruins of an old civilization, the two "extra" crewmen die mysterious deaths, their bodies completely depleted of salt. On Exo III, an icy, barren, craggy world where the inhabitants retreated underground "as the sun dimmed," Kirk is taken hostage and "almost turned into an android" ("What Are Little Girls Made Of?," 1966). On Talos IV, Kirk's predecessor, Captain Pike, attempts a rescue mission of a lost crew. The rocky, sandy, dry planet proves dangerous, however, as a cadre of aliens capture him for their zoo. The aliens manipulate Pike's dreams and memories to try to provide him a pleasant place to stay, but Pike escapes through controlling his thoughts and presenting only strong, negative emotions. The Federation subsequently attempts to limit any other human encounters with Talos IV's indigenous population by instituting the death penalty for visiting ("The Cage," 1964 and "The Menagerie, Parts I and II," 1966).

On their way to Beta VI, the *Enterprise* crew crosses a "star desert," or void in space.[3] The description of the area produces images of Earth deserts for McCoy, who states that the word "conjures up pictures of dunes, oases, mirages." Spock clarifies Bones's romantic view with a textbook definition of desert, describing it as "a waterless, barren wasteland," and continues with his opinion that "I fail to understand your romantic nostalgia for such a place." In the midst of this conversation, the ship encounters a planet, described by Spock's readings as having "no detectable soil or vegetation. Extremely hot, toxic atmosphere, swept by tornadic storms. Continuous volcanic eruptions—deadly to any life forms." Here the crew faces another trying encounter with an alien species. Beaming down to the planet, they encounter "Squire Trelane," who claims to want to study human nature, and refuses to allow the crew to leave. He is revealed eventually as a petulant, overindulged child, but not before placing Kirk's life in danger ("The Squire of Gothos," 1967). Each of these desert planets proves a testing ground for *Star Trek*'s main characters, reflecting views of wilderness prominent in European consciousness even before colonization.

As the American colonies gained their independence from Great Britain and developed a sense of national identity, new ideas about wilderness environments developed. As more Americans participated in the shift from rural areas to urban ones, wilderness areas began to be appreciated for their special characteristics. Early among these groups to appreciate wilderness were the transcendentalists, including Ralph Waldo Emerson and Henry David Thoreau.[4] Far from the mainstream, the transcendental movement portrayed nature as beautiful and worthwhile in its own right, rather than as something to be conquered or dominated. One historian defined transcendentalism as "a movement that anticipated modern environmentalism because it emphasized a holistic and organic natural world, a fundamental human need to remain in contact with nature, a naturalistic ethic" (Opie, 1998: 194–199 [quote from 194]; see also Worster, 1994: 58–111, and Nash, 1982: 84–95).

Emerson and the transcendentalists saw nature as a source of escape and renewal, an antidote to man's everyday urban world bringing them closer to their own souls. "In the woods, is perpetual youth," Emerson began:

> Within these plantations of God, a decorum and sanctity reign, a perennial festival is dressed, and the guest sees not how he should tire of them in a thousand years. In the woods, we return to reason and faith. There I feel that nothing can befall me in life,—no disgrace, no calamity, (leaving me my eyes,) which nature cannot repair ... all mean egotism vanishes.... I am part or particle of God.... In the wilderness, I find something more dear and connate than in streets or villages. In the tranquil landscape, and especially in the distant line of the horizon, man beholds somewhat as beautiful as his own nature [Emerson, 1990: 1473].

As had Emerson, Thoreau expressed views of nature as spiritual and renewing. He stated that:

> [O]ur village life would stagnate if it were not for the unexplored forests and meadows which surround it. We need the tonic of wilderness.... We can never have enough of Nature. We must be refreshed by the sight of inexhaustible vigor, vast and Titanic features, the sea-coast with its wrecks, the wilderness with its living and decaying trees, the thunder cloud, and the rain which lasts three weeks and produces freshets [Thoreau, 1987: 640].

Although the transcendentalists remained a marginalized group until the twentieth century, many other Americans began to appreciate "natural" or "wild" areas as urban areas continued to develop. The attitudes among the general population led Congress to establish several national parks over the course of the century following the emergence of the transcendentalists. Most of the rationale behind these areas (like Yosemite or Yellowstone) tended to be aesthetic: the areas represented America's scenic beauty, a source of pride for the nation. Still, the establishment of parks represented distinct alterations in earlier conceptions of wilderness. This change in attitude reached a high point with the passage of the Wilderness Act of 1964, which designated 9 million acres of federal land as "wilderness," and therefore immune, with certain exceptions, to development (Nash, 1982: 220–227; Runte, 1997: 28–30, 46–47, 264).

Reflecting the influence of transcendental ideas, the original *Star Trek* series portrays pastoral, Eden-like environments as the antithesis to the desert wilderness of dry, craggy, or snowy planets. Rather than a testing ground and place of evil, green, plant-filled environments are places of rest and rejuvenation. Upon landing on a vibrant, plant-filled world in the Omicron Delta region, Kirk orders the crew down for shore leave. Before they arrive, an investigation reveals "a planet remarkably like Earth, or how we remember Earth to be—park-like, beautiful, green, flowers, trees, green lawns, quiet and restful." Sulu comments that the planet has "no animals, no people, no worries," while Spock describes the planet as filled with "peace, sunshine, and good air." The small landing party quickly begins encountering strange things on this Eden-like planet as their thoughts turn into reality. Kirk battles an old nemesis and finds an old flame, Sulu locates an ancient gun and a samurai warrior, and McCoy sees Alice in Wonderland characters. The "caretaker" of the planet soon arrives to explain that the planet was intended as an "amusement park" with "experiences intended to amuse" where visitors' "fondest wishes ... [are] made to happen." Realizing no real danger exists, Kirk orders the crew down for shore leave ("Shore Leave," 1966). *Star Trek* reveals attitudes of "nature," at least in a certain form, as restorative and healthy. Rather than breaking the bonds of its time, and using science fiction as a way to explore different views toward the environment, the original series reflects attitudes toward wilderness posited by Europeans prior to colonization and the transcendentalists in the mid 1800s.

Ideas about Predators: Historical Trends and the Original Star Trek *Series*

Views of predators present perhaps another example, and one of the most striking, of old environmental views prevailing in *Star Trek*'s original series. Generally, *Star Trek* views predators as lower life forms than humans. Predators who present a possible danger to humans are destroyed, even to the point of extinction, by the *Enterprise* crew. In addition, *Star Trek* characters who advocate appreciation or respect for predators tend to be dismissed as weak or unmanly.

For example, in "The Man Trap," an alien life form from the inhospitable planet of M113 comes aboard the *Enterprise*. The alien, which craves salt to survive, assumes the shape of other life forms, including humans. Since it kills humans in the process of absorbing their salt, the alien's presence on the *Enterprise* presents a danger to the crew. Kirk and Spock take an immediate stand to destroy the creature, while Bob Crater, a scientist from M113, and the creature itself (in the form of McCoy) argue for its survival. Crater attempts to persuade the crew of the creature's value, stating that she is the "last of her kind." He and "McCoy" note that the creature is "not dangerous when fed" and is "simply trying to survive by using its natural ability to take other forms," like "the chameleon uses its protective coloring." Despite this attempt, Kirk remains unfazed. "This creature's aboard my ship and I'll have it or I'll have your skin. Or both," he threatens Crater. After Crater makes one more desperate attempt for sympathy, Kirk chides him for being "too pure and noble," and states that Crater "bleed[s] too much." Spock quickly destroys the creature as it attacks both the real McCoy and Kirk. The writers, to dismiss any possible feelings of sympathy for the creature, reveal its true form as its dies— an ugly creature with grey fur, three fingered hands with suckers, and a large, ugly sucker face with purple hair.

Another early episode, "The Galileo Seven" (1967), reinforces this attitude toward other life forms. Forced to crash land on an inhospitable planet named Taurus II, the shuttle *Galileo*'s crew rushes to find an avenue of escape. As two of the shuttle's crew members make a cursory examination of the immediate area, huge, furry ape-like creatures attack them with spears. After one of the aliens kills a crew member, the rest of the crew urge retaliation against the creatures. Spock, senior officer of the mission, attempts to find a logical solution. He states that he is "frequently appalled by the low regard you Earth men have for life," and notes that they have "duties to other life forms." Spock, therefore, orders the crew to fire their weapons merely to frighten, not kill, the creatures. This solution backfires, however, making the creatures angry. They attack the shuttle with rocks, threatening the crew again. McCoy quickly derides Spock's decision as dangerous to their lives, also noting that "respect is a rational process," and these creatures were not capable of such a response. Spock's "logical" response, and respect for the creatures, earn him no respect among his colleagues, and in fact places them in further danger.

This view of predator species reflects an older, well established American policy toward predators. Early Americans tended to see wildlife as yet another resource to be used for gain. Some creatures, especially, tended to be used for profit or food—cattle, buffalo, or deer, for example. Those animals that preyed on "useful" species faced extensive extermination campaigns. Although many settlers simply killed predators like wolves on their own, Thomas Dunlap (1988) notes that "[g]overnment [also] took a hand; Massachusetts Bay and Virginia began paying bounties for wolf scalps in the 1630s" (5). "Wildlife appreciation," on the other hand, really began in the late 1800s, and centered on attempts to preserve certain types of wildlife (most frequently deer) for sport hunters. These early attitudes, which found their way into hunting regulations across the country by 1920, hardly helped the predator, who generally "competed with the hunter for scarce trophies, did it all year round, and did not use sportsmanlike methods" (Dunlap, 1988: 11–13).

Early federal land management and wildlife agencies, around the turn of the twentieth century, also controlled predators and rodents for farmers and ranchers. The Biological Survey and the Forest Service employed various methods, including hiring trappers, passing bounties, lining meat with strychnine, and "in a few cases hand[ing] out free poison" (Dunlap, 1988: 38). These policies had several unforeseen consequences. First, the extensive predator extermination programs also affected the demographics of other animals. Many times the poison set out for predators might be consumed by other species, killing them in turn. In addition, sudden bursts in population of certain animal species could also be traced to a lack of natural predators. The most famous case involved the deer herd in the Kaibab National Forest near the Grand Canyon. In an effort to protect the deer herd, the Biological Survey killed "781 mountain lions, 30 wolves (all that remained) [after years of predator policies], 4, 849 coyotes, and 554 bobcats" in the early twentieth century. By 1924, new problems arose in the area. The deer, growing exponentially in population, ate everything in sight and reach, and, with inadequate food supplies, huge numbers died of starvation the following winter (Dunlap, 1988: 58, 65–69).

During the 1950s and 1960s, as the field of ecology began to develop the concept of the inherent value and worth of any life and environment, as well as the interconnectedness of nature, ideas about wildlife began to change as well. Ecologists and bureaucrats began to understand the place of the predator in natural ecosystems, and to appreciate predators as a valuable part of the natural world's life cycle. The new science of ecology and research involving animal population explosions intersected when the Park Service began policies to protect all wildlife, including predators, in the 1930s. By the 1940s, 1950s and 1960s, even popular nature writing, movies, and television saw that "nature as a web of interdependent organisms linked by food chains connected in trophic levels make predation a neutral phenomenon—one of the mechanisms that kept natural populations in balance. Predators were not evil, even a necessary evil; they were part of the 'web of life'" (Dunlap, 1988: 65–69, 88, 100–103; Worster, 1994: 256–290).

These changes in attitudes spread rapidly to the American population. For example, the number of groups concerned with protecting different types of wildlife expanded in the 1950s and 1960s. These groups' memberships swelled, as did the amount of money flowing into their coffers. Many espoused new ideas about the value of predators in ecological systems, and pressed for many legislative and bureaucratic changes, including stopping the indiscriminate use of poisons, trapping and hunting of predators. Each of these trends flowed into the Endangered Species Act of 1973, which served to protect certain species, including some predators like the wolf, from further damage (Dunlap, 1988: 109, 133, 142–143). As noted earlier, however, these dramatic changes coming to fruition in the 1960s failed to be reflected in the original *Star Trek* series. In fact, *Star Trek* tended to stick doggedly to the view dominant in the early 1800s of predators as "useless" or inherent threats to mankind and its progress.

Modern Environmental Attitudes: Historical Trends and the Original Star Trek Series

Certainly, the original *Star Trek* series presents some views of the Earth's environmental problems and dilemmas prominent in the 1960s. Several episodes point to fears of the Earth's future as a cold, barren, bleak planet, destroyed by atomic weapons during warfare. In "The Naked Time" (1966), Spock and an ensign beam down to a frozen, desolate, cold world to rescue a scientific crew. Spock notes that the planet used to look very much like Earth, and alludes to the planet as a mirror of Earth's future. In "The Menagerie, Part II," the indigenous (and seemingly highly intelligent) life forms have been forced to live well below the lifeless surface because of a devastating war "thousands of centuries ago." The planet is "only now beginning to be able to support life again." In "Balance of Terror" (1966), the *Enterprise* encounters the Romulans for the first time, noting that they possess "primitive" and highly dangerous atomic weapons. One of these weapons explodes, and damages the *Enterprise*, inflicting several injuries from "radiation burns." Nuclear power, and the possibilities it presents, show few benefits in the early *Star Trek* episodes. In fact, the episodes reveal a preoccupation with the possession of such weapons destroying the Earth entirely.

Again, though, these views reflect attitudes seen for over a decade by the time the series began. Fears and knowledge of the devastating possibilities of nuclear power had been prevalent since at least the attacks on Hiroshima, and were well-developed during the 1950s. To a greater degree than from Hiroshima and Nagasaki, contention reached new, more profound levels with the development and subsequent testing of the hydrogen bomb. The public saw the hydrogen bomb as fundamentally different, especially since its radiation and subsequent fallout dangers threatened global proportions (see Divine, 1978; Wittner, 1997; Henrickson, 1997).

H-bomb details and testing prompted increased criticism globally at a variety of levels, drawing support from the liberal, educated middle class, prominent scientists, doctors, religious groups, labor unions and others. Cresting in the late 1950s and early 1960s, the antinuclear activists affected the moratorium of 1958, as well as the disarmament treaties of 1963 and 1968. More importantly, they "helped convince the leaders of the nuclear powers that the waging of nuclear war had become politically impossible" (Wittner, 1997: 466). The antinuclear movement has been credited with prodding the Kennedy administration into signing a ban on atmospheric testing of atomic and hydrogen bombs in 1963 (Wittner, 1997; Boyer, 1998: 61–86). *Star Trek* certainly reflected these well-established fears of nuclear power.

Summary—Original Star Trek *Series*

Overall, the original *Star Trek* series failed to reflect some of the more current concerns and activities of the environmental movement during the 1960s. Views of wilderness and predators on the series remained hopelessly trapped in the 1800s. When environmentalists and Congress legislated changes reflecting ecological beliefs in wild areas and wild animals as useful and part of an ecological whole, *Star Trek* continued to mirror views of deserts as places of danger and predators as creatures to exterminate. *Star Trek* reveals some transcendental-type attitudes toward nature. Despite this, the original series failed to make the leap to an ecological viewpoint developed during the 1960s. Desert environments are never seen as valuable in their own right, healthy, or renewing, for example. On the other hand, some environmental views of the mid twentieth century crept into the series, namely, an overriding fear of nuclear power reflected in the antinuclear movement of the 1950s and 1960s.

Ideas about Wilderness: Historical Trends and the Star Trek *Films*

The *Star Trek* movies, one of the most popular film series in American history, span almost an entire generation, and provide insight into developing environmental views of the late twentieth century. As with the original series, however, the films lag behind emerging ideas within the environmental movement, often by ten to twenty years.

The films continue to develop and use representations of desert and wilderness areas as places of evil or testing grounds, especially in matters of faith. In an early scene in *Star Trek: The Motion Picture* (1979), Spock begins the Kolinahr ritual, a ceremony "through which all emotion is renounced and shed," and where Vulcans "cast out their animal passions." The place of this transformative ritual is an ochre, dusty place with high, craggy peaks and a matching brown sky. Again, after his encounter with death in the third film, Spock returns to the desert of Vulcan, spending time alone and attempting to come to terms with his new life before rejoining the crew of the *Enterprise* in *Star Trek IV: The Voyage Home* (1986). Spock's repeated treks into the Vulcan desert mirror, of course, Jesus's testing of faith in the desert.

The writers pick up this theme of desert as a testing ground for faith in *Star Trek V: The Final Frontier* (1989). When Spock's brother, Sybok, leads the *Enterprise* across the Great Barrier to the planet he believes to be Sha Ka Ree, or heaven, the crew finds another arid, desert planet, with rocky outcroppings, no vegetation and unpredictable rock growths. Sha Ka Ree, again paralleling the desert of Jesus's trial of faith, provides a test of faith and logic for Kirk, Bones, and Spock. Yet again, this formidable environment provides a place of danger and evil, as the "God" Sybok found reveals himself as merely a power hungry alien in need of a ship in order to abandon his planet. Kirk and Spock, through determined questioning, eventually reveal the creature in his true light, destroying him before escaping.

The *Star Trek* movies also use these formidable desert environments as places of testing strength and intelligence, in addition to testing of faith. After being wrongly sentenced to a life imprisonment by the Klingons in *Star Trek VI: The Undiscovered Country* (1991), Kirk and Bones arrive on penal asteroid Rura Penthe to discover a snow desert planet. Warned that "nothing can survive" on the surface, the two watch a man freeze almost instantly when exposed to the weather, and they brave high winds and whipping snow to get to the prison entrance. The dilithium mining planet tests Kirk's physical prowess as he bests a much larger creature fighting for his coat, and later his intelligence as he and Bones struggle to escape.

As with the original series, the films see certain types of landscapes or environments as regenerative, restorative, and healthful, both mentally and physically, continuing the ideas of the transcendentalists as in the original series. While desert environments tend to have negative consequences, green, pastoral ones tend to function in a contrasting way. *Star Trek II: The Wrath of Khan* (1982) reflects this attitude. Beamed down to the center of Regula and abandoned there, apparently by Khan, Kirk admits to feeling "old ... worn out" as he views his rocky, cramped surroundings.

Marcus invites him to see "something that will make you feel young as when the world was new." She leads him to the test area for Genesis, a huge underground cavern with waterfalls, greenery and picturesque mist. As the film ends, the writers reiterate the theme once more. Kirk, faced with the loss of his friend Spock, gazes out a window from the *Enterprise* to the green planet remade by Genesis, and states that he feels "young" again.

Most obviously, *The Final Frontier* reveals this attitude of "nature" as rejuvenating as the *Enterprise* crew vacations at Yosemite on Earth. The national park becomes a place of renewal, where the formalities and responsibilities of command slip away briefly. In *Star Trek: Insurrection's* (1998) case, rural, pastoral settings are literally restorative. The Ba'ku have given up their technology in favor of an idyllic, pastoral life. One Ba'ku notes that "Our technological ability is not apparent because we have chosen not to employ them in our everyday lives. We believe that when you create a machine to do the work of a man, you take something away from the man." Their chosen world, with the "unusual metaphasic radiation" surrounding it, dramatically slows the aging process.

The *Star Trek* films as a whole also continue to privilege certain types of landscapes over others, often with little incorporation of the ideas of ecology. In the films, writers make this hierarchy of environments explicit through the juxtaposition of contrasting scenes. In *The Final Frontier* (1989), the writers effectively contrast the wild desert scenes of Nimbus III, the "Planet of Galactic Peace," with idyllic scenes of the *Enterprise* officers vacationing in Yosemite National Park. Nimbus III provides a ripe environment for Spock's brother, Sybok, as he begins gathering followers in his quest to find Sha Ka Ree. Dry, sandy, and arid, with withered trees and smoking holes in the ground, Nimbus III overflows with poverty and crime. Although the Klingons, humans and Romulans apparently agreed to develop the planet together, settlers had to be "conned into coming" to Nimbus III, and soon began "fighting amongst themselves," presumably for the scarce resources available. Even the three species representatives on the planet regard themselves as "prisoners ... on this worthless lump of rock." Directly following the images of the planet, the writers switch to Yosemite National Park. Visions of green forest, beautiful mountainscapes and deep blue skies contrast with the hazy desert of the alien world. Rather than the danger faced in wilderness environments, Kirk faces no real danger in his rock climbing escapades. When he falls from the impossibly high reaches of El Capitan, Spock swoops in to catch him with the aid of his gravity boots.

Perhaps the most striking use of the hierarchy of environments involves the main story line of the second film, *The Wrath of Khan*. The film opens with the starship *Reliant* searching for "a lifeless planet to satisfy the requirements" of scientists hoping to test a new terraforming technique known as Genesis. Ceti Alpha VI seems to be a perfect candidate, described as having "limited atmosphere, dominated by krayon gas, sand, high velocity winds. Incapable of supporting life forms." Initially excited by the prospect of finding a likely candidate for Genesis testing, Chekov sounds frustrated as he notices "minor energy flux readings" on the planet. Dr. Carol Marcus, the scientist in charge of Genesis, insists on a completely lifeless planet, noting that "there can't be so much as a micron or the show's off," and remains skeptical of *Reliant*'s suggestion that they might "transplant" the life form. In fact, the planet does have life, both human (Khan, abandoned there by Kirk 15 years earlier), and a scorpion-like creature, the "only remaining indigenous life form" of Ceti Alpha V, whose young burrow into human ear canals to survive.

Both the scientist's and the *Reliant* crew's views of Ceti Alpha V/VI indicate, as is common in *Star Trek*, a devaluing of certain types of environments. Because the planet has no valued life forms, it is "worthless," or a "sandheap" with no intrinsic value. No one suggests that the desert planet might have an ecology of its own, valuable in its own right for some reason. Worthless planets are seen as ready canvases for extreme alterations by human scientists. Regula, the planet on which Khan unleashes Genesis, is described a having "various unremarkable ores" and as "essentially a great rock in space." Of the *Enterprise* officers, only McCoy expresses any concern, and not for the "dead" planet, but at the possibility that Genesis may be used as a weapon. Certainly, at this level, ecological views of certain types of environments failed to filter into *Star Trek*'s consciousness.

Modern Environmental Ideas: Historical Trends and the Star Trek *Films*

While the films continue the themes of wilderness in the original series, historical events of the next two decades prompted some new issues in the films. Rachel Carson's *Silent Spring* (1962) demonstrated the negative consequences of pesticides on the environment, causing many people to look at their use of chemicals differently. The oil crisis of the 1970s proved not only that the United States might not be the world power it had been directly following World War II, but also that Americans needed to consider their gross overuse of dwindling natural resources (Opie, 1998; Rothman, 1998). In 1979, a crisis in a small neighborhood in Niagara Falls, New York, fundamentally altered conceptions of the impact of hazardous waste, pollution, and toxic materials on everyday lives. Love Canal prompted reactions from the general public, as housewives fought against the health effects of waste literally being buried in their backyards.

Congress reacted as well, passing the Superfund legislation, in an attempt to make corporations more responsible for their waste (Blum, 2000: 229–284).

It is hardly surprising that *Star Trek* films made during the 1980s would focus on environmental issues. Ronald Reagan's aggressive campaign to roll back environmental gains caused unintended consequences, namely, the increased awareness of many environmental issues and a huge leap in membership for the traditional environmental groups. Having been alerted to the increasing environmental problems of the decade, the general population protested private use of national parks, and opposed relaxed environmental regulations (Gottlieb, 1993; Opie, 1998; Rothman, 1998). As these themes became a more central part of the fabric of American lives, the *Star Trek* movies picked up these issues. However, they still tended to reflect changes, rather than anticipate them.

As the ideas of the environmental movement from the 1960s and 1970s filtered into the popular consciousness, the films incorporated some broader critiques of environmental problems. *The Wrath of Khan* jabs at genetic manipulation, portraying Khan and his group, themselves the product of "late twentieth century genetic engineering," as highly intelligent, but certainly psychotic, power hungry, and evil beings. In *The Final Frontier*, the Klingons litter irresponsibly as they hunt for space garbage to practice shooting, while in the next scene Kirk exhorts his human companions to "pack out your trash," as they abandon the slopes of Yosemite for another space adventure.

Several of the films also deal with the exploitation or overuse of natural resources, a prominent idea within the environmental movement since the 1960s. In *Star Trek VI*, Spock reveals that the Klingon moon, Praxis, exploded because of "over mining and insufficient safety precautions." The destruction of the moon has dire consequences for the Klingon home world. Spock continues that "with the deadly pollution of their ozone, they will have depleted their supply of oxygen in approximately fifty Earth years." Exploitation of natural resources forms a key component of *Insurrection*. The Ba'ku people live peacefully on a planet with a unique natural resource, "unusual metaphasic radiation" which dramatically slows the aging process. Elements of the Federation, along with a group of older Ba'ku known as the Son'a, attempt to remove the Ba'ku to exploit the antiaging properties of the planet by others. Upon discovering the plot, Picard leaps to the assistance of the Ba'ku and saves them from losing their world.

Perhaps the most explicitly "environmental" of the *Star Trek* movies is the fourth film in the series, *The Voyage Home*, in which the crew travels back in time to find a humpback whale to respond to a probe threatening the destruction of the Earth. The film brims with obvious environmental overtones, warning of dire consequences of the extinction of species and the value of nonhuman life forms (Geraghty, 2003: 228–245). Although the probe's message mystifies Earth's human inhabitants, Spock quickly notes that "There are other forms of intelligence on Earth.... Only human arrogance would assume the message must be meant for man." Spock quickly places an ecological context into the film: other life forms have value, a place in the world, and intelligence. Unlike his earlier attempt in the original series, his fellow officers quickly accept this piece of information. After locating a pair of humpbacks in a twentieth century San Francisco aquarium, Spock dives in with the whales to inform them of their mission. Again, the message of the importance of other life and the absorption of ecological values surfaces as Spock notes that "If we were to assume these whales were ours to do with as we please, we would be as guilty as those who caused their extinction." If the message of saving species had not been pounded into the audience enough, the last scenes reiterate the theme once more, as Kirk sums up the adventure by stating, "You know, it's ironic. When man was killing these creatures, he was destroying his own future." Successful in their mission, of course, when they return to the future with the whales, Earth's leaders applaud the *Enterprise* crew, telling Kirk, "You and your crew have saved this planet from its own shortcomings, and we are forever in your debt."

Yet even with this environmental theme, *Star Trek* continued to lag behind the main cusp of the environmental movement. By the mid 1980s, the issue of "environmental justice" had captured the environmental movement. Environmental justice advocates claim that poor, minority neighborhoods suffer disproportionate burdens of environmental pollution. They fight against what they describe as "environmental racism." One scholar activist has defined the movements as referring:

> to any policy, practice or directive that differentially affects or disadvantages (whether intended or unintended) individuals, groups, or communities based on race or color. Racism is reinforced by government, legal, economic, political, and military institutions. Environmental racism is not just a domestic practice. It is global. Environmental racism extends to the export of hazardous waste, risky technologies, and pesticides and the application of nonsustainable and exploited development models to the Third World just as it has been targeted toward people of color, working class people, and poor people in this country [Bullard, 1994: 1037].

Activists of color across the nation struggle against environmental racism by removing polluting industry, landfills, and hazardous waste sites from their communities, or preventing them from being sited in the first place.

The environmental justice movement criticized the "mainstream" environmental movement for a preoccupation with exactly the type of concerns expressed in *The Voyage Home*. Activists in the environmental justice movement describe the mainstream movement as concerned with wildlife over human concerns, landscapes over human problems, and elite recreation over poor working conditions in factories. Grassroots groups, one leader noted, "challenge the 'business-as-usual' environmentalism that is generally practiced by the more privileged wildlife- and conservation-oriented groups" (Bullard, 1993: 7). Hardly alone in this perception, other activists and journalists frequently concur in a view of the environmental movement as elitist and nonhuman centered. One activist in Alabama colorfully stated, "If it does not hoot in the night, or swim upstream, environmentalists are not interested" (Battle, 1994 quoted in Westra and Lawson, 2001: xvii). Judi Bari (1991), an outspoken forest preservation activist in the radical Earth First! group, states that environmentalism failed to reach out to working class people. The problem, she concludes, is "that the environmental movement tends to separate itself from the general social-justice movement in this country. Environmentalists ghettoize themselves among these privileged people and try to limit themselves to wilderness issues that only privileged people can worry about" (73). She continued: "I think traditional environmentalism leaves no room for workers; they're declared immoral because they work in the factory" (75). At the moment when the environmental movement broadened to incorporate a wider critique of society, *Star Trek* revealed its limitations by focusing on the mainstream views ("Save the Whales") seen as increasingly irrelevant to people concerned with urban, human-centered problems.

Even through *The Next Generation* films, the issues of environmental justice failed to take hold of the series, even when the context and problems appeared. In *Star Trek Nemesis* (2002), Shinzon, a clone of Captain Jean-Luc Picard grows up on Remus, the sister planet to Romulus with a dark and light side. The Remans, described as an "undesirable caste" of the Romulan people and later as "slave labor," live on the dark side, engaged in the difficult task of mining dilithium for Romulan heavy weapons production. The Remans present the classic example of "environmental justice": an oppressed people, subject to an increased level of environmental degradation as a part of their oppression. However, despite their plight, no one on the *Enterprise* suggests a raid on the Reman moon to liberate them from their fate on the dark, cold, mining planet. Shinzon's evil nature sullied the fate of the entire Reman people, and, in fact, the audience cheers his destruction. Obviously, the problems of environmental justice had not yet reached the political consciousness of the writers.

Conclusions

Star Trek's original series began just as fantastic, dramatic changes swept across America. The 1960s witnessed far-reaching changes for

African Americans, women, and the environment. Even before affirmative action or the Black Power movement, *Star Trek* absorbed some of the ideas of racial equality, portraying a multicultural crew working together in harmony, well before such changes became close to reality in America. Despite this forward-thinking reflection of race relations, no such "out of the box" thinking persisted with environmental attitudes or issues. *Star Trek* remained mired in much older, persistent values: desert environments reflected danger, pastoral environments renewal. Some more modern ideas crept in, but usually long after their general acceptance, as in the case, for example, of fears of nuclear weapons, or concern over the use of natural resources.

Only tentative conclusions about the impact of the environmental movement can be reached using one science fiction series, regardless of its life span. Perhaps environmental historians have overestimated the impact of the environmental movement's ideas on the general public. Environmental ideas may take longer to reach the general consciousness than expected. Perhaps the lag in views is simply a product of the medium, and the nature of mass produced entertainment. *Star Trek*'s creators, wanting to create a noncontroversial, well-accepted series, may have simply inhibited original, out-of-the-box thinking with regards to many issues, including environmental concerns.

Perhaps, more likely, *Star Trek* simply reflects an accurate picture of the creators of the series. Historians have long accepted that the environment is a culturally constructed concept. Different ethnicities, classes, and genders view the environment differently, and have varying views on its most pressing problems. Wealthy people have different concerns than the poor, as seen in the environmental justice movement, which also reveals demarcations along race lines regarding prominent issues. And, finally, women view the environment and environmental concerns differently from men. Since elite, white men wrote and produced *Star Trek*, the series may simply reflect their dominant view through the last decades of the twentieth century. In addition, as noted, some environmental views have been remarkably longstanding. The conceptions of desert as wilderness and dangerous, for example, have existed among Europeans for well over 500 years. It may be unrealistic to think that even science fiction could override such powerful conceptions, or, perhaps, this may indicate that certain environmental values remain constant over time. Certainly, a more detailed view of other types of popular culture sources, and especially science fiction, could add to the rich panoply of data from *Star Trek*.

Notes

1. Although beyond the scope of this article, the original *Star Trek* series certainly continued to feed certain stereotypes of African Americans. Uhura was frequently seen

as the "musical" crew member, and certainly the writers played off her sexuality to a great degree.

2. Again, although Roddenberry's series attempted to be forward-thinking in race relations, it was hardly a bastion of feminist thought. Women in the original series clutched desperately to men for protection, served coffee and food to the men, or acted as love interests. Effects of the women's movement would take much longer to sink in, as in society in general.

3. This is something of an odd concept, perhaps reflective of the writers' lack of knowledge about the true nature of space itself, which is, generally, characterized by large areas with very low density matter.

4. Emerson and Thoreau's views of wilderness tended toward areas uncultivated by humans. They appreciated forests and nonurban areas for their benefits, and never went as far as advocating that men venture into deserts or ice plains for restoration.

Works Cited

Bari, Judi, and Judith Kohl. "Environmental Justice: Highlander after Myles." *Social Policy* 21, no.3 (1991): 73–75.

Battle, W. "Letter to the Editor." *Faces of Environmental Racism: Confronting Issues of Global Justice.* 2nd ed. Edited by Laura Westra and Bill Lawson. Lanham, MD: Rowman and Littlefield, 1994.

Blum, Elizabeth D. "Pink and Green: A Comparative Study of Black and White Women's Environmental Activism in the Twentieth Century." PhD diss., University of Houston, 2000.

Boyer, Paul. *Fallout: A Historian Reflects on America's Half Century Encounter with Nuclear Weapons.* Columbus: Ohio State University Press, 1998.

Bullard, Robert. "Introduction." *Confronting Environmental Racism: Voices from the Grassroots.* Boston: South End Press, 1998.

_____. "Environmental Racism and 'Invisible' Communities." *West Virginia Law Review* 96 (1994): 1037–1050.

Divine, Robert. *Blowing on the Wind: The Nuclear Test Ban Debate, 1954–1960.* New York: Oxford University Press, 1978.

Dunlap, Thomas. *Saving America's Wildlife: Ecology and the American Mind, 1850–1990.* Princeton: Princeton University Press, 1988.

Emerson, Ralph Waldo. "Nature." *The Heath Anthology of American Literature.* Vol. 1. Edited by Paul Lauter. Lexington, MA: D.C. Heath and Company, 1990.

Foreman, Christopher H. *The Promise and Peril of Environmental Justice.* Washington, D.C.: Brookings Institution, 1998.

Geraghty, Lincoln. "The American Jeremiad and *Star Trek*'s Puritan Legacy." *Journal of the Fantastic in the Arts* 14, no. 2 (2003): 228–245.

Gottlieb, Robert. *Forcing the Spring: The Transformation of the American Environmental Movement.* Washington, D.C.: Island Press, 1993.

Henrickson, Margot A. *Dr. Strangelove's America: Society and Culture in the Atomic Age.* Berkeley: University of California Press, 1997.

Jacobellis v. Ohio, 378 U.S. 184 (1964).

Nash, Roderick. *Wilderness and the American Mind.* 3rd ed. New Haven: Yale University Press, 1982.

Opie, John. *Nature's Nation: An Environmental History of the United States.* Fort Worth: Harcourt Brace College Publishing, 1998.

Rothman, Hal. *The Greening of a Nation? Environmentalism in the United States since 1945.* Fort Worth: Harcourt Brace College Publishing, 1998.

Runte, Alfred. *National Parks: The American Experience.* 3rd ed. Lincoln: University of Nebraska Press, 1997.

Thoreau, Henry David. "Walden." *The Harper American Literature Compact Edition.* Edited by Donald McQuade. New York: Harper and Row Publishers, 1987.

Wittner, Laurence S. *Resisting the Bomb: A History of the World Nuclear Disarmament Movement, 1954–1970.* Stanford: Stanford University Press, 1997.
Worster, Donald. *Nature's Economy: A History of Ecological Ideas.* 2nd ed. New York: Cambridge University Press, 1994.

6

Batter Up!

The Mythology and Psychology of Sports and Games in Star Trek: Deep Space Nine

BARBARA A. SILLIMAN

In *Star Trek: Deep Space Nine* (*DS9*), sports and games are used as metaphors for management style, opportunities for character exposition, and avenues for bonding and self-expression. In a 45-minute episode, during which the primary and secondary story line conflicts are detailed and resolved, ongoing character development is facilitated by the use of games and sports. These clues become part of the continuing relationship between the viewer and the character, and allow for more interesting ways to experience the characters in subsequent episodes of the series. Sports and games allow the writers to infuse into the series serious and weighty subject matter in a more subtle way. One significant subject running throughout the seven years of *DS9* is religion in the form of the Bajoran faith. True spirituality is presented particularly through Colonel Kira Nerys, and the political corruption and personal jealousy many times found in hierarchical authority is presented through Kai Winn, the "pope" of the Bajoran faith.

DS9 is rare in the *Star Trek* franchise, because it treats religion and religious spirituality with respect and acceptance. Religion in *Star Trek* usually has been viewed as a primitive necessity which twenty-fourth century humans no longer need. The Original Series addressed ancient religions with such episodes as "Who Mourns for Adonis?" (1967) wherein Captain Kirk verbally spars with an alien creature who claims to be ancient Greece's sun god, Apollo. In "The Return of the Archons" (1967) computers are used to subdue a society of humanoids by introducing a vengeful god who will punish them if they do not comply with all commands. This atheistic trend is also very evident in *Star Trek: The Next Generation* (*TNG*), whose last one and one-half years ran concurrently with *DS9*. In "Masks" (1994) the *Enterprise* is transformed by a space station archive into a temple, wherein the rivalry between the female sun god, Masaka, and the male moon god, Korgano, of an ancient animistic religion is reenacted. The plot suggests that such religions are primitive and quaint, and the reenactment is an archeological adventure and a puzzle to be solved for Captain Picard. Its religious significance is never discussed. In "Who Watches the Watchers" (1989) the Mintakans, Bronze Age proto-Vulcans, mistake Captain Picard as their Overseer, or god. In this episode Picard calls religion a "belief in the supernatural" and refuses to be a part of a mistake which would force the Mintakan people "back into the Dark Ages of superstition and ignorance and fear."

Similarly, in *DS9*'s episode "Tears of the Prophets" (1998) Benjamin receives a vision from the Prophets warning him not to leave Bajor when he is supposed to lead a task force against the Dominion on Cardassia. Admiral Ross confronts Ben about his obsession with the Prophets and being their Emissary, challenging him: "You are either the Emissary or a Starfleet captain. You can't be both." Religion has no place in the Federation or Starfleet. With *DS9*, the writers begin the series with a placement of religion, religious philosophy and mythology, and religious leadership directly in the center of the continuous story line. The Prophets, the Emissary, the Kai, the Vedeks, and the Orbs are integral parts of the continuing story of *DS9* and its main characters. Many times spiritual and magical events are explained using science and technology. However, at the end of seven years, many lives have been touched by the serenity and strength of Bajoran faith, even as the spiritual leader of that faith demonstrates petty jealousy, personal hypocrisy, and a loss of true faith.

The initial insertion of mythology and religion into the series is with baseball, a commonly played American sport. This game dominates the subtext of *DS9* and is most closely associated with the station commander and his son. Deeanne Westbrook (1996) comments that:

> [B]aseball literature evokes the sense of a universe where time and space may obey the laws of an unknown physics or be measured not in mechanistic terms but in human, psychological ones. There are opportunities in such a world to encounter the sacred, the numinous, the uncanny [2–3].

Although *DS9* is not baseball literature in its strictest terms, it is highly influenced by baseball as a game, a parent-child bonding experience, a group bonding experience, and a metaphor for leadership and teamwork. It also reflects an American sense of mythology, not in religious terms perhaps but certainly in the secular. Odysseus, Hercules, Jason, and King Arthur have been replaced by Babe Ruth, Joe DiMaggio, Hank

Aaron, and Curt Schilling. The heroic quest, formerly the Golden Fleece or the Holy Grail, is now winning the World Series.[1] *DS9* appropriates this tendency toward secular mythology and places it squarely within the character development of the station's Captain Benjamin Sisko. While baseball is presented in its popular usage, its secular mythology blends and reflects the religious mythology of ancient Terran civilizations and the Bajoran people.

Sisko is a military figure who, in the pilot episode, becomes a religious icon for the Bajoran people when he communicates directly with the alien life forms living in the stable wormhole located in Bajoran space. The Bajorans refer to these entities as the Prophets, the god-like figures of Bajoran religious philosophy who, through indirect intervention, seem to lead them. Benjamin becomes the Emissary of the Prophets, a title and position with which, at the beginning, he is very uncomfortable. Thus, the writers of *DS9* make Benjamin part of religious mythology, while demonstrating that he embraces the secular mythology surrounding baseball.

Joseph Campbell (1949) posits that "the mythological adventure of the hero" is an outgrowth of the formula he sees repeated in rites of passage, that is, "separation-initiation-return: which might be named the nuclear unit of the monomyth" (30). As with this monomythic structure, the baseball player performs a mini-rite of passage each time at bat. He separates from his warriors (the team) to face all alone the evil sorcerer (the pitcher) on the pitcher's mound. He uses a magic weapon (the bat) to battle this magician and strike back against his powerful orb (the thrown baseball). His wise mentor or Merlin figure (the team manager) teaches the hero how to fight the sorcerer and then encourages him while he engages in the battle. When the hero successfully disturbs the flight of the magic orb, he must then do battle with the minions of the sorcerer (the basemen and fielders) while running in a ritualistic diamond pattern (the initiation journey through hell). If he is successful, he returns home (literally home plate) to be greeted triumphantly by the cheers of his band of warriors and the whole tribal community (the team and fans). The heroic quest, the ultimate goal and prize, is winning the World Series (see also chapter 7 on the monomyth in the *Star Trek* films).

Benjamin himself fits the hero structure by his separation from the Federation community when he becomes commander of a former minerals processing station on the outskirts (or frontier) of Federation space. He takes on the task of healing and defending the weakened Bajorans whose liberation from Cardassian slavery was, many times, a Pyrrhic victory. He brings with him a small band of warriors (Federation personnel) and his son, Jake, the Telemachus figure (the righteous son of the hero). The warrior death of Jake's mother in a battle against the Borg (a seemingly supernatural enemy) leaves the young boy bereft of a female role model/authority figure. He chooses to bond more strongly to his father. Benjamin's boon companion and mentor is Jadzia Dax who, as Curzon Dax, has known Sisko since he was newly out of Starfleet Academy. Benjamin's heroic quest befits this hero; he must rid the Alpha Quadrant of a lethal, terrifying, and overwhelming enemy, the Dominion (the nemesis and worthy opponent of the hero).

Throughout the course of seven seasons, Benjamin goes through several levels of initiation. He learns the importance of his roles as the Emissary; as the station commander; as an officer representing the political, military, and diplomatic functions of the Federation; and as Jake's father. His greatest initiation will be in the Celestial Temple as a student of the Prophets. His return is anticipated, although it may take a very long time, perhaps as long, if not longer, than Odysseus's 20 years away from Ithaca, thus making Kasidy (his new bride) the Penelope figure and their anticipated child the new Telemachus.

The one link utilized by the writers to join the secular and religious worlds of the station commander of *DS9* is baseball. From the beginning, Benjamin Sisko is closely allied with this very American sport, which—according to *Star Trek* future history—has not been played on Earth (or presumably in the whole Terran system) for about 200 years. The very title of the series reflects the nine positions on a baseball team.[2] He has a baseball significantly displayed on the otherwise uncluttered desk in his office. He plays with the baseball during the informal meetings with his senior officers and also as a stress diffuser when he is dealing with particular problems (e.g., "Honor Among Thieves," 1998). Benjamin is universally identified with his desktop baseball, and it represents him on the station when he is forced to evacuate during a temporary occupation by the Jem'Hadar and the Cardassians. In "A Call to Arms" (1997) when Gul Dukat sees the ball on the station captain's desk he accurately interprets it as a message from Sisko to him that he intends to return and force Dukat from the station.

The baseball serves a different purpose for Bajoran second-in-command Kira Nerys. With the loss of the Orbs of the Prophets and the death of Jadzia Dax, Benjamin takes a leave of absence from the station, returning to New Orleans for rest and a reevaluation of his life's purpose. In "Image in the Sand" (1998) Kira, acting station commander, is put through several difficult situations with Starfleet, the Romulans, and station personnel. She reaches for the empty baseball display stand which Benjamin left on his office desk. Her body language projects her longing for Sisko to return and her desperate search for self-confidence to continue in her forced new role. The missing baseball makes Kira ill at ease, because, for her, it represents the captain—it is a symbol of his merged presence as station commander and as the emissary. Benjamin once defiantly left the baseball behind as a gesture to Dukat that the

Cardassian's tenure on *DS9* was tenuous at best. This time, he has taken the ball, the symbol of his status and presence on the station, with him.

In the premiere episode of the series, "Emissary" (1993), Benjamin uses the game of baseball in his initial discussions with the Prophets to help explain the concept of linear time. In the seventh season episode "Shadows and Symbols" (1998) the baseball clearly represents the sacred Orbs themselves. Benjamin plays an upright piano in his father's restaurant on which he has rested his personal baseball, the one that he had on his desk at the space station. Of its own volition, it rolls off the top and onto the floor. Ben reaches down to retrieve it, initiating the start of a vision from the Prophets. The baseball again becomes symbolic of the merged Sisko—captain and emissary—and acts as a personal Orb, thus giving this simple ball a more religious significance. It is the baseball that marks the hidden location of a true Orb—the Orb of the Emissary. This new, hidden Orb will cleanse the Celestial Temple of the evil Pah-wraiths, allowing the wormhole to open again. The baseball is given a prominence in Benjamin's vision. It is placed in the foreground and fills the visual field. The camera's point of view then shifts to the left, at which time the figure of Benjamin is seen digging rapidly into a section of desert sand. Solidifying its new role for Benjamin as a personal Orb, the baseball initiates a second vision. Duplicating the first vision's genesis, the ball rolls off the piano a second time, but this time it rolls into the hands of a woman who, it is revealed, is Benjamin's real mother, Sara, a Prophet. Benjamin learns from her that he is of mixed parentage, both Prophet and human. Throughout the entire revelatory conversation it is either Sara or Benjamin who holds the baseball, the link between the corporeal and the non-corporeal, the mortal and the immortal, the secular and the divine.

The mythological cycle comes full circle for Benjamin. His character has begun to fulfill the more classical tenets of the hero as listed by Lord Raglan (1949: 178–179), one of which is that the hero is parented by a god and a human. He is on his heroic quest against the forces of the Pah-wraiths, perverse Prophets akin to Judeo-Christianity's devils (aka fallen angels), as well as the Dominion. As he cleanses the Alpha Quadrant of the corporeal superior enemy, he also will cleanse the Celestial Temple of the non-corporeal enemy who were freed earlier by Gul Dukat. At the end of his heroic quest, Benjamin will fulfill the last of the heroic tenets with his mysterious death (while liberating his people from their immortal enemies), his missing and unburied body, and finally his ascension to the Celestial Temple, making him a messiah figure. Thus, secular and religious mythologies are merged by the relic/icon of the baseball itself.

In addition to baseball's mythological elements, Sisko's management style is also very much a part of the baseball tradition. He sets up his hierarchy of authority and his expectations of achievement among his staff using the game as his guide. His command style is very much like that of a Major League Baseball manager. The manager trains his team members to work independently and autonomously at their individual duties according to his design. Their duties are similar but they usually do not overlap. Using National League rules, all players are up at bat when on the offensive, but work at their unique positions (first base, short stop, catcher, etc.) when on the defensive. The manager allows the team members to do their jobs and interferes only when he needs to do so. He will pull players out of the game only when they need to be pulled. Sisko knows these rules clearly and, when asked, pointedly disagrees with the American League's designated hitter rule. On his team, all players should be able to bat, just as all members of Starfleet should know how to defend themselves and their crewmates. Each member of *DS9*'s senior staff works on a dual level, just as in baseball. They each have their own job to do, just as baseball players have their own positions to play. They are all combat trained and, like National League players, they are all able to come up to bat (defend the station) to insure that the team wins. Just like baseball players, they work as a team. They trust each other and work with each other to form a cohesive single unit. Win or lose, they are in it together.

In its secular form, baseball is used as a method of bonding for father and son. Benjamin and his son, Jake, use Quark's holosuites to play or watch games with the greats of the past, especially Harmon "Buck" Bokai of the London Kings, the player who is Benjamin's favorite ("If Wishes Were Horses," 1993). Just like twentieth century fathers and sons, Benjamin and Jake play catch together, which both relaxes them after a strenuous day and strengthens their emotional ties with each other. It is, in fact, the father-son relationship which is a major part of baseball literature. Deeanne Westbrook (1996) points out that typical baseball literature elevates the father-son and diminishes the mother-son. She maintains that "the mythic agenda of much of baseball literature ... [is], by accident or design, to obtain the father's blessing, to become *at one* with him, and in the process, to depict and yet avoid the psychic dangers embodied in the mother" (247). *DS9* maintains that structure, but not at the cost of the mother. With her heroic death during Jake's early adolescence, Jennifer Sisko becomes the good, unobtrusive, marginalized mother. Her status is never diminished, but she is no longer a part of the maturing process. Baseball literature's mother is castrating, "abusive, cruel, unnatural, mad, and sexually flawed" (Westbrook, 1996: 247), but Jennifer is always the good woman who has died before her time and who will never see her son grow and achieve greatness.

Whereas baseball literature's father is a good man who is humbled by society, dead too soon, and gives his blessing begrudgingly to the son to live his own life, he is also a man whose less than stellar memory must be maintained by the more successful son (Westbrook, 1996: 262–3). *DS9* writers also alter that concept. The father in this new paradigm is a great man, successful, even spiritual, and the son lives under a long shadow from which he must remove himself in order to find his own character and destiny. This removal, however, is not traumatic. Quite the contrary, in "Explorers" (1995) Jake is supported by his father when he announces that he does not wish to become a Starfleet officer. After some initial verbal jousting, Benjamin quickly allows for the mature decision-making of his son and supports his decision to become a writer. Jake's role thus changes as he now becomes the Homer to Benjamin's Odysseus, the troubadour singing the songs of the hero's great deeds.

Baseball also establishes a special bond between Benjamin and his future wife, freighter captain Kasidy Yates, the woman whom Jake manipulates to be a blind date for his father in "Family Business" (1995). One major reason Jake feels that Kasidy and Benjamin will enjoy each other's company is that Kasidy is also a baseball fan. Her brother, in fact, lives in a colony on Cestus III which is organizing a grassroots baseball league with other colonists on the same planet. His team is called the Pike City Pioneers. In this episode, Benjamin and Kasidy's first date extends itself when he expresses delight in an audio-only transmission of Kasidy's brother's intramural game which is being broadcast at a specific time that evening. It is at that moment at the beginning of their courtship that these two people discover that they look at life in similar ways and have a mutual interest that they can share.

Baseball many times becomes a metaphor for making choices in life and living with the consequences of those choices. The game itself is a series of possibilities based on which kind of pitch is thrown, how the batter responds to each pitch, and how the infield and outfield react at the moment of impact. A simple missed ball rolling between the legs of a player can become a devastating loss in a game and a World Series.[3] In a pivotal episode in the final season episode, "Take Me Out to the Holosuite" (1998), Sisko is confronted by a Vulcan Starfleet captain who challenges him to a game of baseball to satisfy an old grudge. This game with the Vulcan crew, however, is more than simply baseball. It is a significant learning experience for Benjamin as a leader. He becomes obsessed with winning. He stops seeing it as a friendly rivalry between Starfleet officers, choosing instead to view it as a grudge match between enemies. This game also becomes a rite of passage for Benjamin, a reexamination of himself and of the game he loves. He is David battling Goliath, the *DS9*ers being less experienced and less talented as a team waging war against the Vulcans, who are the superior players. It is evident from the beginning of the episode that the *DS9*ers are no match against the Vulcans. The more disciplined and well-trained Vulcan team is pitted against the untrained and somewhat undisciplined, eclectic *DS9* team of Jake, Quark, Rom, Nog, Leeta (Rom's wife), and *DS9*'s senior officers Ezri Dax, Kira, and Julian, with Security Officer Odo as umpire and Benjamin as team manager (of course). They are the typical multicultural American team doing battle against a unicultural opponent: "The fully constituted [American baseball] team is multiethnic, multi-cultural, and multifarious.... The functional benefit of such multiculturalism is that it helps America as a team to be the best team it can be; let everybody play, and we can beat Japan" (Morris, 1997: 18).

In an effort to strengthen his team, Benjamin removes Rom, a truly terrible baseball player, from the roster. This is an unpopular move among the team, since they see the contest as a bonding experience and a friendly game. Benjamin temporarily loses the respect of his team and his enjoyment of the sport when he places too much value on winning. He has waged so much war against the Dominion enemy that he brings that same attitude to the challenge by the Vulcans and into the ball field. The baseball game should be a safe place to lose, the only place where loss is acceptable. Just being a part of the game is the thrill, and having fun should be the goal. He needs to be reminded that he is at play, in a game, and that war is another reality best left outside the holosuites. It is only after he is ejected from the game by umpire Odo that Benjamin begins to realize how much he has misjudged himself and his team. He sits in the empty stands with Rom seated far behind him. In his epiphany, Benjamin realizes that the game is a group effort of all his people and, win or lose, it is their valiant effort which is important, not the final score. He remembers that they are working best as a team when they are all attempting to achieve the same goal. Benjamin and his team are working counter to each other, thus causing each of them to have less enjoyment. It is only when the team dynamic is reinstated (Rom is re-added to the roster) that the joy of working as one unit attempting a common goal is reestablished (see also Janicker and Geraghty, 2007). Benjamin underlines this renewed joy by informing the computer to insert a cheering crowd in the stands of the holosuite program.

In Quark's bar, while the *DS9*ers joyously celebrate their loss, the Vulcan captain confronts Benjamin, inquiring why they all are so happy about losing. It is Benjamin's delight to inform his logical, unemotional colleague that winning does not matter; it is the joy of the game that is most important. As Jeremy MacClancy (1996) observes:

> One thing that *is* clear is that sports need not necessarily contain any competitive element. The example of the Melanesians—introduced to football by missionaries—who would play the game for days until both sides had come to a draw is already well-known. Native Americans would play lacrosse for days at a time, ending the game only when they had achieved a tie [8].

When lives are at stake, it is more important to know that all hands work with one mind and one goal than it is—singly and isolatedly—to obsess only about winning. Many a war has been won after the warriors have staged a strategic retreat.

The writers of *DS9* have taken character exposition and given it a new dimension by using sports and games to enhance the viewers' knowledge of the characters and to define their personalities. The most obvious game used is baseball, a significant metaphor for the mythic status and leadership style of the commander of the space station, Captain Benjamin Sisko. There is a precision about baseball not found in any other sport. Statistics about the game are routinely memorized by those who love it, and these scores represent in an encapsulated form the life's work of each team member in each league of Major League Baseball. Benjamin would agree with Dodgers pitcher Sandy Koufax when Koufax expresses his opinion that there is a "cleanness" about baseball: "[If] you do a good job, the numbers say so. You don't have to ask anyone or play politics" (quoted in Candelaria, 1989: 115). As with any baseball enthusiast, Benjamin aspires to the perfect game: pitching a no-hitter. In its figurative sense, the perfect game symbolizes any paradigm of perfection in life, whether a grail-like treasure or a pinnacle of achievement sought for either personal or social reasons. The perfect game metaphor may also refer to process, particularly to the process by which the grail or achievement is sought and attained (Candelaria, 1989: 117).

In the final episode, "What You Leave Behind" (1999), Benjamin has triumphed over the almost unbeatable enemy, the Dominion; metaphorically, his team has won the equivalent of the World Series, thus finding their Holy Grail. There are other successes about which the captain can be proud. He has seen his son grow to become a good and honorable man. He has accepted, perhaps even embraced, his role as Emissary of the Prophets. He has married the woman he loves, and she is pregnant with his child. In a solidification of his placement within the Bajoran religious veneration of the Prophets, Benjamin's work is not over quite yet. The Prophets have brought him into their Celestial Temple after his sacrificial death in the Bajoran Fire Caves so that he may continue as one of them, beginning his inheritance as an immortal being, a true child of the Prophets. In this way, Benjamin completes his journey as the messianic hero, as seen in Christian religious mythology. After his death at the hands of his mortal and immortal enemies (both represented in the person of Gul Dukat, a Cardassian who is possessed by a Pah-wraith), his essence is not allowed to die. Instead he literally ascends into the heavenly body of the Celestial Temple to live as one forever with the protectors of Bajor.

After his death, when he has risen to the Temple, Benjamin makes an appearance through a vision. This vision is not shared with any of the male characters who have fought so valiantly and faithfully with him, not even his son, Jake. Rather, just as Christ initially appears only to one special woman at the tomb,[4] so, too, Benjamin appears only to the closest female in his corporeal life, his wife, Kasidy. Much as in the message of the risen Christ, Benjamin comforts her, expresses his love for her, and informs her that he will return to her. As the only Prophet with experience as a corporeal being, he will be essential to the continued benevolent guardianship of the Bajoran people. His personal guardianship, though, will be over Kasidy and their child. Benjamin's baseball takes on an additional, religious, meaning for Kira Nerys after Sisko disappears in the Bajoran Fire Caves. It becomes her personal Orb, a holy relic of the Emissary that she can touch and hold. Baseball is inextricably linked with Benjamin Sisko and is a constant reminder of his essence and his presence. This ball will allow her to feel the presence of Benjamin in her life as she assumes his role as commander of the space station and liaison to the Federation ("What You Leave Behind"). What she does not know at this point is that Benjamin truly is watching over her from his new home in the Celestial Temple. In a sense, Benjamin has been called up to the front office, the administration of the team. From his new position, he will be able to scout the players, intervene when necessary, and look forward to many more winning seasons. Viewers can only hope that Benjamin is allowed some vacation time in order to nurture his new child, playing catch and telling stories of the big game.

Baseball in *DS9* is used as a tool by the writers to center the religious elements within the series and to express the personal life philosophy of Benjamin Sisko. Whether he is conscious of it or not, his life has been formed and informed by baseball, and his command style is strongly influenced by this sport. The mythical qualities that are a part of baseball assist in explaining and in presenting the religious central focus of the series. As a game, baseball is a necessary distraction and good physical exercise for Benjamin. He uses the game to bond with his son, Jake, and to court his second wife, Kasidy. When it becomes necessary, baseball re-instructs Benjamin in the truth about surviving psychologically during wartime. By waging a "safe war" on the diamond, he is able to lose and survive, while he simultaneously initiates a bonding experience for his bridge officers, family, and friends. A concurrent theme—that family and friends are equally important to the military aspects of life in Starfleet—is supported and strengthened by baseball.

While many fans of science fiction in general and *Star Trek* in particular accept the atheistic position that religion becomes outdated in the future and that it represents the primitive nature of humanity, fans of *DS9* also accept the religiosity and spirituality that is a part of this series. The highest Starfleet authority on the space station is also the highest spiritual representative for the Bajoran people. Although Benjamin does not exercise any authority over the religious lives of the Bajorans, his role as the Emissary of the Prophets gives him a significant influence—an influence of which Kai Winn, the Bajoran religious authority, is extremely jealous. Baseball links Benjamin's dual representations and responsibilities. By its own nature, the game has mythological qualities, and it is a perfect way to explain religious observance and spiritual faith while maintaining its secular nature as a team sport.

Notes

1. The Boston Red Sox—whose owner instituted the World Series games in 1903 with the Pittsburgh Pirates' owner, and who handily won that first series ("History: 1903") as well as all five series in which they played up to 1918 ("History: 1918")—were on the quest since 1918 and, in Sisyphean fashion, did not win the World Series for 86 years. Their fans, however, obsessed each year about the possibility of finally breaking the "Curse of the Bambino," until the Sox finally won the World Series in 2004.

The "Curse of the Bambino" refers to George Herman "Babe" Ruth and his years with the Boston Red Sox. Before he was traded to the New York Yankees in 1920, Ruth was a valued player on the Red Sox team, mostly as a left-handed pitcher and in 1919 as a full-time outfielder. After Ruth ("The Babe") was traded, the New York team began an unprecedented winning streak, winning both the American League pennant and the World Series on numerous occasions. In baseball mythology, this phenomenon grew into legend. "Bambino" is the Italian word for baby, in this case referring to the Babe himself, and it was one of several nicknames by which Ruth was known.

2. The nine defense positions in baseball are pitcher, catcher, first base, second base, third base, short stop, right field, left field, and center field.

3. The most infamous case in recent memory occurred in the tenth inning of Game 6 of the 1986 World Series that pitted the Boston Red Sox against the New York Mets. Mets outfielder Mookie Wilson was up at bat at the bottom of the inning with two men on base and with Bob Stanley as Boston's relief pitcher. Wilson struck wild at Stanley's seventh pitch, allowing Kevin Mitchell to bring in the tying run. It was on the tenth pitch that Wilson hit a grounder to Boston first baseman Bill Buckner.

In a seemingly bewitched twist of fate, this simple ground ball rolled between Buckner's legs, allowing Ray Knight to bring in the winning run for the Mets. In a crushing setback, the Mets won Game 6, forcing a seventh game to be played, which the Mets also won, and thus winning the 1986 World Series. As close as the Red Sox were to finally completing the heroic quest, they were thwarted by an inexplicable, almost magical, simple error that cost them the series. Boston fans continue to believe that it was a revisitation of the Curse of the Bambino ("History: 1986").

4. The *New American Bible* gives the following Gospel accounts: Mark acknowledges three women at the empty tomb in Mark 16:1–7 when he talks of Mary Magdalene, Mary the mother of James, and Salome; in Mark 16:9, however, the gospel states that Christ "first appeared to Mary Magdalene"; John 20:1–18 acknowledges only Mary Magdalene at the tomb and as the first person to whom the risen Christ appears; according to Matthew 28:1–10, however, Christ speaks to Mary Magdalene and "the other Mary," telling them not to be afraid; finally, Luke 24:1–12 notes that Mary Magdalene, Mary the mother of James, and Joanna went to the tomb, but Luke does not acknowledge that the women received any revelation at all; instead, the first revelation noted comes to two men walking along a road who were with the disciples but not of the original Twelve (now Eleven after the betrayal and suicide of Judas Iscariot).

Works Cited

"The Babe." *Babe Ruth Biography Page,* available at http://www.baberuth.com/print4.htm (accessed on 22 August 1999).

Campbell, Joseph. *The Hero with a Thousand Faces.* New York: Pantheon, 1949.

Candelaria, Cordelia. *Seeking the Perfect Game: Baseball in American Literature.* New York: Greenwood, 1989.

"History of the World Series: 1903." *The Sporting News: TSN* Archives, available at http://www.sportingnews.com/archives/worldseries/1903.html (accessed on 22 August 1999).

"History of the World Series: 1918." *The Sporting News: TSN* Archives, available at http://www.sportingnews.com/archives/worldseries/1918.html (accessed on 22 August 1999).

"History of the World Series: 1986." *The Sporting News: TSN* Archives, available at http://www.sportingnews.com/archives/worldseries/1986.html (accessed on 30 December 1999).

Janicker, Rebecca, and Lincoln Geraghty. "Playing Hard to Get: Game-Playing and the Search for Humanity in *Star Trek* and *Red Dwarf.*" *Playing the Universe: Games and Gaming as Science Fiction.* Edited by David Mead and Pawel Frelik. Lublin, Poland: Maria Curie-Sklodowska University Press, 2007: 113–126.

MacClancy, Jeremy. "Sport, Identity and Ethnicity." *Sport, Identity and Ethnicity.* Edited by Jeremy MacClancy. Oxford: Berg, 1996.

Morris, Timothy. *Making the Team: The Cultural Work of Baseball Fiction.* Chicago: University of Illinois Press, 1997.

New American Bible. Nashville, TN: Memorial Bibles International, 1971.

Raglan, Fitzroy Richard Somerset (Baron). *The Hero: A Study in Tradition, Myth, and Drama.* London: Watts, 1949.

Westbrook, Deeanne. *Ground Rules: Baseball and Myth.* Chicago: University of Illinois Press, 1996.

PART III

FILM AND TELEVISION

7

The Monomyth in
Star Trek Films

Donald E. Palumbo

Already abstracted from numerous mythological, religious, and fantastic sources, the monomyth has also been repeatedly replicated since Joseph Campbell's 1949 explication in *The Hero with a Thousand Faces*. In addition to serving as the underlying plot structure in the initial *Star Wars* trilogy (Gordon, 1978; Mackay, 1999; Sherman, 1979; Tiffin, 1999), Campbell's monomyth occurs in meticulous detail in several of the most successful SF novels and series and in numerous additional SF films from the second half of the twentieth century (Kimball, 2001; Lundquist, 1996; Palumbo, various; Spinrad, 1990), including all ten *Star Trek* films (Baker, 2001; Reid-Jeffrey, 1982; Roth, 1987). Like the *Star Wars* trilogy, *Star Trek* films may owe much of the impact they have had on the popular psyche to their similar uses of this archetypal material. Yet, more so than in *Star Wars*, each *Star Trek* movie follows the monomyth's essential quest pattern in its entirety: a call to adventure, receipt of supernatural aid, a threshold crossing to an unknown world in which trials must be endured, the acquisition of a boon, magic flight from the unknown world, and a recrossing of the threshold back to the known world—and all incorporate many additional elements of the monomyth as well. Yet, while Campbell's study analyzes the adventure of a solo hero, in *Star Trek* the monomythic hero is most often a composite character—a collective hero combining attributes and experiences of several protagonists who crew the *Enterprise*'s various incarnations—and usually neither Kirk nor Picard, the most prominent protagonists, alone. Thus, the recurring monomythic hero is often the *Enterprise*'s crew as an ensemble and, by extension, the ship itself.

Sometimes the product of a virgin or special birth, the hero may have been exiled or orphaned, may be seeking his father, and may triumph

over pretenders as the true son (Campbell, 1949: 297–334). His mother
may be assumed into heaven or crowned a queen (119–20). He possesses
exceptional gifts, and the world he inhabits suffers symbolic deficiencies
(37). He does not fear death, and he is destined to make the world spiritually significant and humankind comprehensible to itself (388). If a
warrior, he will change the status quo (334–41). If a lover, his triumph
may be symbolized by a woman and accomplishing the impossible task
may lead to the bridal bed (342–45). If a tyrant or ruler, his search for
the father will lead to the invisible unknown from which he will return
as a lawgiver (345–49). If a world-redeemer, he will learn that he and the
father are one (349–54). If a saint or mystic, he will transcend life and
myth to enter an inexpressible realm beyond form (354–55).

    "The standard path of the mythological adventure of the hero is a
magnification of the formula represented in the rites of passage: *separation—initiation—return*" (30). The adventure's "separation" or "departure
stage" entails receiving a "Call to Adventure" in the guise of a blunder
that reveals an unknown world or the appearance of a herald; refusing
the call; receiving supernatural aid; crossing a magical threshold that
leads to a sphere of rebirth; and being swallowed in "The Belly of the
Whale," a descent into the unknown symbolizing death and resurrection
that may involve an underground journey representing a descent into hell
(36). The "initiation stage" includes numerous tests endured in "The
Road of Trials," including the hero's assimilation of his shadow; meeting,
and perhaps marrying, a mother-goddess, who may be the "good mother,"
the "bad mother," or "The Lady of the House of Sleep"; encountering a
temptress; atonement with the father; apotheosis; and acquiring a boon
(36, 110–11). The "return stage" may involve refusing to return; magical
flight from the unknown world; rescue from outside the unknown world;
recrossing the threshold; attaining the power to cross the threshold freely;
and the hero's realization that he is the vehicle of the cosmic cycle of
change (37).

    Only in *Star Trek II: The Wrath of Khan* (1982) and *Star Trek IV: The
Voyage Home* (1986), films in which the monomyth is most prominent,
does Kirk alone exhibit the attributes and enact the adventure of the
hero. Kirk and Picard share the hero role in *Star Trek Generations* (1994),
and only in *Star Trek: Insurrection* (1998) is Picard a solo monomythic hero.
Kirk shares crucial aspects of the hero role with Decker and Spock in *Star
Trek: The Motion Picture* (1979) and with Spock and (to a lesser extent)
McCoy in *Star Trek III: The Search for Spock* (1984), *Star Trek V: The Final
Frontier* (1989), and *Star Trek VI: The Undiscovered Country* (1991), while
Picard shares the hero role with Data (in many ways *The Next Generation*
iteration of Spock) in both *Star Trek: First Contact* (1996) and *Star Trek
Nemesis* (2002) (see Figures 1 and 2).

Qualities of the Hero

Spock is the sole character whose nativity, and literal rebirth, is ever an issue. In *Frontier* his Vulcan half-brother, Sybok, forces Spock to witness their father Sarek's disappointment that Spock seems "so human" at birth. While being half-human and half-Vulcan constitutes a "special birth," Spock's rebirth and accelerated aging on the Genesis planet in *Spock* is far more "special" as well as far more crucial to that film's plot. Because he is only half-Vulcan, Spock in his youth is an exile on his own planet, and by joining Starfleet he had distanced himself even further from his Vulcan heritage and father. In *Spock* the newly reborn Spock is literally in exile from Vulcan on the Genesis planet, which is quarantined.

Circumstances cast Kirk and Picard into several modes of exile in numerous films. As an administrator at the beginnings of both *Picture* and *Khan*, Admiral Kirk is initially in exile from "commanding a starship ... [his] first, best destiny." He forcibly wrests command of the *Enterprise* from Decker in the first film, in the second Spock insists on relinquishing it to him, and in *Spock* Kirk and crew steal the ship to reunite Spock's reborn body with his *katra* (spirit). In *Home* Kirk's initial log entry notes that he and crew have endured three months of "exile" on Vulcan while repairing *Bounty*, their commandeered Klingon bird of prey, and deciding whether or not to return to Earth, where Kirk faces court-martial for violating Starfleet regulations. Already exiled from the *Enterprise* again, from Earth (physically), and from Starfleet (legally) as *Home* begins, Kirk and crew are subsequently exiled from the twenty-third century as well when they travel to and are temporarily stranded in 1986. In *Country* Kirk and McCoy are exiled from the Federation and its justice system when they are tried for murder on the Klingon homeworld and sentenced to imprisonment on Rura Penthe. And in *Generations* a retired Kirk is again without a command and "finding retirement a little lonely." Much like Kirk violating regulations, and producing a similar mode of self-imposed exile from Starfleet, Picard disobeys orders to patrol the Neutral Zone in *Contact* and to leave Ba'ku in *Insurrection*.

Searches for fathers and triumphs over pretenders occur only in the first five films and *Nemesis*, and then primarily through reversal and inversion. V'ger, the antagonist in *Picture*, seeks its "creator" (humanity) to learn the reason for its existence from "a father, a brother, a god"; Sybok, another antagonist, seeks "god" yet finds a false but angry God the Father—a pretender over whom Kirk, Spock, and McCoy triumph—in *Frontier*; and Picard's clone Shinzon, the antagonist in *Nemesis*, seeks Picard, his symbolic father, because he will die without a "transfusion" of Picard's genetically compatible DNA. Kirk unexpectedly encounters his estranged son, David, in *Khan*; and the reborn Spock is reunited with Sarek at *Spock*'s conclusion. In regaining the *Enterprise* in each of the first three films, Kirk triumphs as its true captain over characters depicted as pretenders: fellow protagonists Decker and Spock, in *Picture* and *Khan*, and the *Excelsior*'s less sympathetic Captain Styles in *Spock*. Kirk receives formal command of the *Enterprise-A*, which he retains for the next two films, at the conclusion of *Home*.

The quintessential leader, whose "first, best destiny" is to captain a starship, Kirk exhibits Odyssean ingenuity in outwitting opponents and evading defeat and death. For example, *Khan* reveals that Kirk is the only Starfleet cadet ever to survive the "Kobayashi Maru" exercise, the "no-win scenario" that inevitably ends in simulated death, and he defeats Khan because he knows how to lower another Starfleet ship's shields remotely and is more adept at three-dimensional thinking. His exceptional gift is his genius for captaining the *Enterprise*. Picard is equally capable, but in *Contact* his more specific exceptional gift is having previously been assimilated by the Borg, which enables him to detect their presence, anticipate their behavior, and know their weaknesses.

Kirk faces death without fear on numerous occasions. In *Picture*, for example, all aboard the *Enterprise* recognize that their assignment to intercept V'ger is a suicide mission, and Kirk finally attempts to destroy it by activating the *Enterprise*'s self-destruct sequence; but Decker, who shares the hero role with Kirk and Spock, sacrifices himself instead by merging with V'ger. Spock dies to save the *Enterprise* in *Khan*; both Kirk and Picard sacrifice virtual immortality to duty in leaving the Nexus to save the Veridian system in *Generations*; and Picard relinquishes actual immortality to uphold the Prime Directive in *Insurrection*. After initiating the *Enterprise*'s self-destruct sequence in *Contact*, Picard remains aboard to rescue Data. Similarly, in *Insurrection* Picard initiates the self-destruct sequence on Ru'afo's metaphasic collector even though he believes he cannot escape. He also tries unsuccessfully to use the *Enterprise*'s self-destruct capability in *Nemesis* to destroy Shinzon's battleship, *Scimitar*; but after Picard then transports himself to the *Scimitar* to destroy the ship from within, Data, who shares the hero role, demonstrates that he does not fear death, either, by sacrificing himself to save Picard.

While the threats confronted by the *Enterprise*'s crews in the twenty-third and twenty-fourth centuries do not usually indicate any intrinsic deficiency on Earth or in the Federation generally, these films address the deficiencies of the twentieth and twenty-first centuries either by visiting those eras or by allegorically projecting their shortcomings into the future. Yet even in the twenty-third century it is Federation and Starfleet bureaucracy that Kirk and crew must circumvent in hijacking the *Enterprise* and embarking on their insubordinate quest in *Spock*, and bureaucratic shortsightedness and corruption is an even greater problem for Picard in the twenty-fourth century. Starfleet mistakenly decides to sideline Picard in its decisive confrontation with the Borg in *Contact* because he had previously been assimilated, yet that experience enables Picard to save Earth in minutes after he disobeys orders. And in *Insurrection* Picard must disobey Dougherty's orders to prevent the Federation, seduced by the lure of potential immortality, from violating the Prime Directive.

Insurrection also exhibits an implicit ecological theme, as Dougherty's and Ru'afo's intended crimes against Ba'ku include destroying its ecosystem; but this is a projection into the future of the twentieth century's failure to protect its ecology, and ecological shortsightedness is explicitly twentieth-century Earth's deficiency in *Home*. Because it cannot communicate with Earth's whales, which are extinct, an alien probe is destroying Earth's ecology in the twenty-third century by vaporizing the oceans. Kirk and crew time travel to the twentieth century to capture some whales and convey them to the twenty-third century so that they can communicate with the probe to end its destructive rampage, and during this mission the *Enterprise*'s crew witnesses twentieth century humanity hunting whales to extinction, which Spock observes "is not logical" because, as Kirk points out, in "killing these creatures [man] was destroying his own future" (see chapter 5 on environmental views in *Star Trek*).

In 1991's *Country*, which also features this recurring ecological theme in that the Klingon ecology faces imminent collapse, "the undiscovered country" is "peace." In presenting the Federation's evolving relationship with the Klingons as an allegory of the contemporaneous dissolution of the cold war following the collapse of the USSR, this film projects into the twenty-third century another deficiency of the twentieth century, recurring warfare, just as 1966–69's "classic" TV series often allegorically projected the contemporaneous reality of the Vietnam War into the twenty-third century. Similarly, the evil legacy of war is the deficiency *The Next Generation* crew witnesses in returning to the twenty-first century in *Contact*, as they discover in 2063 a vulnerable humanity that would easily fall to the Borg because its social, political, and physical infrastructures had been destroyed by nuclear war ten years earlier.

The Next Generation crew makes this benighted twenty-first-century world spiritually significant by assuring that "first contact" with the Vulcans occurs, for this encounter will unify and revitalize humanity by giving it purpose and propelling it from dystopian chaos towards the near-utopia of the twenty-third and twenty-fourth centuries. This crew also champions spiritual significance in the twenty-fourth century by upholding the Prime Directive in *Insurrection*, as Picard argues that complicity in the exploitation of Ba'ku is a betrayal of "the principles on which the Federation was founded. It's an attack upon its very soul." Yet the hero's role in making the world spiritually significant is seen only through reversal and inversion in films featuring the "classic" crew. In *Frontier*, for example, Kirk reveals that the "god" Sybok seeks is false.

Spock most pointedly comes to comprehend himself, and particularly his human qualities, in those films featuring the "classic" crew; and Data, through his explicit attempts to be more human, most pointedly comes to comprehend himself and humanity—and thus enables others to comprehend their humanity—in the later films. Reborn in the previous film, Spock is so divorced from the human aspects of his dual heritage as *Home* begins that he is unable to answer the question "How do you feel?" Yet he indicates that he has connected with his humanity during his twentieth-century adventure in saying "I feel fine" at the film's conclusion. In *Generations* Data installs an emotion chip in his positronic brain to understand humor and "become more human." And after Data sacrifices himself to save his captain at the conclusion of *Nemesis*, Picard eulogizes the android by observing that "in his quest to be more like us, he helped us to see what it is to be human."

Both Picard and Kirk, as Klaa and Chang acknowledge in *Frontier* and *Country*, respectively, are professional warriors who repeatedly change the status quo, most often by saving Earth—as in *Picture, Home, Nemesis*, and twice in *Contact*—although they also save the Veridian system in *Generations* and Ba'ku in *Insurrection*. Notorious womanizer Kirk flirts with Gillian Taylor in *Home* and Martia in *Country*, Picard indulges in a more serious romance with Anij in *Insurrection*, and Riker and Troi marry in *Nemesis*; yet the best example of the hero as lover is Decker in *Picture*. As a direct result of stopping V'ger from destroying all life on Earth, Decker, another warrior, merges with the Ilia-probe, a mechanical duplicate of the Deltan crew member with whom he had previously had only a platonic affair because sex with Deltans is fatal to humans. Thus the impossible task of saving Earth leads Decker to an equally impossible bridal bed, however figuratively. While Decker is a world-redeemer once and Kirk and Picard save a variety of worlds repeatedly, the condition that each learns that he and the father are one is met only through inversion. In *Khan* and *Spock* Kirk learns that he is more like David—his son, not his father—than either of them suspects; and Picard learns that he is even more like Shinzon, a clone and his symbolic son, in *Nemesis*. In addition to being a warrior and lover, Decker also satisfies the condition for being a mystic, entering an inexpressible realm beyond form, when he and the Ilia-probe dissipate from this universe at *Picture*'s conclusion.

The Departure Stage

The hero receives a "call to adventure" in the form of a "blunder" that "reveals an unsuspected world" or the appearance of its "herald"— usually "a beast," some shadowy, hooded or veiled, mysterious figure, or someone "dark, loathly, or terrifying, judged evil by the world"—who may literally call the hero "to live ... or ... to die" (Campbell, 1949: 51, 53). This occurs in all ten films; in all but *Insurrection* the "call" is literal and explicit; and in *Picture, Spock,* and *Country* it is temporarily refused. *Picture* begins with a blunder that reveals the unknown to Starfleet when Klingon vessels fire on V'ger and are disintegrated; V'ger then blunders in "mistaking its scans as a hostile act" and destroying space station Epsilon IX. Spock receives a literal "call" in telepathically sensing V'ger "calling from space"; Kirk receives an even more explicit call when ordered to "intercept, investigate, and take ... action" against V'ger; and Scotty temporarily refuses the call in complaining that the refitted *Enterprise* first "needs more work, a shakedown."

Two blunders, a herald, and a similarly literal "call" occur in *Khan.* Seeking a lifeless planet on which to test the Genesis Device, *Reliant's* crew mistakes Ceti Alpha V for Ceti Alpha VI, a blunder that gives Khan— the hooded, dark, reputedly evil herald—an opportunity to capture their ship and lure Kirk to an ambush. Kirk receives a literal call when the *Enterprise* is "ordered to investigate" Carol Marcus' complaint that Starfleet appears to have ordered the *Reliant* to seize Genesis, but his failure to raise shields when the approaching ship does not respond to hails is a second blunder that allows Khan's commandeered *Reliant* to cripple the *Enterprise.* Kirk receives yet another literal call in *Spock* when Sarek implores him to bring Spock and McCoy to Vulcan; Kirk seems to refuse the call in appearing to accept Starfleet's decision not to mount a rescue mission to the Genesis planet, but then tells Sulu and Chekov, "I am ... going anyway." The herald in *Home* is the alien probe whose destructive rampage prompts Kirk and crew to travel to the twentieth century; the blunder is humanity having previously hunted whales to extinction; and the distress signal advising all ships "to avoid ... Earth" is the call.

Sybok, a cloaked and hooded wanderer, is the herald in *Frontier;* his scheme to lure a ship to Nimbus III bears fruit when the *Enterprise's* crew is recalled from shore leave and ordered to recover Sybok's hostages—a recall that is simultaneously a call to adventure and a blunder in that it plays into Sybok's hands. The industrial accident that destroys the Klingon moon, Praxis, is a blunder that, by prompting the Klingons to negotiate with the Federation, calls Kirk to adventure in *Country* when he receives orders to escort Klingon chancellor Gorkon to a peace conference, and Kirk does his best to refuse the call by objecting to the very idea of negotiating with Klingons. Dr. Soran and *Enterprise-D* bartender Guinan are alien heralds who introduce the unknown world of the Nexus in *Generations:* Both are beamed aboard the *Enterprise-B* when the Nexus destroys their El-Aurian transports in the twenty-third century; Soran is also rescued by the *Enterprise-D* after surviving an attack on the Amargosa Observatory in the twenty-fourth century; and the "distress" calls to which these ships respond are the literal calls to adventure. While Picard inadvertently enters the Nexus in trying to save the Veridian system, the fact that the *Enterprise-B* has left space dock without being properly equipped is the blunder that reveals the Nexus to Kirk, who is swept into it while attempting to save the ship by manually adjusting its deflector relays because it has no tractor beams or photon torpedoes.

Contact begins with Picard's nightmare of being Locutus of Borg, this film's herald; and Starfleet's decision to sideline Picard is the blunder that allows the Borg cube to survive long enough to send a "sphere"—which the *Enterprise* pursues—to conquer Earth in the twenty-first century, this film's unknown world. The blunder in *Insurrection* is the Federation's decision to violate the Prime Directive by conspiring with the Son'a to harvest Ba'ku's metaphasic particles; the call is Admiral Dougherty's request for Data's schematics (because the android has run amok on Ba'ku, this film's unknown world), which prompts the *Enterprise* to investigate and to capture Data—who, like Soran and Guinan, is another variant of the herald as "beast" in that he is not human. The call in *Nemesis*—Admiral Janeway ordering the *Enterprise* to the Romulus system (this film's unknown world) because its new Praetor, Shinzon, has requested a Federation envoy—is again literal and explicit. However, like the call in *Frontier*, it is also a blunder in that Shinzon's request is the first step in his plot to destroy life on Earth; this film's herald is Shinzon, who initially appears as a shadowy figure in near darkness and whose ship is equipped with a "perfectly undetectable cloaking device."

After accepting the call, the hero receives "supernatural aid" from an old man or crone, who provides a talisman, or from a guide, teacher, wizard, ferryman, hermit, or smith who offers aid in a context of danger or temptation (Campbell, 1949: 69–72). The *Enterprise* is the talisman in all ten films, and Kirk is given command by three older men successively: Admiral Nogura in *Picture*, Spock in *Khan*; and the Federation council president at *Home*'s conclusion. With few exceptions, crew members serve as guides, teachers, wizards, ferrymen, and smiths. For example, Decker discovers early in *Picture* that he must teach Kirk about the *Enterprise*'s reconfigured systems. Whale biologist Gillian Taylor serves as guide to twentieth century San Francisco in *Home*; Guinan is Picard's guide within the Nexus in *Generations*; and in *Insurrection* Anij is Picard's guide on Ba'ku. Spock reassumes his usual post as science officer, and scientific wizard, in *Picture*. Chief Engineer Scotty is the classic crew's resident smith— yet he is called a "miracle worker" in *Spock* and *Home*, and his legendary expertise often elevates him to "wizard" status—while *The Next Generation* crew's preeminent smith is Chief Engineer Geordi LaForge. The crew person most comparable to a ferryman would be the transporter operator (usually Scotty, but Spock in *Country*), navigator (Ilia in *Picture* and Lt. Saavik in the next three films), or helmsman (usually Chekov, but Ensign Demora Sulu in *Generations*).

The hero next crosses the threshold to an unknown world that leads to a sphere of rebirth and may be defended by a protective guardian or destructive watchman (Campbell, 1949: 77–89). In nearly every film the *Enterprise* goes to warp speed on-screen only twice—at the beginning and end of the adventure—and this is usually a crossing and recrossing of the threshold. To intercept V'ger as quickly as possible, the *Enterprise* engages its warp drive "while still within the solar system" in *Picture*, and this leads to a "sphere of rebirth" (defended by V'ger) in that Decker's climactic merging with the Ilia-probe is seen by Spock as "a birth, possibly the next step in our evolution." In *Khan* the threshold crossing occurs when the *Enterprise* warps to Regula I to investigate Carol Marcus' claim that Starfleet has ordered her to surrender Genesis, which Roth (1987) notes "is a science fiction metaphor for the death-rebirth cycle" (163); and Khan, the destructive watchman, finally triggers the rebirth of the Mutara Nebula as the Genesis planet.

The *Enterprise* crosses a literal threshold in breeching space dock's doors, early in *Spock*, before warping to the Mutara Sector (where destructive watchman Kruge cripples the ship upon its arrival) and its Genesis planet, literally an unknown world on which Saavik and David discover a reborn Spock. *Home*'s crossing occurs when *Bounty* attains "warp 10" to reach the twentieth century—a comically unknown world that Kirk warns is "*terra incognita*" as well as a sphere of rebirth in that the whales found there, one of which is pregnant, enable the rebirth of that species in the twenty-third century. The *Enterprise* evades destructive watchman Klaa's attack at Nimbus III by going to warp speed en route to Sha Ka Ree, reputedly "the place from which creation sprang," in *Frontier*, yet to reach Sha Ka Ree it must also cross a literal threshold—"the Great Barrier," beyond which lies "the unknown." The *Enterprise* again traverses space dock's doors in *Country*, and a destructive watchman in the form of a cloaked bird of prey fires two torpedoes at Gorkon's ship after the *Enterprise* meets it at the "rendezvous point."

The *Enterprise-D* warps to the Veridian system in time to prevent Soran, a destructive watchman, from destroying its sun in *Generations*. Yet this film's threshold is not so much the jump to warp speed as it is the "energy ribbon" that Guinan tells Picard is "a doorway to ... the Nexus," an "unknown world" in which the dead (Kirk, his dog Butler, his nephew René, and Guinan) live again; dual threshold crossings occur when Kirk is swept into the ribbon while saving the *Enterprise-B* and when Picard and Soran are swept into it on Veridian III a century later. The *Enterprise* following the Borg sphere to 2063 is the threshold crossing in *Contact*, the destructive watchmen are the Borg who board and nearly assimilate it there, and the twenty-first century is a sphere of rebirth in that Earth's first contact with the Vulcans, a contact which the Borg attempt to prevent, initiates a new era of peace and prosperity for war-ravaged humanity.

Picard observes that the *Enterprise* is "truly sailing into the unknown" as it warps to Romulus in *Nemesis*; Shinzon's ship, *Scimitar*, is the destructive watchman; and the Romulan system is a sphere of rebirth for Data, who is destroyed there only to be symbolically reborn in the form of his physical double, B-4.

In the departure stage's final episode the hero is "swallowed" in "the belly of the whale," a death-and-rebirth experience that is often a literal or symbolic underground journey representing descent into a literal or figurative hell that may contain devils, flames, or *memento mori*; the hero may also enter a temple guarded by gargoyles and might be literally or symbolically mutilated, dismembered, or killed (Campbell, 1949: 90–92). Variations occur in each film except *Generations* and *Contact* and are often elaborately convoluted. The *Enterprise* is swallowed by a "wormhole" early in *Picture*, for example, and subsequently penetrates V'ger's energy cloud, in which it is seized by a "tractor beam" and drawn through an "aperture" that closes behind it, leaving it "trapped" and, in McCoy's words, "looking down their throats"—swallowed again.

Khan features the series' most extensive variety of literal and figurative underground journeys and is most explicit in portraying them as symbolic descents into hell that signify death and rebirth, the film's central motif. The opening sequence seems to depict a "training mission" that appears to end with the *Enterprise* "dead in space" and Spock and his crew dead as well; yet everyone rises again as Kirk enters to reveal that this has been a simulation, the infamous Kobayashi Maru exercise. The film's literal underground journey is the protagonists' descent "deep inside Regula ... underground," where Khan gloats that he will leave Kirk "marooned for all eternity in the center of a dead planet, buried alive." Kirk had resurrected Khan and his followers from centuries of cryogenic freeze fifteen years earlier; and they are resurrected again when Khan tricks the *Reliant's* crew into beaming them "up" from the nearly lifeless desert that the planet on which Kirk had deposited them has become. Echoing Khan's symbolic resurrection from Ceti Alpha V, Kirk also employs a ruse to signal Spock to beam him and his companions "up" from Regula. Chekov then seems to die, but later turns up inexplicably alive. While Regula's transformed interior is an underground Eden rather than a symbolic hell, Khan—whose "pride" is his undoing and who swears he will "chase [Kirk] around perdition's flames"—is nonetheless the film's symbolic devil. He initially presides over the hellish Ceti Alpha V and at the conclusion of the battle between the *Enterprise* and *Reliant* declares, "From hell's heart I stab at thee!" as he triggers the Genesis Device in the Mutara Nebula, the film's other symbolic hell.

Spock then sacrifices his life in repairing the *Enterprise's* warp drive so that it can escape the "Genesis wave," and his body is "buried" in space on a trajectory that takes it to the Genesis planet. In *Spock* David and

Saavik beam down to Genesis and discover a "regenerated Captain Spock"; as the planet destroys itself in a series of volcanic eruptions that identify it as this film's symbolic hell, Kirk fights Kruge, its devil, who plunges to his death in molten lava. Spock is resurrected from the dying planet when he and the remaining *Enterprise* crew are beamed aboard Kruge's abandoned bird of prey. Scheduled to be "decommissioned" at *Spock*'s beginning and destroyed at its climax, the *Enterprise*, too, is resurrected as the newly rebuilt *Enterprise-A* at the end of *Home*, which also features a comic inversion of being "swallowed" in "the belly of the whale" when Scotty beams two whales aboard the *Bounty*.

The two symbolic hells into which the *Enterprise*'s crew descends in *Frontier* are Nimbus III, whose devil is the seductive Sybok, and Sha Ka Ree, whose devil—more pointedly and allusively—is an alien who (like Lucifer) wants to be worshipped as "god." Kirk, Spock, McCoy, and Sybok are symbolically swallowed when trapped by "god" in rib-like spires of rock that spring from Sha Ka Ree's desert floor to form a cave-like prison that combines the visual imagery of being inside a carcass and being underground. In *Country* Kirk and McCoy endure a literal underground journey that is likewise a symbolic descent into hell when they are imprisoned in Rura Penthe's mines, "the alien's graveyard" that fellow-prisoner Martia terms a "hell hole." In *Insurrection* Picard leads Ba'ku's inhabitants to refuge in a series of mountain caverns where he and Anij are trapped by a cave-in. Yet in *Nemesis* it is his clone Shinzon, not Picard, who had spent ten years underground in the symbolic hell of the Reman mines; and it is Data's double B-4, not Data, who is literally dismembered when initially found on Kolarus III.

The Initiation Stage

The monomyth's initiation stage begins with "the road of trials," a series of tests in which the hero is assisted by the talismans, advice, or agents of those who had offered supernatural aid and may also assimilate or be assimilated by his shadow "by swallowing it or by being swallowed" (Campbell, 1949: 97, 108). Each film involves tests and trials, and in all but *Home, Generations*, and *Insurrection* a protagonist assimilates or is assimilated by his shadow. The most explicit tests and trials include Decker sacrificing his humanity in *Picture*; the Kobayashi Maru exercise in *Khan*; stealing the *Enterprise* in *Spock*; recovering whales from the twentieth century, as well as Kirk's court-martial, in *Home*; Kirk, Spock, and McCoy unmasking "god" and, with Scotty, resisting Sybok's seductions in *Frontier*; Spock unmasking the conspiracy to assassinated Gorkon, as well as Kirk and McCoy standing trial for the murder and then escaping Rura Penthe, in *Country*; Picard and Kirk preventing Soran from destroying

Veridian in *Generations*; defeating the Borg in both the twenty-fourth and twenty-first centuries in *Contact*; Picard rebelling against Starfleet Command to uphold the Prime Directive in *Insurrection*; and Picard and Data preventing Shinzon from sterilizing Earth in *Nemesis*, which also features the clearest example of a hero being aided by a helper's talisman when Data uses the "emergency transport unit" Geordi had given him to switch places with Picard just before the *Scimitar* explodes.

As V'ger strives to evolve beyond the state of "no emotion, only pure logic" to which Spock aspires through the Vulcan rite of Kolinahr, they are shadows at the beginning of *Picture*. Khan is Kirk's shadow in *Khan*, and Spock and McCoy are the crucial shadows in *Spock*: McCoy's emotional secular humanism is juxtaposed with Spock's reserved scientific rationalism throughout the classic TV series as well as in each of the first six films, and McCoy both assimilates and is assimilated by Spock when he receives Spock's *katra* at *Khan*'s climax, must bear it throughout *Spock*, and as a consequence often appears to be possessed by Spock until he returns it at that film's conclusion. Spock's shadow in *Frontier* is Sybok, the half-brother who "was banished from Vulcan" for renouncing the Vulcan logic Spock embraces. Kirk's shadows in *Country* are Chang—as both are warriors who oppose any rapprochement between the Klingons and the Federation, yet Kirk thwarts Chang's conspiracy to prevent it—and Martia, a shape-shifter who assumes Kirk's appearance, fights him in that guise, and is killed because she is mistaken for Kirk while betraying him and McCoy during their escape from Rura Penthe.

The Borg Queen, a woman who has almost entirely become a machine, and Data, an android who aspires to be human, are shadows in *Contact*, in which Data disintegrates what remains of her humanity after resisting her offer to cover him with human skin. And Data's shadow in *Nemesis* is B-4, the "prototype" he replaces, as Shinzon's captive, but who finally replaces him at the film's conclusion. Yet the series' most obvious shadows are Picard and Shinzon, the clone he kills in hand-to-hand combat.

The hero might also encounter a goddess, a temptress, or both. The goddess—with whom he might have a mystical marriage in a special location—may assume the guise of the "good mother," who is bliss, perfection, and the combination of opposites; the "bad mother," who may threaten castration and may be absent, unattainable, forbidding, punishing, or the locus of forbidden desire; or "the Lady of the House of Sleep," who is "the reply to all desire, the bliss-bestowing goal of every hero's ... quest" (Campbell, 1949: 109–11). To Kirk the true goddess is and always will be the *Enterprise*, as he acknowledges in *Generations*; yet females appear as versions of the goddess or temptress, however perfunctorily, in each film. In *Picture* Ilia is the goddess to Decker, with whom she has had only a platonic romance. As sex with Deltans is "forbidden" and allegedly fatal,

Ilia possesses attributes of the "bad mother"; yet to Decker she is "the Lady of the House of Sleep," as merging with her simulacrum at the core of V'ger's energy cloud is the mystical marriage that is a reply to his desires and literally the goal of his quest.

In *Khan* Kirk encounters the goddess as "good mother" in Dr. Marcus, the mother of his son and originator of the life-creating Genesis Project who shows him a subterranean cavern she has transformed into a lush paradise. Roth (1987) argues that this "metamorphosis of grave into womb ... recalls the mythic hero's encounter with a fertility goddess who helps reclaim him from the underworld" (164). In *Spock* the reborn Spock appears to have at least a mystical marriage on Genesis with Saavik, here the goddess as "good mother" who helps him survive *pon farr*. His human mother, Amanda, is the "good mother," who wants Spock to get in touch with his "feelings" at the beginning of *Home*, in which Kirk later flirts with Dr. Taylor, whose ecological concerns suggest that she is another symbolic nature goddess. Uhura plays comic temptress twice in *Frontier*. While under Sybok's influence she repeatedly flirts with Scotty—who implores her "to wait until I'm a wee bit stronger"—and later seduces Sybok's followers into abandoning their posts by dancing in a skirt of fronds atop a sand dune. Martia, a more dangerous temptress in *Country*, seals with a kiss her pact to help Kirk and McCoy escape from Rura Penthe, but this offer of aid is merely a ploy to entrap them in an escape-attempt ambush. In *Generations* Guinan is a "Lady of the House of Sleep" who explains the dream-like nature of the Nexus to Picard; in *Contact* the Borg Queen is a temptress who fails to seduce Data into divulging the *Enterprise*'s encryption codes; and Picard enjoys a mystical marriage with Anij in *Insurrection*. The "bad mother" in *Nemesis* is Tal'aura, who murders everyone in the Romulan Senate, while the temptress is Commander Donatra, who fails to seduce Shinzon.

The hero next experiences atonement with the father or a father figure who may be "the initiating priest through whom the young being passes on into the larger world"; yet this could be a negative encounter and can entail an initiatory rite of circumcision that might also contain "a dramatized expression of the Oedipal aggression of the older generation; and the ... patricidal impulse of the younger" (Campbell, 1949: 136–39). Thus, the father can be or appears to be a tyrant or ogre, and "the two are atoned" only after the hero sees beyond this negative manifestation and "beholds the face of the father" (147). As the superior officer who wrests command of the *Enterprise* from him, Kirk is father figure as tyrant-ogre to Decker in *Picture*; yet, as both (with Spock) share the hero role in this film, their atonement when Kirk permits Decker to merge with the Ilia-probe is a partial inversion. *Khan* completely inverts this dynamic in that Kirk is both the hero and the father as tyrant-ogre who is atoned with his son, David, who initially vilifies Kirk for having abandoned him but finally faces Kirk and confesses, "I'm proud ... to be your son."

At *Spock*'s conclusion Sarek shares the role of initiating priest in imploring a Vulcan priestess to perform the *fal-tor-pan* ceremony that will reunite Spock's *katra* and body; at *Home*'s conclusion the two are atoned when Sarek faces Spock and acknowledges him as "my son"; and *Frontier* depicts Sarek as an ogre-father who had disparaged Spock at his birth for being "so human." Spock's and Sarek's reconciliation in *Home* occurs immediately after Kirk is atoned with the Federation council president, a father figure who essentially exonerates Kirk for violating Starfleet regulations. And *Frontier* also exhibits two additional negative encounters: McCoy recalling that he took the father he could not cure off of life-support, only to learn "not long after [that] they found a cure," and a false "god"-the-father smiting Kirk and Spock with energy bolts on Sha Ka Ree. Picard killing his symbolic son, Shinzon, at *Nemesis*' climax is an inverted negative atonement.

The initiation stage's penultimate episode is apotheosis—transcending one's humanity to become god-like—which symbolizes attaining enlightenment, involves an annihilation of consciousness representing loss of ego, and is characterized by a symbolic transcendence of duality signaled by the unification of such apparent opposites as time and eternity, birth and death, male and female, self and other, or flesh and spirit (Campbell, 1949: 149–71). While significant conjunctions of opposites occur at the conclusions of each of the first four films—and while apotheosis is suggested in *Generations* by the association of nirvana with the Nexus (where "time has no meaning" and Soran anticipates "an appointment with eternity") and, more mundanely, by the valorizations of Kirk, Cochrane, and Data at the conclusions of *Home*, *Contact*, and *Nemesis*—the most literal apotheosis occurs at *Picture*'s climax, when Decker transcends his humanity and loses his ego (while simultaneously unifying male and female, self and other, birth and death, and time and eternity) in merging with the Ilia-probe. Life and death also merge at *Khan*'s climax when Khan's suicidal attempt to destroy the *Enterprise* with the Genesis Device transforms the Mutara Nebula into the vital, life-bestowing Genesis planet as Spock simultaneously chooses death to enable the rest of the crew to outrun the Genesis wave and live. In *Spock* the fal-tor-pan rite unites Spock's flesh and spirit via yet another merging of opposites in melding Spock and McCoy; and in saying "I feel fine" at *Home*'s conclusion Spock signals a unification of self and other, which he embodies, through the integration of his human emotions and Vulcan logic.

Receiving the boon, which is "the means for the regeneration of [the hero's] society as a whole," is the final episode in the initiation stage. The highest boon is enlightenment, that "perfect illumination" symbolized by apotheosis, but the hero usually seeks such lesser gifts as immortality, power, or wealth (Campbell, 1949: 38, 189). While the boon is literally the regeneration of twenty-first century society in *Contact* and is most often a symbolic regeneration in the form of Earth's or another planet's salvation, which implies immortality of the species, the boon in some films also involves specific revelations or explicit intimations of immortality. In addition to halting the prospective extermination of life on Earth, another boon gained through Decker's apotheosis in *Picture* is knowledge, for V'ger also transmits to humanity all the data it has gathered in three centuries of exploring the universe; moreover, Spock discovers that "logic and knowledge are not enough" in this film and therefore abandons his attempt to attain Kolinahr. Continued immortality is explicitly the boon granted Ba'ku's inhabitants in *Insurrection*.

The Return Stage

In the return stage the hero could refuse to return or to give the boon to humanity, his return could be opposed or furthered by "magic" means, his attempt to return could end in failure, or he could be rescued from outside the unknown world. In crossing the return threshold he might convey new wisdom to the known world, experience a dilation of time, encounter dangers that require him to "insulate" himself, or return with a talisman of his quest; and on returning the hero may become "master of the two worlds," by acquiring the ability to pass freely between them, or he might achieve "freedom to live" by divesting himself of anxiety or by realizing that he is a vehicle of the cosmic cycle of change (Campbell, 1949: 193–243). In *Picture* Decker acquires the boons only by merging with V'ger and thus refusing to return, much as Spock refuses to return in sacrificing himself to save the *Enterprise* in *Khan* and Data refuses to return in sacrificing himself to save Picard in *Nemesis*. Although the boon of peace is attained, the crew refuses to return twice in *Country*: Rescuing Kirk and McCoy from Rura Penthe involves ignoring orders to return the *Enterprise* to space dock; and at the film's conclusion Kirk ignores that order again in instructing Chekov to set course for the "second star to the right and straight on 'til morning." As it is destroyed, the *Enterprise* itself does not return in *Spock* or *Generations*. In leaving the Nexus to prevent the Veridian system's destruction in *Generations*, Picard and Kirk reject the boon of personal immortality to bestow the boon of extended life on others. And in a similar partial inversion in *Insurrection*, Picard— who had refused to return earlier in ignoring orders to leave the system— also refuses to give the boon of immortality to his society, the Federation, in assuring that Ba'ku's inhabitants retain it.

In *Frontier* McCoy and Spock are rescued from outside the unknown world when Scotty transports them from Sha Ka Ree to the *Enterprise*.

	Motion Picture	Wrath of Khan	Search for Spock	Voyage Home	Final Frontier	Undiscovered Country	Generations	First Contact	Insurrection	Nemesis
Monomythic Hero(es)	Decker, Kirk, & Spock	Kirk	Kirk, Spock, McCoy	Kirk	Kirk, Spock, McCoy	Kirk, Spock, McCoy	Kirk & Picard	Picard & Data	Picard	Picard & Data
Special Birth			Spock	Spock						
Mother a Queen										
Exile or Orphan	Kirk has no ship	Kirk has no ship	Kirk & Spock	Kirk & crew	Spock as a youth	Kirk & McCoy	Kirk is retired	Picard disobeys orders	Picard disobeys orders	(Shinzon: Picard's clone)
Seeking His Father	(V'ger seeks creator)	Kirk (inverted)	Spock & Sarek reunited		Sybok (seeks "god")					(Shinzon seeks Picard)
Triumph over Pretenders	Kirk over Decker	Kirk over Spock	Kirk over Styles	Kirk made captain						
Exceptional Gifts	Kirk as captain	Kirk as captain	Kirk as captain	Kirk as captain	Kirk as captain	Kirk as captain	Picard as captain	Picard's Borg history	Picard as captain	Picard as captain
No Fear of Death	Kirk, crew, Decker	Kirk & Spock	(David Marcus)		Kirk, Spock, McCoy		Kirk & Picard	Picard	Picard	Picard & Data
World's Deficiencies			bureaucracy	bureaucracy & ecology		war & ecology		war & bureaucracy	bureaucracy & ecology	

	Motion Picture	Wrath of Khan	Search for Spock	Voyage Home	Final Frontier	Undiscovered Country	Generations	First Contact	Insurrection	Nemesis
Spiritual Significance	(V'ger)				Kirk (inverted)		Kirk	Picard: Vulcan contact	Picard: Prime Directive	
Make Humanity Comprehensible	Decker seizes his destiny	Kirk understands himself	Spock understands himself	Spock understands himself	Spock understands himself		Kirk makes a difference	Data installs emotion chip		Data as exemplar of humanity
Hero as Warrior	Kirk & Decker	Kirk defeats Khan	Kirk defeats Kruge	Kirk saves Earth	Kirk outwits "god"	Kirk outwits Chang	Kirk & Picard	Picard defeats Borg	Picard saves Ba'ku	Picard defeats Shinzon
Hero as Lover	Decker to Ilia			Kirk to Gillian Taylor		Kirk to Martia			Picard to Anij, (Troi & Riker)	(Troi & Riker)
Hero as Ruler										
Hero as World-Redeemer	partial: Decker	Kirk, inverted	Kirk, inverted	partial: Kirk		partial: Kirk	partial: Kirk & Picard	partial: Picard	partial: Picard	Picard, inverted
Hero as Saint or Mystic	Decker									

Figure 1: The Qualities of the Hero in Star Trek Films

	Motion Picture	Wrath of Khan	Search for Spock	Voyage Home	Final Frontier	Undiscovered Country	Generations	First Contact	Insurrection	Nemesis
Call to Adventure	Spock & Kirk	Kirk	Kirk & McCoy	Kirk & crew	Kirk & crew	Kirk	Kirk, Picard, crews	Picard & crew	Picard & crew	Picard & crew
Call Refused by	(Scotty, temporarily)		Kirk (as a ruse)			Kirk, temporarily		Picard, inverted		
Supernatural Aid Provided by	Nogura, Decker, Spock, & Ilia	Spock, Saavik, McCoy, Chekov	Scotty, Chekov, Uhura, & Sulu	Scotty, Spock, Gillian, President	Scotty, Chekov	Spock, Chekov, & Valeris	Guinan, Demora Sulu, & Geordi	Geordi LaForge & Dr. Crusher	Anij, Dr. Crusher, Data, & Worf	Geordi, Riker, Troi, & Crusher
Crossing the Threshold	To/into V'ger cloud	To Regula I	To Genesis planet	Back to 20th century	To Sha Ka Ree	Leaving space dock	Into the Nexus	Back to 21st century	To Ba'ku	To Romulan system
In "Belly of the Whale"	Wormhole, V'ger	Regula I, Mutara Nebula	The Genesis planet	Whales on *Bounty*	Nimbus III, Sha Ka Ree	Rura Penthe mines			Caves on Ba'ku	(Shinzon in mines)
Road of Trials	V'ger/ Decker, Spock	Khan Shadows Kirk	McCoy shadows Spock	Kirk's court-martial	Sybok shadows Spock	Kirk's Klingon trial	Picard saves Veridian	Borg Queen/ Data	Preserve Prime Directive	Shinzon Shadows Picard
Meeting with the Goddess	Decker with Ilia	Kirk & Carol Marcus	Spock with Saavik	Kirk & Gillian Taylor			Picard with Guinan	Picard with Lily Sloane	Picard with Anij	(Tal'aura as "bad mother")
Woman As Temptress					Uhura (& to Scotty)	Martia to Kirk		Borg Queen to Data		(Donatra to Shinzon)

	Motion Picture	Wrath of Khan	Search for Spock	Voyage Home	Final Frontier	Undiscovered Country	Generations	First Contact	Insurrection	Nemesis
Atonement with the Father	Decker/Kirk, inverted	David/Kirk, inverted	Spock with Sarek	Spock with Sarek	Spock/Sarek, negative					Shinzon/Picard, negative
Apotheosis	Decker, (V'ger)		Spock & katra	Kirk valorized			Nexus = nirvana	Cochrane valorized		Data valorized
Receiving the Boon	Earth saved, data	Lives of crew saved	Genesis not a weapon	Earth saved again	(Sybok is undeceived)	peace with Klingons	Veridian saved	Earth saved twice	Ba'ku is saved	Earth saved again
Hero Refuses to Return	Decker	Spock	(the Enterprise)		(Sybok)	crew & Kirk disobey	Captains reject boon		Picard disobeys orders	Data
Magic Flight	Ship & crew	Ship & crew	Kirk & crew	Ship & crew	Kirk	Kirk & McCoy	Kirk & Picard	Picard	Picard & crew	Picard & crew
Rescue from Outside					McCoy, Spock, & Kirk	Kirk & McCoy				Enterprise & crew
Re-crossing Threshold	V'ger As talisman	Dilation insulation talisman	Spock/ Bounty: talismans	Dilation insulation talisman			Time dilation, talisman	Time dilation	Time dilation, talisman	B-4 As talisman
Master of Both Worlds	Decker & Kirk	Kirk acquires ship	Kirk acquires ship	Kirk acquires ship			Picard	Picard disobeys orders	Picard disobeys orders	
Freedom to Live		Kirk		Kirk	Kirk	Kirk	Kirk & Picard	Picard	Picard	Picard

Figure 2: The Stages of the Adventure in *Star Trek* Films

Kirk's return is then opposed by Klaa's attack; but Kirk, too, is finally rescued from outside the unknown world when he is beamed to a Klingon bird of prey. In *Country* Kirk and McCoy are rescued from outside the unknown world when Spock transports them from Rura Penthe to the *Enterprise* after their escape has been both furthered and opposed by Martia's shape-shifting. In *Nemesis* both the *Enterprise* and Picard are rescued from outside the unknown world—by Romulan battleships and Data, respectively—and these rescues are repeatedly opposed and furthered by an inelegant jumble of extraordinary means. In all the remaining films, however, the return is simply opposed and furthered—or, more simply still, merely furthered—by extraordinary means, as when V'ger returns to Earth with a captive *Enterprise* inside it in *Picture.*

These heroes often experience a dilation of time in the unknown world, sometimes encounter dangers in returning that necessitate "insulation" in the form of precautions, and frequently return with a sentient being (or several) as talisman. V'ger is the talisman in *Picture.* In *Khan* the ruse Kirk employs to escape Regula's core involves only a figurative dilation of time, but Spock transfers his *katra* to McCoy as a form of psychic insurance before sacrificing himself to save the *Enterprise,* and the ship leaves the Mutara Nebula with Carol and David Marcus aboard as talismans. In *Spock* Spock's body is the living talisman retrieved from Genesis and returned to Vulcan on *Bounty,* a second talisman acquired after the *Enterprise* is destroyed. In *Home* the crew returns to the twenty-third century a few minutes before they had departed, yet spend a day or so in 1986, and *Bounty*'s cargo of whales serves as both "insulation" against the danger posed by the alien probe and, with Gillian Taylor, as talismans. Similar dilations of time occur in *Generations*—in which Picard leaves the Nexus with Kirk, the talisman recruited there, minutes before Picard and Soran enter it—and in *Contact,* in which *Enterprise* returns to the very moment it had left the twenty-fourth century after having spent several days in 2063. The most literal dilation of time occurs when Anij slows time for Picard in *Insurrection,* in which Data is the talisman retrieved from Ba'ku, and B-4 is the talisman retrieved from Kolarus III in *Nemesis.* Kirk becomes "master of the two worlds" by literally gaining the freedom to cross the threshold of space freely when he regains command of the *Enterprise* in *Picture, Khan, Spock* and, and *Home.* He wants "to make a difference" in *Generations,* and his and Picard's repetitive world-saving makes each of them conscious that he is a vehicle of the cosmic cycle of change.

In depicting ten science-fiction quests that recapitulate the monomyth's essential departure-initiation-return structure, these films collectively symbolize the monomyth's intrinsic theme, transcendence, in imagery especially appropriate for their times. Henderson (1964) argues that "at the most archaic level" of the symbolism of transcendence the hero reappears as "the shaman ... whose ... power resides in his supposed ability to leave his body and fly about the universe as a bird," and he specifically identifies "space rockets" as contemporary "symbols of release or liberation ... for they are the physical embodiment of the same transcendent principle, freeing us at least temporarily from gravity" (151, 157). It is symbolically appropriate, therefore, that space flight is the essential, common element in this series of films that repeatedly recapitulates the monomyth and is initiated by a film in which one hero, Decker, explicitly transcends his humanity. Yet to be freed from the constraints of time and, even more, from the physical universe itself are far more fantastic liberations than to be freed from the constraint of gravity; and these still-more-fabulous symbols of transcendence each occur once in both the classic *Trek* and *The Next Generation* films: when the *Bounty* and *Enterprise-E* travel through time in *Home* and *Contact*, respectively, when Decker transcends this universe by evolving into a "higher form of consciousness" that can access "higher dimensions" in *Picture*, and when Kirk and Picard enter the nirvana-like Nexus (as well as travel forward and backward in time, respectively, when they exit it) in *Generations*.

Works Cited

Baker, Djoymi. "'Every Old Trick Is New Again': Myth and Quotations in the *Star Trek* Franchise." *Popular Culture Review* 12, no. 1 (2001): 67–77.

Campbell, Joseph. *The Hero with a Thousand Faces*. 2nd ed. Bollingen series XVIII. Princeton, NJ: Princeton University Press, 1949.

Gordon, Andrew. "*Star Wars*: A Myth for Our Time." *Literature and Film Quarterly* 6 (1978): 314–26.

Henderson, Joseph L. "Ancient Myths and Modern Man." *Man and His Symbols*. Edited by Carl G. Jung et al. Garden City, NY: Doubleday, 1964.

Kimball, A. Samuel. "Not Begetting the Future: Technological Autochthony, Sexual Reproduction, and the Mythic Structure of *The Matrix*." *Journal of Popular Culture* 35, no. 3 (2001): 175–203.

Lundquist, Lynne. "Myth and Illiteracy: Bill and Ted's Explicated Adventures." *Extrapolation* 37, no. 3 (1996): 217–23.

Mackay, Daniel. "*Star Wars*: The Magic of the Anti-myth." *Foundation* 76 (1999): 63–75.

Palumbo, Donald E. "The Monomyth as Fractal Pattern in Frank Herbert's *Dune* Novels." *Science-Fiction Studies* 25, no. 3 (1998): 433–58.

_____. "The Monomyth in Alfred Bester's *The Stars My Destination*." *The Journal of Popular Culture* 38, no.2 (2004): 333–368.

_____. "The Monomyth in *Back to the Future*: Science Fiction Film Comedy as Adolescent Wish Fulfillment Fantasy." *Journal of the Fantastic in the Arts* 17, no.1 (2006).

_____. "The Monomyth in Daniel Keyes' *Flowers for Algernon*." *Journal of the Fantastic in the Arts* 14, no.4 (2004): 427–446.

_____. "The Monomyth in Gene Wolfe's *The Book of the New Sun*." *Extrapolation* 46, no. 2 (2005): 189–234.

_____. "The Monomyth in James Cameron's *The Terminator*: Sarah as Monomythic Heroine." *The Journal of Popular Culture* (forthcoming).

_____. "The Monomyth in Time Travel Films." *The Celebration of the Fantastic: Selected Papers from the Tenth Anniversary International Conference on the Fantastic in the Arts*. Edited by Donald E. Morse, Marshall B. Tymn, and Csilla Bertha. Westport, CT: Greenwood Press, 1992.

Reid-Jeffrey, Donna. "*Star Trek*: The Last Frontier in Modern American Myth." *Folklore and Mythology Studies* 6 (1982): 34–41.

Roth, Lane. "Death and Rebirth in *Star Trek II: The Wrath of Khan*." *Extrapolation* 28, no. 2 (1987): 159–66.

Sherman, Marilyn R. "*Star Wars*: New Worlds and Ancient Myths." *Kentucky Folklore Review* 25 (1979): 6–10.

Spinrad, Norman. "Emperor of Everything." *Science Fiction in the Real World*. Carbondale and Edwardsville: Southern Illinois University Press, 1990.

Tiffin, Jessica. "Digitally Remythicised: *Star Wars*, Modern Popular Mythology, and Madam and Eve." *Journal of Literary Studies* 15, no. 1–2 (1999): 66–80.

8

"Blow Up the Damn Ship!"

Production Redesign and Special Effects Reuse in the Star Trek Films

MICHAEL S. DUFFY

On the surface, *Star Trek* has been a successful franchise for forty years, or at least since the debut of *Star Trek: The Motion Picture* in 1979, though its industrial and creative development has always held unique problems. Most *Trek* fans have detailed knowledge of the innumerable creative gestations that the franchise has gone through. As I wrote this, fans were celebrating *Star Trek*'s 40th anniversary as a franchise (marked with various conventions throughout 2006), yet the prevailing mood of both the industry and the mainstream public seemed muted, almost *non-chalant*, even disinterested.[1] With no current television series on the air, and new directions reportedly being explored in the feature film franchise, *Star Trek* as a franchise seems at a distinct turning point. It is at this critical time in the franchise's history that I think it is worth reflecting on *Trek*'s often ignored cinematic aesthetics. In this chapter I will introduce one possible theory as to how *Trek* is differentiated visually from other science fiction texts, and in particular, how its feature film entries have achieved a stylistic continuity through industrial fabrication.

Paramount Studios, having shepherded *Star Trek* since its beginnings, has regularly encountered criticism from *Trek* fans for its alleged "treatment" of the franchise, both industrially and creatively. The studio seems to have a unique relationship with its long-lasting property, which has been interpreted as both possessive and aloof, comparable in many ways to MGM and Eon Productions' development of the James Bond franchise. Paramount has seen that *Trek* can be successful given the right combination of creative elements; yet fan communities persistently argue that Paramount frequently fails to "have faith" in the industrial areas of the film franchise in particular. Much of this criticism has had to do with regular budgetary restraints which were prescribed during production of the first six feature films, which forced each successive film production to reuse and redesign sets, props, and more interestingly, previously constituted special effects shots. Paradoxically, the fan communities that criticize the early "lack" of studio and budgetary "support" simultaneously find pleasure—or at the very least, intellectual interest—in identifying, collecting and analyzing details of specific effects shots and production elements that have been introduced and "reused."

I am taking this notion one step further, and will argue that these supposed budgetary "limitations" (primarily in the original series feature films I–VI) in fact helped create a greater design aesthetic within the *Star Trek* film franchise, providing a stylistic link which enhanced the gradual expansion of the "journey to new worlds," and complemented both the "filmic" and real-life aging of the central characters/actors. There is an interesting "franchise effect" to be documented here, which also parallels the development of special visual effects throughout the 1980s and 1990s, and the gradual transition from "original" physical effects to the "next generation" of digital and computer-generated models. Paramount's long-lasting relationship with the *Star Trek* film franchise is unique, initially producing feature films with modest budgets, yet selling them as "blockbusters" during the 1980s era of financial and creative excess in filmmaking.

While there has always been academic interest in the *Trek* franchise as a whole, much of this focus has leaned towards analysis of the various television series, rather than their feature film counterparts. My recent choice of study therefore came about as I realized both a *lack* of aesthetic and historical-industrial inquiry into the *Trek* feature films, and an *increasing* interest in online *Trek* fan communities in discussing the industrial and cultural impact of the feature films. Curiously, Michele Pierson notes that "Over the years, the various art directors, production designers, and effects supervisors involved in rendering the *Star Trek* universe for television and cinema screens have been quick to point out that the aesthetic demands of fans do feed back into production and effects design" (2002: 56). Additionally, Pierson points to how Henry Jenkins' conversations with students about *Star Trek* often revealed "a detailed knowledge of how the special effects were done, how much different types of effects cost to produce, and the relative strengths and weaknesses of different designers" (Jenkins cited in Pierson, 2002: 56). It seems logical, then (if you'll pardon the pun), to introduce my ideas about special effects reuse in the *Trek* films with a focus on current fan community response to these production choices.

A recent discussion thread on an online *Star Trek* message board was titled, "Ok, What's the greatest Movie Special effect?"[2] A poster, "jon1701," of Manchester, UK, originated this thread in which they state, "Obviously this is open to interpretation and personal preference, but what were the special effects that had the biggest impact on you—the ones that blew you away at the cinema—the ones that made you rewind the VCR?"[3] Many posters then proceed to make jokes about "the 25-minute long introduction" of the *Enterprise* starship in *The Motion Picture*, yet have no problem calling it "beautiful." Treker4747 chooses to vocally "dis-clude" *The Next Generation*-era movies, and emphasizes the "practical" effects in the original series films. Does this last comment indicate something about *Trek* fans' and science fiction audiences' sensibility towards different "generations" of effects? It takes nine posts in the thread before someone says "depends on what kind of effect" you're talking about. It is a fundamental question, often given little thought in online "talkbacks"—or, as yet, in academic discourse on special effects.[4]

In order to fully focus on the "effects" in the *Star Trek* films themselves, it is appropriate here to briefly bring into discussion the nature of science fiction as a genre, and particularly, the meaning of "images" within it. Vivian Sobchack agrees that "There has been only minor consideration of the nature of [sci-fi] images and their function in the creation of a film genre which in photographic content is unlike any other" (2004: 4). Indeed, my discussion here in a wider sense is concerned with how sci-fi images "in content and presentation function to make [sci-fi] film uniquely itself" (2004: 4). *Star Trek*, as a science fiction-based franchise, has charted its own particular journey through special visual effects. The *Trek* film series is a creative and industrial reflection, and abstraction, of the film industry's general technological development, and I will argue that *Trek* films in this context have taken an aesthetic path as yet uncharted in film studies discourse.

Beyond its decidedly humanist, democratically driven character dynamics, hopes of utopia, and "those pointy ears," *Star Trek*'s most recognizable visual and narrative element must surely be that *ship*—namely, the Starship *Enterprise*. It is through, for, and because of "the ship" that most of the major conflicts take place in the *Trek* films. The consistent and near-constant presence of the *Enterprise* gives it iconographic meaning in the science fiction universe, where normally, Sobchack argues, spaceships "do indeed evoke the genre, but [are] specifically and physically not *essential* to it" (2004: 4). In many of the films, the *Enterprise* becomes a cipher through which the main characters emote. And if one can ever believe the oft-stated production designer's tagline, "in this film, the environment really *is* a character," then it must be noted that before the onset of digital visual effects, the original *Trek* films fully embraced the idea of ship = environment = character. If, as Scott Bukatman argues, "cinematic style (as well as authorial consistency) can be located in the fields of art and effects direction" (2003: 82), then the *Star Trek* film series has a definite visual effects aesthetic, and it was achieved in a decidedly unspectacular fashion.

The first foray into feature films for the crew of the original *Star Trek* series, *Star Trek: The Motion Picture*, was in fact rewritten from a second television series pilot, tellingly titled "In Thy Image," and also developed as bare-bones B-grade feature, before arriving at its more epic final incarnation on film screens. Still, in an effort to save costs, many sets built for use in the proposed second television series, *Phase Two*, were simply used for the feature film with little alteration. Arguments vary as to whether *The Motion Picture* was actually put into production because, or rather in spite of, the success of *Star Wars* (1977), though arguably the film reflects more of *2001: A Space Odyssey* (1968) in tone and sensibility.[5] This is where the first *Trek* film found difficulties with the studio, fans and general audiences. In choosing a design aesthetic for the film, producers and special effects handlers were at a crossroads. In a larger sense, as actor Leonard Nimoy recalls, "[The studio was] preoccupied with this idea that it must have size and stature. Although everyone [at Paramount] seemed to have an idea about what a *Star Trek* movie should *not* be—a magnified television episode—no one could agree on what it *should* be" (Nimoy cited in Hughes, 2001: 26). With creative heads already at odds, the *Trek* film franchise began an aesthetic journey that would find itself shaped on the very ideas of consistency and difference.

Star Trek: The Motion Picture, in any version viewed (there are at least three official edits: theatrical, television/video, and a 2001 "director's edition"), differs greatly in visual design from the nine *Trek* features that follow. Yet there are visual cues and meanings created in the film which manage to survive throughout most of the other original series films. Sobchack, when speaking of iconographic symbols in the classic western film genre—of which *Trek* creator Gene Roddenberry often saw his show as an update, a "wagon-train to the stars"—notes that "[in westerns] the railroad is not merely its physical manifestation; it *is* progress and civilization" (2004: 5). Comparing this identification to the spaceship in science fiction, she argues that "there is no consistent cluster of meanings provoked by the image of a spaceship.... Because there is no consistent meaning, there is little accumulation of 'emblematic power' carried by the object from movie to movie" (2004: 5). This, I will argue, is where the *Trek* films differ, and this iconographic signification begins with *The Motion Picture*.

In its regeneration of the original *Star Trek* television series aesthetic (and by consequence, the original *Enterprise* ship design), *The Motion Picture* attempts to restore and simultaneously enlarge the fabric of meaning associated with the original show, ship and crew members. While some design changes in costume and ship "fitting" took place for the big screen debut, there is clearly an attempt in *The Motion Picture* to adhere to an *image and a setting* that is recognizable to *Trek* fans (i.e., "the same, but different"). In visual approach to the *Enterprise* itself, *The Motion Picture* takes its cue from many other sci-fi films such as *Conquest of Space* (Byron Haskin, 1955), "with its lavish treatment of takeoffs, maneuverings and landings" (Sobchack, 2004: 6). Films like these, Sobchack describes, "visually celebrate the spaceship and dwell on its surfaces with a caressive photographic wonder" (6). Much has been made of the sequence in *The Motion Picture* featuring Captain Kirk's arrival at the refitted *Enterprise*, how the camera lingers on its outer surface, so much so that even actor William Shatner himself seems in awe of it all. The scene functions as a moment of both spectacle and narrative, a big-screen gift to *Trek* fans; the *Enterprise* here is an object at once aesthetically meaningful and, as Bukatman would have it, "hilariously fetishized" (2003: 96).

There is another thread to this analysis, however. Most of *The Motion Picture*'s special and visual effects were supervised by Douglas Trumbull, who is possibly better known for his effects work on *2001: A Space Odyssey*, *Close Encounters of the Third Kind* (1977) and *Blade Runner* (1982). Bukatman notes that Trumbull's effects design and sequences "are rooted in an ambivalent relation to new technologies, [and] they depend on new technologies for their very effect(s)" (2003: 83). Still, Trumbull's work, in Bukatman's opinion, most frequently constitutes "less the description of an object than the construction of an environment" (2003: 94). The myriad of lighting and optical effects Trumbull used in *The Motion Picture* to construct the open-space environments and the outer structure of the V'ger probe are surely notable, but equally as interesting here are the aesthetic choices for the *Enterprise*'s warp speed takeoff.

Bukatman, in his book *Matters of Gravity*, draws a comparison between cinematic special effects of this era and nineteenth century "luminist" American painting, which concentrated on the relationship between nature and human destiny (2003: 97).[6] Luminist painting evoked "the sublimity of the American landscape," Bukatman explains, "defined by its representation of light: a cool, hard, palpable light (not diffuse) spread across a glassy surface" (98). Like the *Enterprise*'s warp speed signature, in luminist painting "the linear edges of reality are pulled taut," "strained almost to the point of breaking" (Novak, 1995: 27). For *The Motion Picture*, Trumbull applied lighting through optical effects to achieve a red, white and blue visual of the warp engine wave of the *Enterprise* as the ship speeds off. The conspicuously colored warp signature simultaneously evokes the American flag and the dream of a "new frontier" that *Star Trek* was founded on. In these moments in *The Motion Picture*, there is, like the luminist paintings, "the sense of vast stillness verging on an imminent crescendo of light and sound" (Wilmerding cited in Bukatman, 2003: 100).[7]

Though Trumbull did not work on any of the successive *Trek* films, his "especially contemplative" visual aesthetic (as Bukatman calls it) is present throughout, if not in outer space environments, than at least through the continuing use and refinement of the *Enterprise*'s bright colored warp speed signature (2003: 95). Indeed, the reuse of these very shots from *The Motion Picture*, those featuring the *Enterprise* blasting off into warp speed, and departing from space dock, are what arguably begins to give the *Enterprise* the "emblematic" power that it acquires throughout the *Trek* film series. Trumbull also contributed major work in fine-tuning specific scenes for *The Motion Picture*, writing, directing and reshooting a pivotal effects-heavy sequence in which Spock enters the V'ger probe from space.[8] Trumbull's extensive involvement during production of *The Motion Picture* provides an early example of special effects producers establishing an aesthetic approach, and an authorial presence, not just in post-production, but on-set. Despite *The Motion Picture*'s troubled production, its last-minute completion, and its mixed box office reception, a decision was made to continue the franchise, a choice that is as interesting for its aesthetic consequences as it is for its industrial ones.

For *Star Trek II: The Wrath of Khan* (1982), a decision was made produce the film through Paramount's television division, and reuse many ship models and props from *The Motion Picture*[9] reflecting the original film's attempt to reuse its own production "history." Given a much-reduced budget, and a script that focused much more on personal interaction than "contemplative" space travel, the production crew on *Wrath of Khan* opted for creative "reuse" rather than reconstruction, an approach that would soon define the franchise. This reuse was paired with a change in authorial approach, emphasizing a belief that perhaps a different "direction" with the same elements could indeed prove more aesthetically and financially successful. Despite being notable for one of the first uses of computer-generated technology in a feature film, during a scene depicting a computer-mapping of the planetary-changing "Genesis effect," *Wrath of Khan* more prominently displays its reliance on reused and reincorporated special visual effects, in sequences featuring the Enterprise leaving space dock, and blasting into warp speed. The choice to employ a different director, lighting design, costumes and composer from the first film, coupled with the film's aesthetic reuse of previous design and effects elements, moved *Wrath of Khan* into a different "phase" than its predecessor. With these merging of production elements, and the first attempt to "battle-damage" the *Enterprise*, *Wrath of Khan* acquired a new stylistic approach that would remain *"in continuity"* until the original crew retired from the franchise.

Star Trek III (1984) finds the *Enterprise* crew struggling in *The Search for Spock*; late in the film they choose to sacrifice (self-destruct) their ship in order to save themselves and gain a tactical advantage. This dramatic moment, rendered with models and optical effects by Industrial Light &

Magic, constitutes an admission of and adherence to what many find appealing in science fiction films—not just an exploration of new worlds, but a reliance on fate-determining cosmic battles and explosions (despite there being no sound in space). As Barry Keith Grant explains, "The genre's primary appeal has been the kinetic excitement of action—that 'sensuous elaboration' which Susan Sontag describes as 'the aesthetics of destruction ... the peculiar beauties to be found in wreaking havoc, making a mess'" (Grant and Sontag cited in Sontag, 1966: 212). The notion of the *Enterprise*'s destruction equating to the full emergence of grand spectacle in the *Trek* films is not necessarily illuminating; what is interesting here is that at this point the *Trek* films begin to become visually intertextual, almost optically *riffing* on themselves.

The original conception for the *Enterprise*'s destruction was apparently to have it detonate entirely in space,[10] yet the final film version has the ship exploding its primary hull in space, while the bottom half of the ship disintegrates into a nearby planet's atmosphere. (This choice interestingly provides an extra character-building moment at the conclusion of the film in the form of a shot showing Kirk, McCoy and Scotty watching the ship falling through the atmosphere, as they contemplate their choice; "What have I done," Kirk sighs.) The initial visual effects sequence was completed according to the *early* conception, however, and, again due to budgetary limitations, a completely new shot could not be created, so the producers reconstituted the shot by *reusing* the original first half of the explosion, and only commissioning new images for the atmosphere burn-out. *Wrath of Khan* and *Search for Spock* used previous *Enterprise* footage both in their films *and* their theatrical trailers, creating in essence a thematic and visual through-line by way of special effects.

While digital technology interfaces have, since the early 1990s, provided the ability to reconstitute all manner of shots using various kinds of visual effects, in the 1980s film layering optical effects was generally the only option available to accomplish complex matte shots such as the *Enterprise*'s destruction in *Search*. That the *Trek* production teams were able to promote and manufacture globally viable and successful science fiction films with reconstituted and reused special effects footage is notable. More importantly, the visual aesthetic achieved for the *Enterprise* through this "textual poaching"[11] of previous films equates to something singular and astute. The production teams' technical ingenuity is arguably the audience's (and scholar's?) advantage; the *Enterprise*, as image, effect and iconography, becomes the communicator by which lives are lived, loved and lost by the producers, actors and fans. The portrayal of the *Enterprise* in the *Trek* films seems to exemplify film scholar Annette Kuhn's notion that science fiction cinema's "distinctive generic traits" may "have to do in large measure with cinematographic technologies and with the ways in which these figure in the construction of diegetic and spectatorial

space." She argues that "while science fiction films may certainly tell stories, narrative content and structure *per se* are rarely their most significant
features" (Kuhn, 1999: 11).

Kuhn's ideas are borne out most obviously in the middle three original series *Trek* films. When Kirk reunites with Spock at the end of *Search*,
he tells him, "You saved the ship," even though it is now lost. Of course,
Kirk's statement has multiple meanings: Kirk means to convey to Spock
that his sacrificial actions helped save most of the *Enterprise*'s crew, but
the comment also seems directed at longstanding *Trek* fans who have kept
the franchise alive, conveying to them that while in the characters' world
the iconic *Enterprise* vessel may be gone, it, like the franchise, forever has
the possibility of being resurrected. In *Star Trek IV: The Voyage Home* (1986),
though the crew is without the *Enterprise* for the entire film, specific visual
and thematic use is still made of the ship. In the film's opening scenes,
the filmmakers find a way to incorporate the previous film's footage of
the *Enterprise* exploding, by putting Kirk and crew on trial for their dis-
obedience. Again, the *Enterprise* is the focus of reuse and reconstitution,
for dramatic effect, this time from the very beginning of the film. Jan
Johnson-Smith agrees with me here:

> Notably, the pivotal points in [*Star Trek II, III* and *IV*] do not lie only in the
> death, funeral and resurrection of Mr. Spock ... but rather in their parallel.
> The films linger respectively upon the destruction of the *Enterprise* at the
> planet Genesis, and its rebirth at Earth's starbase as the *Enterprise NCC
> 1701A*. The death and rebirth of the vessel is thus given equal dramatic
> weight to the death and rebirth of its First Officer [Johnson-Smith, 2004:
> 272].

When the *Enterprise* finally does *re*appear at the close of *Voyage Home*, it is
"given" to the crew as a gift from Starfleet, the interplanetary organization within which the crew operates. It is a brand-new ship, yet appears—
at least on the outside—to be in the exact style and design of the original.
While some audiences possibly interpreted the appearance of a near-
identical ship as a marginalization of the previous ship's destruction, the
move was apparently a more popular choice than giving the crew the
Excelsior, a more advanced and bulkier model, which itself was initially
planned to be the crew's new ship for future films.[12] Also, the production
of *Voyage Home* offers more proof of just how much industry, technology
and aesthetics are beginning to coalesce. Production diaries of the film
state that Kirk Thatcher, hired at the beginning of the film as a "production assistant" for "visual effects," in fact became so involved in the overall creative approach that he was given an "associate producer" title on
the film by the close of production.[13]

In *Star Trek V* (1989), the crew attempt to meet *The Final Frontier*, but
instead encounter a god-alien pretender who doesn't want any of their

culture or intellect, only their ship. In this film, however, the grandiose nature of the plot is especially hurt by effects work which arguably renders the *Enterprise* closer to the (even cheaper) original TV series model than ever before. During production, a decision was made to bypass the previously successful working relationship with the prominent visual effects company Industrial Light & Magic, and contract the special effects work out to a few smaller companies, Associates & Ferren[14] and Peter Wallach Enterprises (Fields, 1989). One production article on the film gleefully claims, "Feature film effects have truly gone 'where no man has gone before'—namely this New Jersey town on the Hudson across from Manhattan, where New York-based production company Peter Wallach Enterprises recently set up shop in a warehouse adjacent to Hoboken High School" (Fields, 1989).

ILM did still get to "work" on the film in some capacity, as a few effects shots of the *Enterprise* in space-dock, originally completed by the company for *Voyage Home,* were reused here. In a moment late in the film that seems to reflect these production dilemmas, the god-alien, like a petulant child (or possibly an angry fan), badgers Kirk, "Bring me the ship"; "I must have the ship"; "Now, *give me what I want.*" Adding to the aesthetic aloofness of the film was the decision to use and multipurpose the sets of *Enterprise*'s sick bay and various corridors from the then in-production *Star Trek: The Next Generation* television series—set some 80 years later.[15] Interestingly, the "next generation" *Star Trek* television series then adopts this aesthetic of reuse for themselves: in 1996, the series *Star Trek: Voyager* reused effects shots from *Star Trek VI: The Undiscovered Country* (1991) in a flashback episode featuring the "original series" character Sulu (played by original actor George Takei). As the *Enterprise* sets off under Kirk's command for the final time in *The Undiscovered Country,* we see more of the interior of the *Enterprise* than we ever have before, including a kitchen(!), yet Trumbull's visual echo remains in the tricolored warp speed generation of the *Enterprise*'s engines

This visual-thematic/aesthetic intertextuality continued into the 1990s, when the original crew finally passed the torch to the "next generation" cast in the film *Star Trek Generations* (1994), which itself reused many sets from the just-completed television series (and, consequently, previous *Trek* films), as well as effects shots of both the *Excelsior* and a Klingon ship explosion—lifted frame-for-frame—from *Country.* As *The Next Generation* cast and crew took over the film franchise (having already established themselves through seven successful years on television), a distinct change was happening in the film industry itself. Because of the success of films like *Terminator 2: Judgment Day* (1991) and *Jurassic Park* (1993), digital technology was moving into the forefront, most prominently in the areas of special visual effects and compositing. The interesting thing about *Generations,* however, is that despite its attempt to shift the franchise forward both narratively and thematically—and its "passing the torch" to a new crew both on screen and off—it retained, in its production approach, the "old-fashioned" production and design aesthetic of the previous *Trek* films, despite the fact that digital approaches were quickly being adopted throughout the industry. Though some computer-generated imagery was used, most notably in a stunning sequence featuring "stellar cartography," the majority of visual effects work was handled with scale models and traditional film compositing [layering one image over another] (anon, 1995). Yet the importance of visual effects in selling the *Star Trek* franchise to the public remains interestingly important. *TNG* producer Rick Berman allegedly could not accommodate actor Leonard Nimoy's overtures to rewrite parts of the *Generations* script (that Nimoy was interested in directing) *because special effects companies had already been booked for specific sequences.*[16]

Star Trek Generations* again finds the crew being forced to sacrifice their ship, except this time we not only see it destroyed in space, we also witness its crash-landing on a planet's surface. This adoption of what one could call an expanded "aesthetics of destruction" clearly is meant to signal to the audience that "you're not going to see this on television." Paramount and the filmmakers were aware that *Generations* needed to be something altogether "different" yet "recognizable," just as the television series it was based on differed ever so slightly from its original series counterpart. More importantly, it needed to be *spectacular* in a way that the television show never was; indeed the very nature of the blockbuster industry itself contributed to what Roberta Pearson calls the "historically specific conditions of production and reception that [would] result in a higher degree of spectacle in *Trek* cinema than television" (Pearson and Messenger-Davies, 2003: 105). While *The Motion Picture* adhered very closely to the original television series in visual design and narrative approach, *The Next Generation* films, by contrast, were forced to "up the ante" more noticeably and quickly, to both separate themselves from their television origins, and compete with the contemporary blockbuster environment. With these ideas in mind, it becomes easier to understand why every one of the four *TNG*-era films featured the *Enterprise* either being destroyed or nearly destroyed. More importantly, it becomes clear that the *Star Trek* image that had been "carefully forged" over previous decades now includes an aesthetic visual style of *destruction.*[17]

The *Enterprise* in the *Star Trek* films, through its constant birth, destruction, rebirth, and reuse, reflects the film franchise's creative and financial imperatives. It is simultaneously both loved and hated by its crew on-screen; it is often malfunctioning greatly, yet its crew (and especially its captains) are clearly happiest when aboard and in operation. "Don't let them promote you," Kirk tells Picard in *Generations*, "don't let them do anything that takes you away from that chair!" The ship's consistent reappearance, with minimal design changes, and despite "generations" of crews, arguably forms a centerpiece for the film franchise, keeping it accessible and recognizable. While it has been noted by Michele Pierson and others that the tension between spectacle and narrative in the 1990s becomes even more pronounced and complicated, *Trek* film history interestingly parallels this rise in use of new, copious amounts of special effects for spectacular impact. The *Star Trek* filmmakers gradually embraced the "next generation" of visual effects technology by re-rendering most of the archetypal ships and recognizable visual cues with new digital technology. However, this transition did not occur suddenly or quickly; the franchise's first use of completely computer-generated ships was not achieved until the ninth film, *Star Trek: Insurrection,* in 1998.

Despite *Star Trek*'s consistent move towards appealing to blockbuster sensibilities, Roberta Pearson notes that by the mid-1990s most film critics still "[didn't] expect *Trek* films to be as spectacular as others in the sci-fi genre," which leads her to ask "whether spectacle functions differently in these films than in other sci-fi blockbusters," a notion that I have indeed been arguing throughout this chapter (Pearson and Messenger-Davies, 2003: 104). The *Trek* films have always contained what Steve Neale calls "textual" and "institutional" events, in both dialogue and visual approach—"a remark addressed to the spectator by the film, and by the cinematic apparatus, about the nature of its special effects," all of which constitutes a distinct "awareness on the part of the spectator" (Neale, 2004: 11). Nowhere is this idea more apparent than in *Star Trek: First Contact* (1996), the eighth film in the series. *First Contact* self-comments on the franchise's use of the *Enterprise* in an almost phallic worship. As the *Enterprise* is nearly lost once again, Captain Picard argues with Lilly, an idealistic human civilian from the past, whose proper place in history is revealed as she forms a greeting party for the first alien spaceship to set down and make "first contact" with Earth. Faced with undeniably depressing odds, Lilly pleads with Picard to abandon his pride and sacrifice the *Enterprise* for the greater good. "Jean-Luc, blow up the damn ship!" Lilly cries in desperation, as Picard screams "Noooo!" and smashes a rifle through a display case of miniatures of previous *Enterprise* ships. "You broke your little ships," Lilly exclaims dourly. One needn't think too long before coming to an obvious assertion: old-fashioned models are *out,* digital technology is *in.* The meaning is clarified as Picard visits the bridge one last time, in preparation for the ship's self-destruction. As the ship's doctor intones "So much for the *Enterprise-E,*" Picard, who could be resigning himself to the potentialities of digital technology, replies—almost with a smirk—"Plenty of letters left in the alphabet."

In contrast, *Star Trek: Insurrection,* in lieu of self-destructing the entire ship, takes the route of *merely* ejecting the "warp core" yet again, as in *Generations.* Despite facing an enemy that comes across much less threatening on-screen than the previous film's Borg collective, Picard and crew again face the imminent almost-destruction of the *Enterprise*. Technological language overtakes the film, where around every corner there is a holographic projection or a "transport inhibitor." *Insurrection* features the first full transition into computer-generated modeling for visual effects crews "rendering" the famous *Enterprise* (anon., 1998). Watching the film, one gets the strange feeling that digital technology has not only taken over the film's special effects, but also its narrative. "Didn't we used to be explorers?" Picard laments in the beginning of the film.

    Star Trek Nemesis (2002) visualizes the ultimate parallel between such diametrically opposed themes of technology and humanism that Vivian Sobchack describes in her writings on science fiction. Picard is literally matched when he encounters a heretofore unknown clone of himself, Shinzon. The Remans, the antagonists in the film, pilot the *Scimitar*, a ship that is graphically and structurally the opposite of the *Enterprise* and seems to conform to Sobchack's description of the "demonic side" of a spaceship. Sobchack explains:

> [In] many films it is a trap from which there is little hope to escape. Its sleekness is visually cold and menacing, its surfaces hostile to human warmth. It functions mechanically and perfectly, ignorant of its creators and operators—or it malfunctions with malice, almost as if it could choose to do otherwise but prefers to rid itself of its unsleek and emotionally tainted human occupants. Instead of glowing like a night light, it coldly glitters like the blade of a stiletto. Instead of humming, it ticks. It evokes associations not of release, but of confinement. The womb-like and protective warmth of a positive visual treatment is nowhere apparent; rather, the ship is seen negatively, viewed with antitechnological suspicion, the images of it suggesting a tomb-like iciness, a coffin-like confinement. Its corridors and holds echo the sounds of human isolation or provide a haven for alien and lethal dusts and slimes; in unseen corners the subversion of human life begins [2004: 6].

    Tinted in green and dark blue, the *Scimitar* becomes everything that Sobchack describes, and adequately serves as the ultimate physical and graphical "nemesis" to the *Enterprise*. In *Nemesis*, the franchise seems to have reached a creative and aesthetic stopgap, wherein the best option available for presenting a "spectacular" conflict on-screen seems to be in creating a mirror opposite of the smooth and sleek *Enterprise*, and for the epic conclusion, have these two mechanistic titans simply collide with one another. Surprisingly, it is the *Enterprise*, under Picard's orders, that takes the initiative. With definitions of space exploration and visual effects constitution being literally smashed into oblivion, it is indeed arguable that in *Nemesis* (as the film's marketing tagline so aptly put it) "a generation's final journey begins."

    Some have suggested that the *Star Trek* franchise overall has lacked in "aesthetic innovation"; however I believe that, at least in the film series, the aesthetic visual style is actually more one of continuity, before journeying towards fabrication and dissonance. The early apparent "lack of innovation," forged through visual effects reuse, in fact helped establish a visual style unique to this franchise, and to science fiction film in general. The *Star Trek* film series defiantly plays with the notion of what Scott Bukatman has called the "awe" and "play" of special effects sequences. "The effect is possessed of its own hypnotic grandeur," Bukatman claims, "it is designed to inspire awe, but always within a reassuring sense of play" (2003: 109). Coupling with this is Jan Johnson-Smith's assertion that "in thirty years we will doubtless laugh at 1990s [digital visual] effects in the same way as we mock the rubber monsters, polystyrene rocks and 'red shirt' alerts of 1960s *Star Trek*" (2004: 7). True, but at some point in the future, when we can no longer tell the difference anymore between what is "real" and what is "digital," when we look back at images of the past, will we even know *why* we're laughing? It is already happening to our visual senses, as Sobchack so interestingly explains:

> Inevitably, then, we must be led away from a preoccupation with a search for consistent visual emblems into more ambiguous territory. It is the very plasticity of objects and settings in [sci-fi] films which help define them as science fiction, and not their consistency. And it is this same plasticity of objects and settings that deny the kind of iconographic interpretation which critically illuminates the essentially static worlds of genres such as the western and gangster film [2004: 10].

While this chapter is not necessarily, in Bukatman's words, an "attempt to situate authorship around the visual designers of a film" (2003: 235), it is a move towards viewing and studying special visual effects, particularly those related specifically to science fiction's iconographic potentialities, in a way that, hopefully, illuminates a meaning beyond simply how the "effect" works within a film's narrative or how it becomes "spectacle." The *Enterprise* performs a unique function in science fiction films, as a visual object that moves in space and time, never becoming unrecognizable, creating a galaxy-wide nexus of meaning that has yet to be fully interpreted. Through its continuous destruction and rebirth by way of narrative and visual effects technology, the ship delivers visual appeasement and inspiration to an audience of knowledgeable fans and outside observers, "traveling to new worlds" while simultaneously retaining a "blockbuster" sensibility.

It has been my argument that the "look" of the *Star Trek* films has developed in parallel to industrial, technological and aesthetic movements in contemporary Hollywood cinema of the last few decades. While this may seem an obvious assertion, I think that a deeper investigation of the *Trek* films' production history and creative intentions reveals that the

150 Part III: Film and Television

original series films were, by virtue of their very limitations, forced to place their visual aestheticism within a concrete narrative and character-based structures which precluded any visual effects misuse. Given minimal resources in technology and capital to accomplish their goals, producers of these films successfully created a minimalist visual and aesthetic "style" in their constant use and reuse of the popular visual effects involving the *Enterprise*. The "next generation" films, conversely, operated on an increasing economy of scale in budget and "blockbuster" anticipation, which, in tandem with the rapid expansion in Hollywood of digital techniques for special effects in the 1990s, caused this second set of films to form a much more ambiguous relationship between studio, actors and audiences. Throughout the film series, filmmakers attempted to successfully incorporate new technologies while reusing existing approaches, until widespread industry adoption of digital technologies became absolutely *paramount* to the visualization of special effects and production design with blockbuster purpose. The shift and transformation from one "generation" to the "next," therefore, has encompassed more than simply a change of production crew and cast. This move in cast and crew also reflects the complex institutional and artistic changes taking place in the New Hollywood, and the intense struggle for *Trek* to remain a "contender" in the mainstream feature film marketplace, despite the proliferation (and subsequent lagging) of its television counterparts.

Notes

1. Though there have been a few false starts. Paramount reportedly commissioned a script in early 2005 delving into the *Trek* universe's origins, tentatively titled *Star Trek: The Beginning*. Planned to be an epic "restart," and set in a different era than the most recent *Trek* "prequel" television show, *Enterprise: The Beginning* as of early 2006 had seemingly been shelved, as initial reports about it were not followed up, its entry was removed from the Internet Movie Database, and Paramount claimed to have "no feature film in active development." Yet, in April 2006, Paramount announced rather surprisingly that writer/director J.J. Abrams (who had just completed *Mission Impossible III* for the studio) had made a deal with the studio to develop and possibly direct a new *Star Trek* feature for release in 2008. Early reports indicated that the film might still be set as a "prequel" to the original television series, though Abrams and his producing partners have not revealed specifics. Initial interviews with *The Beginning*'s script writer, Erik Jendreson, in March and August 2005, still exist on *Star Trek* Website TrekWeb, available at http://www.trekweb.com/stories.php?aid=422f8a4f0754e (accessed 15 February 2006), and http://www.trekweb.com/articles/2005/08/26/430f1c48c18bd.shtml (accessed 15 February 2006).

2. "Ok, What's the greatest Movie Special effect?" *Trek BBS* message board [online], available at http://www.trekbbs.com/threads/showflat.php?Cat=&Number=4728803&page=0&view=collapsed&sb=5&o=7&fpart=1 (accessed 15 July 2005). Obviously one could interrogate the subliminal meanings of the very specific spelling choices of this Internet message board post—namely which words are capitalized, or not, and why might that be? Why are "Movie" and "Special" emphasized, while "greatest" and "effect" made less so? (Though the poster's lack of grammatical sense in the use of "one's" gives a clue that this might all simply be overinterpretation on my part.) While one might simply chalk these

choices up to quick random thinking and relaying of thoughts on a message board community, that fact remains that specific communicative choices such as these reveal our direct and indirect concerns with what we say, how we say it, and who we say it to (lately, online); these choices tell us about who we are, what we know and what we are implicitly concerned with in the various arts that fascinate us.

3. While it might surely be interesting to trace the implications of Mancunian interest in *Star Trek* or special effects, that is not, unfortunately, my primary concern in this chapter.

4. In a witty display of *Trek* fans' self-mocking humor, an earlier thread on the message board, "I figured out what the worst *TNG* Movie effect"—again note the grammatical and punctuational inconsistencies—features the priceless quote: "Personally, I think the worst *TNG* movie effect is Shatner's toupee in 'Generations.'" (The poster is referring to *Star Trek: Generations* (1994), the seventh feature film in the *Trek* franchise, and likely the last to feature William Shatner as Captain James T. Kirk.)

5. For slightly differing accounts of this argument, see Edward Gross et al. (1995), *The Making of the Trek Films*, and William Shatner (1995), *"Star Trek" Movie Memories*.

6. Bukatman's full quote relating to my point is as follows: "In the nineteenth century, America revealed its obsession with the relationship between nature and human power and human destiny in prose, paint and politics."

7. Referenced in Bukatman (2003: 100), quote is from John Wilmerding, writing about the paintings of Frederick Church (Wilmerding, ed. 1980: 121).

8. See audio commentary by Trumbull, and retrospective special features, on *Star Trek: The Motion Picture—The Director's Edition*. Robert Wise, 1979 (2001 DVD) Paramount Pictures.

9. According to different sources, 65 percent of the film was apparently shot on the same set:

> Space Station Regula 1 was the space station from [*The Motion Picture*] ... turned upside-down. The sets of *Reliant* were actually the *Enterprise* with different lighting, camera angles, and different seat covers. The *Enterprise* Torpedo Room and Spacelab transporter sets were originally parts of the Klingon bridge built for the first *Star Trek* movie. The Spacelab model is that of the orbiting space office turned upside down and with some cosmetic changes from the first *Star Trek* movie. The computer ship diagrams when the shields are being raised are actually from the aborted 1978 *Star Trek: Phase II* TV show.

Star Trek II: The Wrath of Khan (film entry), *Internet Movie Database* (Website), available at http://www.imdb.com/title/tt0084726/trivia (accessed 5 May 2005); also Shatner's *"Star Trek" Memories*, and other informational Websites such as *Word IQ*'s *Star Trek II* entry, available at http://www.wordiq.com/definition/Star_Trek_II:_The_Wrath_of_Khan (accessed 10 May 2005), and Shatner (1995).

10. It was originally intended to be "a massive matter/anti-matter explosion," one fan notes. *Star Trek III: The Search for Spock* (film entry), *Internet Movie Database* (Website), available at http://www.imdb.com/title/tt0088170/trivia (accessed 15 May 2005). See also Michael Okuda's text commentary on *Star Trek III: The Search for Spock*, special edition, Leonard Nimoy, 1984 (2002 DVD), Paramount Pictures.

11. If I may borrow Henry Jenkins's book title and term here.

12. Or so claims *WordIQ*: "The filmmakers initially intended for the crew to receive the USS *Excelsior* (NCC 2000) (possibly renamed to *Enterprise*), but an unexpectedly large outcry caused this idea to be dropped." *Star Trek IV: The Voyage Home* (film entry), *Word IQ* (Website), available at http://www.wordiq.com/definition/Star_Trek_IV:_The_Voyage_Home (accessed 15 May 2005) (writing content originated in 1986). Also see Michael Okuda's text commentary on *Star Trek IV: The Voyage Home*, special edition, Leonard Nimoy, 1986 (2003 DVD), Paramount Pictures.

13. See: *Star Trek IV: The Voyage Home* (film entry), *Internet Movie Database* (Website), available at http://www.imdb.com/title/tt0092007/trivia (accessed 15 May 2005); also Michael Okuda's previously mentioned text commentary on the *Star Trek IV* DVD.

14. "The special effects work was also hampered by the budget cuts. Instead of using the special effects studio used for earlier *Trek* films, Industrial Light & Magic, the crew

went with the much smaller Associates & Ferren. The special effects supervisor, Bran Ferren, publicly admitted he didn't care about the quality of the effects work, and the end results were predictably poor." *Star Trek V: The Final Frontier* (film entry), *WordIQ* (Website), available at http://www.wordiq.com/definition/Star_Trek_V:_The_Final_Frontier (accessed 10 February 2006).

    15. *Star Trek V: The Final Frontier* (film entry), *Internet Movie Database* (Website), available at http://www.imdb.com/title/tt0098382/trivia (accessed 10 February 2006). Also see Michael Okuda's text commentary on *Star Trek V: The Final Frontier, special* edition, William Shatner, 1989 (2003 DVD), Paramount Pictures.

    16. *Star Trek Generations* (film entry), *WordIQ* (Website), available at http://www.wordiq.com/definition/Star_Trek:_Generations (accessed 10 February 2006).

    17. Eric Chauvin, CGI matte artist for the television series *Star Trek: Voyager,* in an e-mail interview with Jan Johnson-Smith (Johnson-Smith, 2005: 108).

Works Cited

Anonymous. "Paramount's 'Star Trek: Generations' special effects leverage Wavefront software; Santa Barbara Studios creates cutting-edge effects with DYNAMATION and COMPOSER." *Business Wire* (December 21, 1995). http://www.findarticles.com/p/articles/mi_m0EIN/is_1994_Dec_21/ai_15952631 (accessed 10 February 2006).

Anonymous. "Viewpoint Boldly Goes Where No Modeling Team Has Gone Before Helping Create First all-CG Starfleet for *Star Trek: Insurrection.*" *Business Wire* (December 21, 1998). http://www.findarticles.com/p/articles/mi_m0EIN/is_1994_Dec_21/ai_15952631 (accessed 10 February 2006).

Bukatman, Scott. *Matters of Gravity: Special Effects and Supermen in the 20th Century.* Durham and London: Duke University Press, 2003.

Fields, Gaylord. "Peter Wallach explores 'Final Frontier' of Hoboken for 'Star Trek V': N.Y. effects house does motion control for film." *Back Stage* (June 1989).

Grant, Barry Keith. "Sensuous Elaboration." *Against Interpretation.* Edited by Susan Sontag. New York: Delta, 1966.

Gross, Edward, et al. *The Making of the* Trek *Films.* Image Publishing, 1995.

Johnson-Smith, Jan. *American Science Fiction TV: "Star Trek," "Stargate" and Beyond.* London: I.B. Tauris, 2005.

Hughes, David. *The Greatest Sci-Fi Movies Never Made.* London: Titan Publishing Group, 2001.

Kuhn, Annette. "Introduction to Part One: Cultural Spaces." *Alien Zone II.* Edited by Annette Kuhn. London: Verso, 1999: 11–15.

Neale, Steve. "'You've Got To Be Fucking Kidding!': Knowledge, Belief and Judgment in Science Fiction." *Liquid Metal: The Science Fiction Film Reader.* Edited by Sean Redmond. London and New York: Wallflower Press, 2004.

Nimoy, Leonard. *I Am Spock.* New York: Hyperion Books, 1995.

Novak, Barbara. *Nature and Culture: American Landscape and Painting, 1825–1875.* New York: Oxford University Press, 1995.

Pearson, Roberta E., and Maire Messenger-Davies. "'You're not going to see that on TV': *Star Trek: The Next Generation* in Film and Television." *Quality Popular Television.* Edited by Mark Jancovich and James Lyons. London: British Film Institute, 2003: 103–117.

Pierson, Michele. *Special Effects: Still in Search of Wonder.* New York: Columbia University Press, 2002.

Shatner, William. *"Star Trek" Movie Memories.* New York: HarperTorch, 1995.

Sobchack, Vivian. "Images of Wonder: The Look of Science Fiction." *Liquid Metal: The Science Fiction Film Reader.* Edited by Sean Redmond. London and New York: Wallflower Press, 2004: 4–10.

Sontag, Susan. "The Aesthetics of Destruction." *Against Interpretation.* Edited by Susan Sontag. New York: Delta, 1966.

Wilmerding, John, ed. *American Light: The Luminist Movement, 1850–1875.* Washington D.C.: National Gallery of Art, 1980.

9

Star Trek: Popular Discourses

The Role of Broadcasters and Critics

PAUL RIXON

On the twelfth of July 1969, the BBC screened its first episode of *Star Trek* (often now referred to as the Original *Star Trek* (OST), an appendage begat to it by later productions in the franchise). This first episode signaled the start of *Star Trek*'s extended run on British television; never has a decade gone by without it yet being shown. It has, in many ways, become as much part of British television culture as *Doctor Who*, a longer running and more British variant of the television science genre. As with most programs, the way *Star Trek* has come to be understood and accepted by the audience, the way it has been talked about and culturally assimilated, has been informed and shaped by a public discourse. Those engaging in such a discourse include the general viewers, fans, broadcasters, producers, distributors, stars and television critics. This discourse is not of course fixed, new perceptions of a program might emerge and gain credence over time. For example, while *Charlie's Angels* (1976–81) might have been viewed as exciting television when it was first screened by ITV in the 1970s, and as such it was used in prime time to attract a mass audience, it is now viewed in a more ironic way, very much as a program of its time, and is more likely to be shown in an afternoon or late night slot, often as typical example of 1970s retro-chic (Gough-Yates, 2001: 94–97).

In this chapter I will explore the interplay between two important groups in the shaping and development of the early public discourse around *Star Trek* in Britain. These groups include the broadcasters, in this case the BBC, and the television critics. I will start by analyzing and reflecting on the early attempts of the BBC, in the late 1960s and early 1970s, to enter into a public discourse to create a particular understanding of *Star Trek*. To do this I will analyze some of the publicity material sent out to the media in 1969 and a number of resulting stories which appeared in the BBC's listing magazine, *Radio Times*, in the early 1970s. I will then look at the role of the critics in this discourse as they articulated their particular views of *Star Trek* at this time. Of particular interest is the way that the critics' views of *Star Trek* have changed over time and the different coverage, or lack of coverage, provided by the tabloids and broadsheets. I will begin, however, by exploring, at a more abstract level, the concept of the narrative image and the roles played by British television critics in the wider public discourse surrounding television programs.

Broadcasters and Television Critics: A Public Discourse

In some ways, the two groups with the most resources to articulate their views publicly about television, who often struggle over the framing and overall acceptance and meaning of a program, are the industry (including both those that own and those that broadcast television programs), and television critics (those that critically review and write about television). While the critics use the airwaves, magazines and newspapers, and now the Web, to articulate their views, broadcasters use trailers, advertising and their own listing magazines to create an official view or framing of the program or series in question—though, they also, as we shall see, try to influence the views of the critics.

The broadcasting industry is eager to engage in such a public discourse as it tries to construct and maintain an image beneficial for the program and their channel. To do this they take account of the forum they are using, the past history of the genre in question, the view of critics, feedback from viewers, how they wish to use the program, accepted perceptions of their channel and existing views on the particular program or series. In this way they engage constructively and interactively in the developing public discourse around a program. This is not to say that such an image or view will necessarily be accepted or understood, but it does provide us with an understanding of how broadcasters try to direct or influence the public discourse. One way to think about the way they try to shape the public perception of a program is through the concept of the "narrative image."

The concept of the narrative image, as developed by John Ellis, was originally applied to cinema and the way studios advertise and sell an individual film by constructing a particular image to attract an audience: "An idea of the film is widely circulated and promoted, an idea which can be called the 'narrative' image of the film" (Ellis, 1982: 30). However, for Ellis, because television programs are produced mainly as series and serials, and are shown over a number of weeks and consumed in a casual basis in the domestic environment, they are not marketed in the same way as film (Ellis, 1982: 24–33).

Miller (2000), however, develops and extends the concept to television, suggesting that, in a certain way, broadcasters and others in the industry do engage in creating a narrative image of certain programs. This has become more important for broadcasters operating in an increasingly competitive environment where, with hundreds of channels, there is a need to increase the public's awareness of a channel's programming, and this is especially true for programs in which large amounts of money have been invested. Through expenditure on marketing and promoting a program broadcasters attempt to create a narrative image, a pre-image, a way of understanding the program or series before and during its run (38–39). This is important because broadcasters can, by presenting a particular way of viewing, attract audiences that might not otherwise watch, while providing a viewpoint for those who would have watched anyway. They might also be able to adapt the image of a program during its run, taking account of the changing public discourse about it. Broadcasters will, in this way, tailor the image of a program to be relevant to an audience or the market they are trying to target. This, of course, will differ for any program in relation to the broadcaster showing it and the national market they operate in or target. Therefore, the way *The Avengers* was "sold" to the American market and the resulting public discourse was different from the way its image was constructed and marketed in Britain (Miller, 2000: 56–60).

However, as noted above, broadcasters are not the only powerful and well placed group active within the public arena; there are also the television critics. For John Fiske, such public debates about television operate along an axis. At one end are the broadcasters seeking to woo the audience, to make the program succeed in a particular way; at the other end are the critics, those who are able to provide the public with a more thoughtful and critical viewpoint. Halfway between the two sit the fan and cult magazines, those that are not completely under the control of the broadcasters and that are keen to develop and present their views of the programs but, at the same time, are often reliant on the producers and broadcasters for access to the stars, background information and gossip from the industry (Fiske, 1992: 118–19). However, as Poole argues, the television critics are not isolated from the media world, they work for the media and depend on broadcasters for their living: "One would have to say that journalists and critics writing about television operate under the double institutional hegemony of the electronic and print media and this determines what they can and, often more significantly, what they cannot say" (1984: 52). The critics might well, because of lack of time and the wish to maintain good relations with the broadcasters, tend to initially reproduce and maintain the view of a program as presented by broadcasters. Also, as critics cannot stand outside of the social and cultural world, they are unable to provide independent critical reviews of programs. As with all of us, in different ways, they take up a variety of positions, dominant, popular or subversive, within the wider shared cultural field as they produce their reviews.

Therefore, television critics are important in such a public discourse not because they determine the way the public view, understand and value programs but because they, unlike the public, are able to articulate their views, or those of a certain social and cultural perspective, on a regular basis through the media. They are able, through their criticism, or reports, as Jack Gould, the American television critic, called them (Gould, 1996), to help shape a framework for understanding programs; they help create and sustain a hierarchy of what is considered to be "good" programs, programs to watch and programs to miss; they highlight popular debates surrounding certain programs, debates they nurture and engage with; they provide pleasure for the public in the reading of the reviews and criticisms, as well as presenting new ways of enjoying and engaging with the programs themselves. As Fiske notes in relation to the role of secondary texts, such as television criticism, "[they play] ... a significant role in influencing which of television's meanings may be activated in any one reading...." (Fiske, 1992: 118).

Therefore, to explore how a program takes on a certain meaning or acceptance within a particular context at a particular time requires some comprehension of the surrounding public discourse, one in which broadcasters and critics play an important role. Such an interplay tells us something of the needs of the industry, its history, the development of different television genre, the critical discourse around television at that time and the wider cultural, social and political context within which television operates. It does not tell us how the audience understands or views such programs; it does, however, tell us something of the struggle by different powerful groups over such an understanding and viewpoint.

Star Trek: Creating a Narrative Image

When a broadcaster purchases a series like *Star Trek* they will have to decide how to use the program, who its intended audience is, how best to market it and when and where it should be scheduled. Likewise, reversing this logic, looking at how a program was scheduled, provides some indication of how the broadcasters viewed the program. For its first season on British television *Star Trek* (season in terms of how it was shown on British television rather than in terms of how it was shown in America) was broadcast on Saturdays at 5:15 P.M.; after this, throughout the 1970s, it was mostly shown in an early evening slot, often around 7:00 P.M.

This Saturday slot was traditionally thought of as a family slot, one also occupied by *Doctor Who*; this was a time when it was thought the whole family, including small children, would watch together. It would seem that those working at the BBC thought *Star Trek* was a family show, one with enough elements to keep all ages watching. It is also interesting to note that the BBC decided to begin screening *Star Trek* on BBC1 in July 1969, the very moment that *Apollo 11* was returning from space. It would seem that the BBC was using the interest engendered in such a mission to launch this topical series. The two space stories, the fictional ones of the Starship *Enterprise* and that of the American space program, seemed to dovetail nicely. The interaction between the two space programs, can be seen, in that after episode two of *Star Trek*, shown on 19 July 1969 ("The Naked Time," 1966), the BBC scheduled an *Apollo 11 Update*.

To help promote and market the program, to help create a particular narrative image, the BBC, as with most of its shows, released a "promotion sheet" on 20 May 1969. Such information, along with stills, was sent out to various television critics; this included "2 colour transparencies [being] sent to Mr. D. Dick, Radio Time" (T66/6/1, 20 May 1969). Alongside this information the BBC also had at its disposal "[t]wo general trailers and for the following ten episodes, all in colour" (Ibid.). The promotional sheet, while providing running information and suggesting a billing title, *Start Trek,* also presented the premise of the series and introduced the cast of characters and actors.

This material makes clear, from the very start, that this series is set in the future, that the then current attempts to travel to the moon are of long ago:

> Over a century has passed since Man [*sic*] took the first tentative space-step to the moon and the primitive, cramped capsule which made that historic journey bore little resemblance, if any, to the United Spaceship *Enterprise,* the largest and most modern of the "Star Ship Class" fleet in the service of Earth and the federation [Ibid.].

A linkage is being made here to the historic steps being witnessed at the time in space travel and where they might eventually lead the human race. However, at the same time, it would seem that the role of a ship has not changed much over time, as this spaceship, like earthbound ships before, is often on patrol, "assisting colonists, aiding scientific exploration, putting down conflicts, regulating trade, engaging in diplomatic missions etc" (Ibid.). This idea would be familiar to most in Britain who were used to the role the British navy played in protecting the then declining British Empire. (Compare this to the original opening narration as discussed in chapter 1.) In more modern times, this is a role more associated with the American navy, which, strangely, shares the same abbreviation prefix as that before the *Enterprise*'s name—USS. While, for the

U.S. Navy it stands for United States Ship, here, in this series, it stands for United Spaceship (Roberts, 2000: 65).

Of course, *Star Trek* is a series set in the future when conflicts between earth nations and ideologies then currently occurring in countries like Vietnam have long gone. It was an idealistic series, a rare form of optimistic science fiction, one that suggests things could work out, that the basic American values of democracy, as espoused by the *Enterprise* and its crew, are important, as much as now as in the future (Barrett and Barrett, 2001: 10). *Star Trek* presents a vision of a time when the earth has combined with others planets to create a federation to promote peace. Where people from many planets work together, the *Enterprise* crew, reflecting the makeup of the federation, is "international in origin and multi-racial ... one third female [and] initially only one part-alien, Mr. Spock." This future is one that many in the 1960s hoped would develop, a world where everyone can live and work side by side (Roberts, 2000: 127). While this promotional material talks about *Star Trek* in terms of the future it also highlights terms associated with the past, colonists and federation, begging the question of the degree the series still reaches back to the specific colonial struggles of the American nation against Britain. Indeed, when watching the series it is noticeable that the crew mostly seems to be white Americans (Roberts, 2000: 127–8).

Throughout the BBC's promotional leaflet, attempts are made to provide an understanding of various futuristic aspects of the series in relation to what the audience or critics would then understand; this has often been achieved by using and stressing nautical terms, found within the series itself. For example, the *Enterprise* is compared to being "bigger than a naval cruiser of the twentieth century" and Captain James Kirk is described as a "[s]pace-Age Captain Hornblower" (T66/5/1, 20 May 1969). There is also an attempt to provide the scale of the *Enterprise*'s landing deck by noting that it is "big enough to take a fleet of twentieth-century jet liners." While set in the future it would often appear, with the sickbeds, bridge and captain's log, that this series is connected to earth's seafaring (and air transport) past, a point also made in more detail by Michèle and Duncan Barrett (2001: 9–51).

As with much science fiction, the underlying technology is an important part of this series (Roberts, 2000: 146–180). Therefore, it is not a surprise that descriptions of the technology and the ship dominate the BBC's publicity material. Two pages focus on describing the ship, its size and shape, the ship's power, its computer, main viewing screen, armaments, sensors, deflectors, tractor beams and transporters as well as the personal hand-phasers and communicators (T66/6/1, 20 May 1969). Throughout, there is an attempt to provide rational explanations, to provide a realistic understanding of such technology. For example, when describing the main means of propulsion, it is noted that the *Enterprise* "use[s] matter and anti-matter for propulsion, the annihilation of dual matter creating the fantastic power required to warp space and exceed the speed of light—some 670,000,000 miles an hour" (Ibid.). The verisimilitude of the series is viewed as being important for the program; as Walter M. Jefferies, art director of the series is quoted as saying:

> We spent more than four months building the model ship and the interior sets. There isn't a button or a panel in it that isn't there for a logical, functional reason and based on scientific research and projection of what is now being done within the area of space travel [T66/6/1, 20 May 1969].
> Indeed, "scientists from the famous Rand Corporation acted as consultants for the series" [Ibid.].

Star Trek was first shown in Britain at a time of great technical advances, at the end of a decade that had started with the British Prime Minister, Harold Wilson, looking towards the future benefits of the "white heat of technology" (Wilson, cited in Goodman, 1995). It was the time of new solid-state technology, the product of the space program, leading to advances in computer, telecommunication, medicine and satellite technologies, among many other developments. It would seem that, at this rate of development, *Star Trek*, which was set, according to the BBC, 100 years in the future, might well be reachable. Though, as Roberts points out, "[I]t [*Star Trek*] ... purports to be set in the 23rd century ... [b]ut it is also, and at the same time, egregiously dated, in a rather quaint and unmistakably 1960s' fashion" (2000: 35). While, at the time, it have might have appeared as futuristic, this quickly changed and the show often began to reflect more the style and fashions of the time in which it was made than that of the future.

To support the view that this is a well produced, crafted and scripted series, the BBC's publicity material focuses on the quality and experiences of the actors and producers and the awards and nominations gained by the series. Hence we read that *Star Trek* was "given five Emmy nominations" and that it was awarded the Photoplay Award for "the most popular television series of 1967" (T66/6/1, 20 May 1969). We are then also provided with some background to the actors themselves, partly, it would seem, to stress their experience and standing. We are told that William Shatner has worked with Sir Alec Guinness, Anthony Quayle and James Mason; James Doohan (Scotty) is a "veteran radio performer with over three thousand, five hundred shows to his credit"; and that Nichelle Nichols (Lt. Uhura) used to be a vocalist with Duke Ellington and Lionel Hampton's bands (Ibid.). This, it would seem, is a talented group of actors. Likewise, we are treated to a mini biography of the series creator, Gene Roddenberry.

Here we read about his experiences in the war as a pilot and, after this, that he was awarded the highest award for a civilian pilot, and how, as he worked as a policeman in the Los Angeles police department, he was writing television scripts for various police series, such as *Dragnet*. It would seem that he "has made full use of his exciting experiences in his work as a television writer and producer," as he helped create one of "the best science fiction series yet made for television" (Ibid.). The seminal nature of the series was also signaled when the "Smithsonian Institute asked for the pilot program for its space museum"; NASA was also noted as virtually shutting down when *Star Trek* was shown.

The BBC's publicity material highlights particular characteristics of the series. *Star Trek* is a realistic, futuristic program set in space. Its technologies are plausible, though way in advance of that being used by NASA. The program is one of the most realistic science fiction programs yet, one watched and liked by many in the science world. This program set in the future was still connected to the past and the endeavors of humankind to explore, colonize and live together. The series was very successful in America, gaining a huge fan following and creating stars out of two of the main characters. It was not a run-of-the-mill American series; the actors had pedigrees and the creator unique experiences to draw on. This was a series that was topical, relevant and, in America, developed a strong fan following. This was, the BBC suggested, a program to watch.

The Role of the Listings Magazine: The Radio Times

The BBC has, since the 1920s, operated its own listings magazine, called the *Radio Times*. This magazine not only lists what is shown and when on BBC's radio and television channels, and more lately on all channels available in Britain, but also presents reviews and articles about a select number of these programs. In many ways it has been used as a means of publicizing and framing the narrative image of the BBC's programs. While the broadcasters do not have direct control over such magazines, they have some input into what programs might be publicized and how—indeed, they have in the past helped select the cover stories (Patterson, 1990: 37).

Star Trek appears in the *Radio Times* on two notable occasions in the early years of its first screening on the BBC, in the 27 June to 3 July 1970 (North) and the 20 to 26 January 1973 (North) editions. Near the end of the 1970 *Radio Times*, there is an article where Daniel Yergin talks to Gene Roddenberry, "the creator of the *Star Trek* series—the strip cartoon of television" (*Radio Times*, 1970: 48). It is titled "How Gene Roddenberry got the world to love a freak with pointed ears and no emotions." In terms of layout the piece covers four sides, one of which is a cartoon strip depicting various characters from the series, and the *Enterprise*, with Captain Kirk saying to Spock, "Is there anyone on this ship who looks even remotely like Satan?" and Spock replying, "I am not aware of anyone who fits that description, captain." It would seem that there was some acceptance of the almost playful feel to the series, its "strip cartoon" element, where action occurs quickly, often with little character development, a point also noted by critics of the time.

On the next page is a full-page color photograph of Captain Kirk, seemingly "Favourite No. 5" of *Radio Times*. This is one of the publicity stills for the series, and it has Kirk looking moodily out of the photograph wearing his yellow *Star Trek* uniform; the background is out of focus but in the foreground, emphasizing the space theme, is a globe. This is a serious photo—Kirk is not smiling but looking thoughtful—while also presenting Kirk in a typical romantic hero pose; he looks very much the captain of a spaceship. Countering this, interspersed throughout the rest of the text, are little diagrams of toy flat pack games and models, stressing the childish or fan nature of the series, as well as the developing merchandising tie-ins. It would seem that, while the diagrams and cartoon strip stress the playful entertainment quality, the picture of Kirk plays with the notions of adoration, of fan worship and an older more romantic engagement with the series and its stars. For this reason, it is interesting to note that this is one of the first science fiction programs that, for a variety of reasons, became popular with the female audience (Roberts, 2000: 95). For example, Penley has argued that many female viewers have been attracted to *Star Trek* by the implicit sexual relationships hinted at within the program, whether between male, male and female or human and alien characters. Some viewers, many of whom are heterosexual women, often referred to as "slashers," but writers in the genre, have gone further by fictionalizing an off screen relationship between Kirk and Spock (Penley, 1997: 103; Bacon-Smith, 1992: 44–80).

The interview itself starts by introducing Gene Roddenberry and something of his own philosophy of the world, suggesting some linkage between his view of the world and *Star Trek*; to study one is to understand the other. It then goes on to note how *Star Trek* differs from most other American programs of the time which, while they "look to be assembled by committees of advertisers and executives, reaching for standard parts from the shelves in the supply room of tired and safe ideas ... Roddenberry was creator-writer-producer of a show that was unmistakably original" (*Radio Times*, 1970: 48). According to this article, not only was Gene Roddenberry a remarkable person but he had also created a series that was equally unique. Gene Roddenberry stands outside of the American television system, the article said, a system that is driven by commercial needs. Indeed, while *Star Trek* is a story set in the future, there is also the story of the fight to make the series in the 1960s, a story of the past. This is a show created by an artist, someone with vision. In the classic view of the artist, he is there struggling against the system to create something different. As Gene Roddenberry noted, "I wanted to do the best science fiction that had been done up till that time" (Ibid.).

The article continues: "*Star Trek* is not like other American programs; it is not just a standard science fiction series, but is also a form that allowed Gene Roddenberry to circumvent the American censors, to explore the problems facing American society of the day by setting them in the future. As he noted, it allowed him to "make statements about sex, religion, Vietnam and unions, politics and intercontinental missiles. Indeed we did make them on *Star Trek*, we were sending messages, and fortunately it all got by the network" (Ibid.). This was a show with high values but, as the interview notes, was one that took note of the intelligence of the audience, such that Gene Roddenberry argued that, "I insisted that we start with something and then be true to that thing all the way through" (Ibid.). As Jenkins and Tulloch in a similar way note, Roddenberry saw *Star Trek* as a program that "allowed him to reach an audience intelligent enough to comprehend his thinly veiled allegories" (1998: 7–8). To help create a program that lived up to these ideals, Roddenberry sought advice from a physicist and help from the military. They had to think about how such a ship would fly at faster than light speed, as well as the design of various aspects inside the ship, the living quarters, sick bays and bridge.

Visually this article seems to suggest that the program is like a strip cartoon, a bit of fun, while the interview stresses its cerebral nature, that it is not a run-of-the-mill series. It had been conceived by a creative genius able to work against the American commercial system, someone who had a lifetime of experiences. The program was a product of love, produced with an eye to detail. It had developed into a "cult" followed by a large number of fans. It was a program as much about the future as it was the current situation: a program with a message. The article ends with a list of ten upcoming episodes on the BBC.

The other main article around this time about *Star Trek* in the *Radio Times* appeared in the 20 to 26 January 1973 issue. This article is a one and a half page spread near the front of the magazine. The left hand page is one of the few pages in the *Radio Times* that is in color; it is entitled "The *Star Trek Enterprise* voyages on." The two color photos are of William Shatner and Leonard Nimoy, shown in everyday activities, rather than dressed as Captain Kirk and Mr. Spock. William Shatner, sporting a moustache, is wearing a checked shirt and is shown reading a newspaper, while Leonard Nimoy, dressed in a more colorful, even psychedelic, shirt, is holding a small dog. Only on the next page do we see a black and white still from the show, a picture from that night's episode showing Captain Kirk dressed as a Nazi officer confronting someone else dressed in a similar fashion (from "Patterns of Force," 1968); a linkage is being made here between the actors, William Shatner and Leonard Nimoy, and *Star Trek*, the program.

This article focuses on the success of the series, though no longer produced, which has gained a cult following and the views and lives of the two main stars, William Shatner and Leonard Nimoy. It is a timely reminder that the new season starts that night and of its developing cult status. As the subheading notes, "[T]hree years after its final journey, *Star Trek* still has a fanatical following." It then notes that Peter McDonald, in this article, "talks to two ex-crew members" (*Radio Times*, 1973: 8); it does not say actors or characters; it confuses and conflates their "real" and "reel" lives. It is as if they have left the Starship but, somewhere, it continues to travel across the universe with a different captain and second officer.

This series is now a cult series; indeed, we are told that more and more fans are gathering each year to pay homage, that *Star Trek* has become a huge booming business, that *Star Trek* lives on, helped partly by reruns (Ibid.). Both William Shatner and Leonard Nimoy are asked to reflect on this success and devoted following that has developed for the series. They provide, in this way, an interaction of their "real" and "reel" lives, of William Shatner talking about being Captain Kirk, of his life in the show and outside, and Leonard about being Spock and what he is now doing. Leonard Nimoy suggests, as Gene Roddenberry had noted in the previous article, that *Star Trek*'s success is linked with its connectedness with the issues of the day, that it "broached subjects such as the world's future, racism, even Vietnam" (Ibid.). William Shatner says less about why the show was successful and instead talks of being "impressed by the loyalty of the fans": "It is the same everywhere I go. The wish to see the show returned to production is undiminished and I understand that the studio has been averaging some 500 letters a week" (Ibid.: 9).

Most of the article focuses on the careers of Shatner and Nimoy after *Star Trek*, the "real" lives of these two actors. However, in many ways, and especially for the fans, it is giving some insight into the lives of two actors who cannot fully be separated from the characters they played in *Star Trek*. We learn about Nimoy wondering if he should have been a politician rather than an actor and that, as a son of an immigrant Russian barber, how he had to struggle some 17 years for the success he is now having; he sounds contrite and surprised, in some ways, with the adoration he now attracts. He also talks about his "sense of responsibility to my fellow men which would be as great if I was not an actor." Indeed, it is noted that "[m]any of the issues close to Nimoy are the same as those dealt with in allegory in *Star Trek* and they form an important factor in the cultism surrounding the show" (Ibid.: 8).

As much as Captain Kirk and Mr. Spock had different traits within the series, so, it appears, do the actors playing them. While Nimoy talks about having a responsibility to other men, William Shatner talks very much about himself, how *Star Trek* has given a boost to his career and has "provided that security and momentum, and since its end he has been enjoying the luxuries of acting for acting's sake in repertory theatre, between carefully selected films and directing television plays" (Ibid.: 9). We get a sense of William Shatner's ego, that he feels able to take up any challenge and succeed: "Here in America just last year I went into the mountains to hunt dear, wild boar and goat with a bow and arrow" (Ibid.). For those fans in the know, some actors in *Star Trek*, supposedly, did not get on well with William Shatner, with some suggesting that he was arrogant. In some ways we get a similar impression from this article; Nimoy (Spock) is considered, rational and thoughtful, while Shatner is impulsive, full of confidence and self-belief.

This article not only reminds us that *Star Trek* is back, but that it has developed a fanatical following; that it has turned very quickly into a cult. This is a program that means a lot to many people, many who look towards the stars that appeared in it for some greater understanding of the show, if not the world around us. It is more than just a series; it presents a way of viewing, understanding and coping with the developing and changing world around us. The article helps the reader explore the fine dividing line between the reel (fictional lives) and real lives of the characters and actors, though, by the end, we start to wonder how much of the actor went into the character and vice versa. As Ellis argues:

> The television performer appears in subsidiary forms of circulation (newspapers, magazines) mostly during the time that the series of performances is being broadcast. The result is a drastic reduction in the distance between the circulated image and the performance. The two become very much entangled, so that the performer's image is equated with that of the fictional role (and vice versa) [cited in Pearson, 2004: 62].

As we move through the 1970s this thin dividing line is hard to separate, as Shatner for many is Captain Kirk and Nimoy is Mr. Spock. As Pearson suggests, "William Shatner will forever and always be Captain James T. Kirk and nothing else at all" (2004: 66). While the original publicity material introduces *Star Trek* to the critics, providing background information, often talking about it in a playful way, these two later articles, published in the BBC's listings magazine, *Radio Times*, highlight a shift in the BBC's narrative image of the program. It is as if they are adapting their view in line with the success of the program and the developing public discourse. The first stresses the cerebral nature of the program, its uniqueness, while the second highlights the developing cult nature of the program and explores the lives of the two main stars.

Television Criticism: Coverage of Star Trek, *1969–1979*

Looking at the reviews of the late 1960s and early 1970s one is struck not so much by how *Star Trek* is covered by the tabloid or broadsheet papers, or whether it was by the serious, neo or popular critics, but more by the lack of coverage altogether. Beyond the small blurb that many of the papers provided about the programs being shown that night, there is only a handful of mentions or reviews of *Star Trek*. This can be put down to a number of reasons: it was an American series and many of the reviews tended to focus on popular homegrown product; initially *Star Trek* appeared to be a run-of-the-mill television series, with nothing too much out of the ordinary to review, that as, in its first season, it ran in the late afternoon, it attracted less critical attention than if shown in prime time. However, within a decade or so, with the almost continual runs of *Star Trek*, its developing cult status, the development of new television series in the franchise, such as *Star Trek: The Next Generation*, and a series of Hollywood films, *Star Trek* became a recognizable institution. Indeed, the names of Kirk, Spock, and Scotty and various catchphrases became part of British shared culture. This is true to such an extent that, even though *Star Trek* was made forty years ago, when actor James Doohan recently died there was extensive coverage of his role in *Star Trek* as engineer Scotty, and references to his overused catchphrases relating to beaming crew members up or lack of power that could be provided by his warp engines (Callaghan, 2005), coverage that rarely happens to the same degree when other minor North American television actors die.

One of the first reviews of *Star Trek* appeared in *The Daily Mirror* on 14 July 1969. Here, the association of *Star Trek* with a "comic" is suggested, when it notes, "BBC-1's new imported space comic, takes everything on the shoulder." The review then continues comparing this series to other adventure heroes and strip cartoons, such as "Tarzan, King Kong and Captain Marvel," suggesting that it exhibits a certain simplicity in its form and content; it does, however, note that this form "enables the implausible to mingle with the mundane" (*Daily Mirror*, 14 July 1969). The program is described in simple terms of good and bad, where, "[a]s in all science fiction they are in deadly peril of being taken over by machines" (Ibid.); where the "forces of light are the old-fashioned moralities—love, fellow feeling, respect for life..." (Ibid.). It is a program where the dialogue is rather simplistic, where they have to "'re-energise' the engines, take their fingers off the buttons that 'activate the contracts that blow the impulse banks up.'" However, while the review paints a picture of a simple program, where good and bad are easily separated, "*Star Trek*'s crew have their hearts in the right place" (Ibid.).

It would seem that the critics in the early reviews of *Star Trek*, unable to build on viewers' knowledge of the program, attempted to associate it with other existing forms known to the viewer, such as the comic strip, or made references to existing British science fiction programs, for example, *Doctor Who* (Dean, 1969). There is little mention, in the informal way that they would be referred to later in the decade, to the characters such as Scotty, Kirk or Spock. And while there are comments about the scenery as being made up of "scraggy planetary terrain made rather obviously of painted tarpaulin and plastic flowers" (*Daily Mirror*, 12 July 1969), it is without the irony that later reviews would utilize.

Several of the reviews in this early period directly take up from the BBC's initial publicity material, illustrating how successfully the broadcaster's attempts at shaping the initial perception of a program can be. For example, a number of articles focus on "Mr Spock, the ship's second officer, who is half human, half Vulcan and has long, pointed ears" (*Evening Standard*, 12 July 1969: 10), which is directly referred to in the BBC's publicity, "[t]he other is a character with long pointed ears—Mr Spock, the ship's second officer, half human, half vulcanian" (T66/6/1, 20 May 1969). Reviews also often mentioned the cult following and the authentic feel of the series: "The American-made series *Star Trek* has been hailed as the most authentic science fiction series ever produced for television" (*Daily Mail*, 12 July 1969) and "[I]t has got two principal characters who have become 'cult' characters in America—Captain James Kirk, commander of the space ship, and a Mr Spock, the ship's second officer" (*Evening Standard*, 12 July 1969: 10). These are similar to the BBC's publicity descriptions of the cult status of Spock with his "cult personal following," and the hailing of the series as "the best science fiction series yet made for television" (T66/6/1, 20 May 1969).

However, later in the 1970s, it is obvious in the television reviews that *Star Trek*, in some way, had taken its place more firmly within the psyche of the nation. The reviewers, and those writing the listings, are now able to refer to the main characters by one name only: "Spock's first independent command looks like being his last, lost on an unexplored planet and attacked by its weird residents, but Kirk and the *Enterprise* are also engaged in conflict" (*Daily Telegraph*, 31 October 1979). They even feel able to play on a wider knowledge of the program by making jokey references to the well known introduction to the program, "Boldly go Captain Kirk and his merry men in this resurrection of the first *Star Trek*" (*Evening Standard*, 24 September 1973). This is a program that is now known by the public, that has developed a substantial following and, in some ways, a more complex set of meanings for those who watch it.

It must also be noted that the way critics working for different types of papers have written about *Star Trek* could be viewed as being related to their relative position in the cultural field. For those writing for the quality papers, such as *The Times*, there is little or no coverage for most of the 1970s, for the more popular tabloid papers, the coverage in the 1970s is less critical than reflective of the popularity of the program. A review notes in the *Daily Mirror*, "[a]s in all good science fiction they are in deadly peril of being taken over by machines.... [the] *Star Trek*'s crew have their hearts in the right place" (14 July, 1969). Later coverage by Clive James in the *Observer* provides a more satirical view of the series:

> How, you might ask, can anyone harbour a passion for such a crystal-draining pile of barbiturates as Star Trek? The answer, I think, lies in the classical inevitability of its repetitions. As surely as Brunnhilde's big moments are accompanied by a few bars of the Valkyries' ride, Spock will say that the conclusion would appear to be logical, captain. Uhura will turn leggily from her console to transmit information conveying either (a) that all contact with Star Fleet has been lost, or (b) that it has been regained [James, 1973].

In the limited reviews that appear in this decade, which start by introducing the viewers to *Star Trek*, there are attempts to present it as a strip cartoon, stressing its entertainment value. The reviews note the quality of the series, the nomination for awards and the cult following in America. They help, in this way, to create a feeling that this is an interesting program, slightly above the ordinary, which is topical and has a growing fan base. Later in the decade, however, reviewers are able to utilize the shared understanding of *Star Trek* as they make references to its story lines, scenery, special effects and its crew (stars); Mr. Spock is now Spock, Captain Kirk is Kirk, the viewers know what the "captain's log" is, they know about Scotty and his engines and have a grasp of the basic technologies and terms found in the program. This was a program that had become part of British television culture, which had developed a fanatical following by those known as Trekkies and had started to take on a more complex meaning than that initially provided by the BBC's original publicity material. Indeed, even the BBC found itself affected by the developing assimilation of such a program into British culture. For example, at Caversham, the BBC's archive, one of the folders is subtitled "Log," in reference to Captain Kirk's weekly log. This was now a cult program, a popular mass viewed program, both an entertaining and multilayered program, a program that was now noticed, that had become part of British television culture.

Conclusion: The Public Discourse around Star Trek

Star Trek appeared in Britain with few realizing how it would, over the next four decades, become the cult classic that it has. The BBC, as any broadcaster would, attempted to shape the narrative image of the program as best it could. This material it aimed at the general public and at those most active in the public discourse, the television critic. The BBC presented a view of a program that was a cult hit in America, that was unique in standing out from the usual American programs, a program that could be associated with the American space program. It suggested that this was a topical, well made, exciting science fiction series, like *Doctor Who*, a program watchable by families. It was both a "strip" cartoon for the children, and a program able to provide stimulating views of the world for the older audience; it was a program not only with interesting stories but also populated by a range of characters, some of which were becoming stars.

The television critics taking up on this material at first tended to use these views in their work, though not all the papers could be bothered to review such a program. Such reviews stressed the nominations for awards, the program's verisimilitude, the topicality of the program, the cult characters, especially Spock and the strip cartoon quality. Over time, however, they were more able to develop a shorthand and to play with the audience's knowledge of the program. Sometimes, as with Clive James, *Star Trek* began to be reviewed in quality papers, but often in an ironic way, where James both enjoyed and criticized such programs.

Around all programs a dynamic public discourse develops. Many groups struggle over such a discourse, trying to articulate their views as loudly and as powerfully as they can. The broadcasters and critics are, at least in the first days of a new program being shown, powerful players in such a discourse. In terms of *Star Trek*, in the days before the development of the domestic videocassette player, the BBC seemed able to shape some of the early reviews, or at least to get some of its themes picked up and used. Later on, however, as the critics got more accustomed to the program, and as the public, likewise, began to assimilate and articulate various views of the program, the narrative image of *Star Trek* changed. By the end of the 1970s, the perception and understanding of *Star Trek*, as found within the public television discourse, had become more complex and multilayered than what had been presented by the BBC.

Works Cited

Bacon-Smith, C. *Enterprising Women: Television Fandom and the Creation of Popular Myth.* Pennsylvania: University of Pennsylvania, 1992.
Barrett, M., and Barrett, D. *Star Trek: The Human Frontier.* London: Polity, 2001.
Brooker, C. *Screen Burn: Television with Its Face Torn Off.* London: Faber and Faber, The Guardian, 2005.
Callaghan, D. "*Star Trek*'s Scotty sparks out of this world tussle." *The Guardian* (August 2005): 2.
Dean, B. "Now Doctor in the House Goes on TV." *Daily Mail* 12 July 1969.
Ellis, J. V*isible Fictions: Cinema; Television; Video.* London: Routledge & Kegan and Paul, 1982.
Fiske, J. *Television Culture.* London: Methuen, 1987.
Goodman, G. "Leading Labour beyond pipe dreams." *The Guardian,* 25 May 1995.
Gough-Yates, A. (2001), "Angels in Chains? Feminism, femininity and consumer culture in *Charlie's Angels.*" *Action TV: Tough Guys, Smooth Operators and Foxy Chicks.* Edited by B. Osgerby and A. Gough-Yates. London: Routledge, 2001: 83–99.
Gould, J. "Early criticism, like early television, grappled with the same problems as today." *Quill* 84, no. 10 (1996). http://web33.epnet.com (accessed 20 May 2005).
James, C. "Drained Crystals." *Observer,* 16 September 1973.
____. *Visions Before Midnight.* London: Picador, 1981.

____. *The Crystal Bucket.* London: Picador, 1982.
____. *Glued to the Box.* London: Picador, 1983.
Jenkins, H., and J. Tullock. *Science Fiction Audience: Watching* Star Trek *and* Doctor Who. London: Routledge, 1998.
Lealand, G. *American Television Programs on British Screens.* London: Broadcasting Research Unit Working Paper, 1984.
Miller, J. *Something Completely Different: British Television and American Culture.* London and Minneapolis: University of Minnesota Press, 2000.
Paterson, R. "A suitable schedule for the family." *Understanding Television.* Edited by A. Goodwin and G. Whannel. London: Routledge, 1990.
Pearson, R. E. "'Bright Particular Star': Patrick Stewart, Jean-Luc Picard, and Cult Television." *Cult Television.* Edited by Sara Gwenllian-Jones and Roberta E. Pearson. Minneapolis: University of Minnesota Press, 2004: 61–80.
Penley, C. *NASA/Trek: Popular Science and Sex in America.* London: Verso, 1997.
Poole, M. "The Cult of the Generalist: British Television Criticism 1936–83." *Screen* 25, no. 2 (1984): 41–61.
Purser, P. *Done Viewing: A personal account of the best years of our television.* London: Quarter Books, 1992.
Radio Times. Star Trek 30 years. Official Collector's Edition. London: BBC, 1996.
Roberts, A. *Science Fiction: the New Critical Idiom.* London: Routledge, 2000.
Shelley, J. *Interference: Tapehead Versus Television.* London: Atlantic Books, 2001.
Worsely, T.C. *Television: The Ephemeral Art.* London: Alan Ross, 1970.

NEWSPAPERS AND MAGAZINES

Evening Standard, 12 July 1969.
____. 24 September 1973.
The Daily Mirror, 14 July 1969.
Daily Mail, 12 July 1969.
Radio Times, 27 June to 3 July 1970 (North).
____. 20 to 26 January 1973 (North).
Daily Telegraph, 31 October 1979.

CAVERSHAM, BBC

T66/6/1. "TV Press Office *Star Trek*: 1969–1994." 20 May 1969.

PART IV

THE FANS

10

Star Trek: The Franchise!

Poachers, Pirates, and Paramount

SUE SHORT

Of all the TV shows that tend to be associated with fan culture, *Star Trek* serves as one of the most notorious examples. The series' global appeal has been chronicled in Jeff Greenwald's *Future Perfect: How "Star Trek" Conquered Planet Earth* (2000), providing a fascinating insight into the diverse cultural interest that has been taken in the show; its production history has been charted by various contributors, including the original producers, Herb Solow and Robert Justman, the series creator, Gene Roddenberry, and a number of cast members, each relating the debt owed to fans in keeping the series on the air in its difficult early years (see chapter 2 for an alternative view of this period in franchise history); and its legendary fan loyalty has even been affectionately lampooned in *Galaxy Quest* (1999) and the documentary film *Trekkies* (1997). Academically, while some critics have elected to explore ideological issues within specific episodes—tending to reiterate the ways in which *Star Trek* is seen as sexist, racist, and pro-American (often without acknowledging how it has also attempted to challenge such ideas), others have concentrated instead on determining what the series means to its followers, assessing the enormous appeal the *Trek* universe has generated among audiences, and making numerous claims about the fans' status as renegades, poachers and textual pirates, claims that have been made with an equivalent degree of fervor as those attacking *Star Trek* yet which similarly warrant closer analysis. It is just such an examination this chapter undertakes, questioning whether the critical assertions that have been made about *Star Trek* and its fans demand to be reconsidered in light of the sheer scale of the franchise today and the manner in which it has openly targeted fans, both as consumers and alleged copyright thieves.

I would like to state, from the outset, that my interest in *Star Trek* is very much that of a category *D* fan, situated many rungs below those who attend conventions, dress as their favorite characters, or attempt to learn Klingon, yet positioned nonetheless with some appreciation and understanding of both the franchise and its appeal. Far from wishing to humiliate fans, or to overtly champion them, I intend to go where few critics have ventured before, aiming to explore beyond the simple stereotypes that have been created in popular culture and academic discourse in terms of *Star Trek* fandom. I am all too aware of the potential stigma involved in expressing any attachment to the show, recalling the look of sympathy I have received from certain people who have raised their eyebrows and reduced their expectations of me accordingly when I have made my interest known. By the same token, however, I have also experienced a genuine sense of inclusiveness when meeting fellow fans, feelings that are often claimed to be of great significance within the fan community. Nevertheless, shared enthusiasm does not necessarily constitute blind adoration or unthinking acceptance. Neither does it preclude the ability to be critical of specific texts or the way in which the franchise is operated. The show is far from uniformly understood or appreciated by fans, any more than they themselves can be neatly slotted into a particular category or list of characteristics, and it is in attempting to unveil some of these complexities that this chapter chiefly concerns itself.

A somewhat polarized view has been formed about *Star Trek*'s enthusiasts. On the one side there is the "Trek-nerd," summed up by Henry Jenkins as "nerdy guys with glasses and rubber Vulcan ears" (Jenkins, 1992: 9). This is still a prevalent stereotype, despite the efforts Jenkins and others have gone to in demonstrating the prominence of female fans within *Trek* culture (see, for example, Camille Bacon-Smith's *Enterprising Women*, 1992), as well as the relatively high status many occupy. Indeed, although the series has attracted interest from men and women alike, and despite the number of high-achieving professionals who consider themselves fans, the Trek-nerd is typically conceived of as a social misfit who is unable to live in the "real world," fixated with a show that preaches universal tolerance and understanding, and willing to literally buy into this fantasy by purchasing any amount of merchandising Paramount makes available to them. The fan as fantasist and gullible consumer is thus writ large into the image of the "typical" *Star Trek* fan, and it was chiefly in order to refute this stereotype that Henry Jenkins was galvanized into providing an alternative. As he puts it, feeling that the images of "vulnerable consumers were so at odds with my highly social, engaged, empowered and creative experiences as a fan ... I got tired of being told to get a life and decided to write a book instead" (see Jenkins' Website).[1]

The result was *Textual Poachers*, a study of various fan cultures written from the position of an engaged insider, one who was keen to note that critical appreciation could not only afford a level of innovation on the part of audiences, but also supply a host of potential meanings. Jenkins straddles the positions of academic and fan, yet is principally concerned with heightening the status of the latter group at the expense of the elitism exercised by professional scholars, arguing that "everyday people develop theories to explain their own relationships to media and these theories can be as sophisticated on their own terms as those produced within the scholarly community" (Ibid.). Against the derogatory image of the "Trek-nerd," Jenkins provides the "Textual Poacher," a figure who, far from uncritically consuming media products, utilizes elements to fulfill certain needs, including that of community and creativity. Refuting the stereotype of the socially inept loner, Jenkins emphasizes the level of kinship afforded within fandom, as it unites people from diverse backgrounds via a common interest that he views as being politically progressive. Furthermore, rather than buy up any official merchandise in a disconcerting demonstration of commodity fetishism, Jenkins points out that fans have generated their own products, including fanzines containing original fiction and artwork, thereby achieving the status of artists rather than mere consumers.

Similarly aiming to correct the popular image of *Trek* fans as unthinking geeks in thrall to the industry, Michelle Erica Green points out that fan activities existed long before the commercial culture that later engulfed the franchise, even in the relative absence of marketing and related merchandise. As she argues in her online article, "The Selling Out of *Star Trek*":

> We Trekkies have never needed new Trek materials to keep us going. Our fandom thrived in the mid-70s, when no new episodes were in the works ... who needed mass marketing? We had fan conventions, pen pal clubs, home-produced newsletters (this in the days before the home computer) and fanzines" [Green, 1991: 1].

Interestingly, while she deplores the consumerism that later emerged in the wake of new series, films and tie-in books, and particularly the way in which fans were positioned as a ready market for collectibles, Green is also wary of academic appropriation, even the relatively sympathetic interest taken by the likes of Jenkins, whose ostensible celebration of fan activities she views as "patronizing." In her assessment the academic intellectualizing of fan pleasure "seems worse than its commodification.... Between the capitalists and the Marxists, Trek gets lost. The mainstreaming of *Star Trek* may have gotten it out of the closet and into the academy, but it's costing fan culture its soul" (Green, 1991: 2).

The detraction suggests an interesting rift on presumed grounds of ownership, one that echoes larger debates over who truly owns *Star Trek*. While Jenkins comes from within the fan community, like Green, and commends fan interests in much the same way that Green does in other articles (see for example her Web article "Fans Connect and Create Online"), he has nevertheless met with criticism from both fans and academics alike who variously argue that he misreads, misappropriates, or unduly exaggerates the power fans have. I endeavor to explore these claims and the conflicts they invoke. Academics are often uncomfortable with their fan interests, and either attempt to justify their favorite shows and films at all costs (often by asserting them to be subversive in some way) or guiltily pick them to pieces. These are pitfalls I intend to avoid. While I may have a vested interest in terms of the pleasure afforded to me by *Star Trek* this does not exist at the expense of my critical faculties. Neither, would I add, does it do so for most admirers of a given media product, for just as theory-making occurs outside the academy, as Jenkins notes, so does an attendant level of skepticism. Although I admire the show, know enough about preferred nomenclature to use the term "Trekker" over "Trekkie," and would openly claim myself to be a fan, I am also very aware that the franchise primarily exists as a commercial entertainment venture irrespective of its origins, innovations, or the interests it has fostered. Despite the progressive ideals espoused within its narratives, the favored value-system is often as inconsistent and contradictory as the assessment that tends to be made of its fans—figures who have been caught between two opposing realms of understanding (or, rather, misunderstanding): the credulous victim of mass entertainment, and the renegade resistance fighter using *Trek* as a means of gathering the troops.

Star Trek fans have attracted so much attention (whether positive or otherwise) because they offer such interesting examples of fan involvement, including the man who transformed his flat into an *Enterprise*-style apartment complete with sliding electric doors and blinking light panels; communities who meet up to sing "filk" songs about specific characters and relationships; and viewers who not only re-view taped episodes but also edit scenes together to form an entirely new narrative. It is just such "enterprising" activities that Jenkins uses to exemplify his theory of fandom as a "DIY activity," one that appropriates elements from consumer culture for its own purposes. Drawing on the work of Michel de Certeau, Jenkins takes the term "poaching" to describe how fans raid images from mainstream media for their own ends, arguing that "Their activities pose important questions about the ability of media producers to constrain the creation and circulation of meanings. Fans construct their social and cultural identity through borrowing and inflecting mass culture images, articulating concerns which often go unvoiced within the dominant media" (Jenkins, 1992: 23). By adapting popular fictions to discuss ideas about identity and society, Jenkins argues that fandom provides "a space within which fans may articulate their specific concerns about sexuality, gender, racism, colonialism, militarism and forced conformity" (Jenkins, 1992:

283). Where serfs once poached food from wealthy landowners as an illicit survival tactic, a means of counterbalancing an economic system in which they were at a disadvantage, the intellectual equivalent, according to Jenkins, can be found in fans who similarly take what they need as a means of collective social criticism and communication.

This argument challenges the "cultural dope" theory that views audiences as unthinking consumers. The active, rather then passive, model has gained prominence within media theory, inspiring a level of optimism (even presumed radicalism) among many theorists involved in reception studies, who often celebrate what they perceive as "resistance" in their subjects' appropriation of texts. Far from being indoctrinated or pacified in a manner summed up by *The Matrix* (1999) and its image of recumbent bodies tied to a vast machine, the differing ways in which audiences read meaning into chosen media images is itself seen as a politically charged activity. As John Fiske (another key influence on Jenkins) has stated, "The creativity of popular culture lies not in the production of commodities so much as in the productive use of industrial commodities. The art of the people is the art of 'making do.' The culture of everyday life lies in the creative, discriminating use of the resources that capitalism provides" (Fiske, 1989: 27–28).

Although such claims make a welcome change to the pessimistic doom-mongers that would decry us all as one-dimensional zombies, the resourcefulness championed by the likes of Jenkins and Fiske is nevertheless in danger of distorting the context in which fandom operates today, underestimating the ways in which fans are actively courted from a series' first inception, targeted as a means of securing network approval for a new show, and thereafter continuously exploited via a steady stream of tie-in products. This is not to deny the fact that fans freely select what they will watch—or buy—but to question whether, given the ways in which fan cultures have altered and that industry strategies towards them have changed, we may have to adjust Jenkins' view of "textual poachers" as those who make and distribute their own fanzines to include those who, far from initiating products, simply provide a willing market for any ancillary goods corporations wish to add their series logo to. The fact that Paramount has rigorously patrolled its corporate ownership of *Star Trek* in order to circumvent "poaching," while encouraging fan interest via such ventures as the *Star Trek Experience* theme park in Las Vegas suggests that, far from the Do-It-Yourself activities praised by Jenkins, fandom now operates in a commercial climate that has a keen eye on what it can get out of, rather than offer, viewers (see chapter 12). What is clear in the resulting territorial dispute surrounding fans, their activities, and their motivations is that the media industry and its audiences have a virtually symbiotic relationship that needs to be better understood.

As is now legendary, the continuation of the original series owed its existence to fans who campaigned to save *Star Trek* from cancellation after both its first and second season. Roddenberry took advantage of the interest launched by Bjo and John Trimble's famous letter writing campaign in 1967 (enlisting the additional recommendation of SF writers such as Harlan Ellison and Isaac Asimov) to make the studio aware that a loyal fan base was following the series, with a combination of phone calls, demonstrations, and mail by the thousands uniting to convince NBC that *Star Trek* was worth saving. By signaling their approval in this way fans initiated a new level of audience feedback that defied the numerical data provided by relatively poor Nielsen ratings, introducing a qualitative response that has subsequently proved invaluable for those endeavoring to launch new television ventures today. Just as Roddenberry played a crucial part in keeping his show on the road, even getting production company Desilu Studios to foot some of the bill for the campaign, the ever expanding fan base surrounding the franchise has been further capitalized on by Paramount in various ways, from the four spin-off series and ten feature films that have descended from the original series to the games, T-shirts, calendars, books and other merchandise that is now available.

One relatively recent product seems to sum up how fandom has altered from the climate in which Jenkins and Fiske first enthused about fan-produced texts. In addition to its other publications, Paramount launched the *Star Trek Fact Files*, in which *Star Trek*'s complex universe was presented in a ready-made scrapbook of glossily printed sheets filled with episode guides, technical specs and cosmological details which eventually fit into a handsome collection of lever-arch files. The product seems designed for the stereotypical Trek-nerd, providing piecemeal details that elaborate the show's fictional world. In doing so it corroborates what Sara Gwenllian-Jones (2003) describes as "world-building for profit," a means of expanding upon fictional domains in order to perpetuate audience interest (166). Signaling that the industry has taken note of fan activities and carefully reproduced them, the *Fact Files* evade the need to "Do It Yourself" because they have effectively done it for you. As she states:

> The merchandising industry that surrounds cult television series imitates the text-producing practices of fans. Instead of fan-authored trivia files and cultural criticism, commercial culture produces episode guides and glossy magazines. Instead of "filk" music, it produces CDs of soundtracks. Instead of fan fiction, it produces novelisations, comics and, sometimes, spin-off series that extend the metatextual logics of fan readings. It sells fans shinier versions of their own texts, all stamped with an official seal of approval [167–168].

This is not to say that fans do not continue to produce their own texts but to question the context in which this now occurs. While fan activities have moved to the Internet in recent years, an ongoing tug of war exists in terms of intellectual copyright and commercial interests. Paramount's parent organization, Viacom, did not hesitate in issuing "cease and desist" letters to "unofficial" *Star Trek* sites that formed in the mid-1990s, and continued harassment led to the Online Freedom Federation for those attempting to preserve some creative freedom. As the site's legal advisor, John Pisa-Relli, has stated, "Paramount's ingratitude toward *Star Trek* fans, its intolerance toward modest commercial or even non-profit fan activities, and its general mishandling of the franchise demonstrate an appalling lack of good business judgment" ("Paramount's Book Warpath"). It would seem that it is precisely this sense of "good business judgment" that has prevailed of late, with a more tolerant attitude to fan sites seemingly prompted by the belated acknowledgment that they essentially provide free publicity. Legal disclaimers now accompany any sites related to *Trek*, reiterating that "*Star Trek*—in its many incarnations are all property of Paramount Pictures," and as long as the sites do not infringe upon these rights, or attempt to sell any products, they are generally allowed to continue. While this apparent tolerance clearly suits the corporation, with these sites maintaining audience interest in the franchise at no cost to themselves, it also indicates an interesting shift in power relations—a negotiated settlement, if you will, in the murky quadrant of cyberspace. Jenkins has noted these online conflicts, including the relative powerlessness held by fans against corporate interests, yet remains determined to celebrate online fans as "shock troops in a struggle that will define the digital age" (Jenkins, "Digital Land Grab").

The sites themselves tell a different story, as those that remain are also the least likely to upset corporate watchdogs. STARFLEET—claimed by the *Guinness World Records* as the largest independent fan organization in the world—introduces itself to online visitors with a stirring message, arguing that "*Star Trek* taught us that we can control mass media—we do have a say over our environment and destiny." However, this power is questionably demonstrated. Despite charitable endeavors intended to emulate Roddenberry's humanistic ideals, the main impetus of STARFLEET seems to be greater immersion into the fictional world of *Star Trek*, with doctorate degrees available in disciplines including "Alien History and Culture." Despite its obvious reference to *Star Trek*'s origins, and the part played by fans in keeping the show going, the claimed ability to "control the mass media" becomes a somewhat empty assertion in a site that complements the corporate selling of *Star Trek* rather than challenging it in any way.

Even when they do produce texts for themselves, Gwenllian-Jones maintains that the idea of the heroic resistive fan is greatly exaggerated, arguing that "Many fan-produced texts are adoring or whimsical and exhibit little in the way of politicised engagement with their beloved cult object,"

going on to cite K'Tesh's Klingon Recipe Pages and its assembly of culi-
nary trivia from various *Star Trek* series to exemplify her point that "extraterrestrial gastronomy does not qualify as 'resistant'" (2003: 164). While
she notes that more politicized examples of fan cultures exist, particularly in online discussions where fans "debate issues of identity or other-
ness," she adds that they are not resisting the cult text itself, but using it
to oppose "wider sociocultural forces" (Ibid.). Nevertheless, such appropriation indicates that fans do politically engage with the world at large,
rather than seeking to escape from it, and accordingly prove that they
are capable of distancing themselves from texts that Gwenllian-Jones
largely assumes represent a "desire for immersion" (167).

    As Jenkins notes, fan responses involve "not simply fascination or
adoration but also frustration and antagonism" (Jenkins, 1992: 23).
Rather than remain content to live in the fictional world brought to them
via Paramount, or necessarily approve of the worldview invoked, *Star Trek*
fans often voice their detractions. Thoughtful ideological readings routinely surface in message board discussions, including reading the Borg
"against the grain" as representatives of an imperialist USA (see Short,
2004, and chapter 4 in this volume), noting various ways in which the
United Federation of Planets is coercive in its practices, and generally providing an articulate refutation of the official narrative intentions of the
show. Far from yearning to live in the imaginary future presented, many
such posters discern contemporary relevance within narratives and show
themselves to be a far cry from the conventional Trek-nerd who is all too
willing to suspend disbelief in order to fully inhabit a fictional realm.

    Clearly, not everyone will wish to expose the franchise to this level
of scrutiny, just as behind the scenes exposes and blueprints from the technical manual will be of little interest to some. Indeed, it seems fair to
assume that what viewers get out of *Star Trek* is very variable, partly because
the show is deliberately designed that way. Scripts contain elements of
humor, drama, romance, and adventure as each aim to provide different
modes of appeal for its diverse market. Underwriting it all, and possibly
the reason why the franchise has generated such global interest for an
astonishing four decades, is its optimistic espousal of future social relations, reiterating ideals that remain very appealing, no matter how flawed
they are sometimes shown to be (see chapter 1 on the franchise's utopian
premise). Michael Jindra (1994) argues that *Star Trek*'s faith in the future
and its belief in humanity's goodness are key reasons for fan devotion,
which he aligns with religious belief in terms of tapping into a core value
system. An equivalent faith in scientific discovery adds an interesting ratio-
nalist touch to the show's utopia. Things can and will get better, we are
told. Humans can triumph over their most destructive capacities and even
prove to be a force for universal liberation and enlightenment. The problems come when we start to ask how inclusive this notion of "we" actually

is, for despite its purported multiculturalism, despite the fact that we have seen a woman and an African-American man in positions of command, or that various alien "orphan" figures have been accepted by Starfleet, there are limits to the show's egalitarianism (see chapter 4 on mixed heritage adoptees in the franchise). The options available for dissent, as proven by the Maquis—a group of rebels introduced toward the end of *The Next Generation,* indicate that assimilation is the favored method for dealing with potential detractors, and the same tactic might be said to operate in *Star Trek's* corporate response to fans also.

While lawsuits are filed against authors such as Samuel Ramer, whose book on *Trek* trivia, *Joy of Trek,* was banned from sale and subjected to a $22 million claim for breaching copyright, popular fan fiction authors have been invited to write official tie-in novels, indicating a sense of corporate pragmatism in recruiting talent from within the fan community— and keeping any profits to be had. A similar acknowledgment occurs in monitoring fan feedback, as is now conventional practice, even if ideas are not always approved. While Paramount firmly denied any romance between Data and Tasha Yar in *The Next Generation,* despite this subject being of intense concern among fans, the relationship between Odo and Kira was allegedly developed in *Deep Space Nine* as a response to fan speculation.[2] This suggests that a growing level of reciprocation has emerged between writers, producers, and the fan community. This is not always the case, however. Campaigns to introduce a gay character met with little official acknowledgment, a fact that George Takei's recent decision to "come out" ironically highlights. Although fans will occasionally make a difference in the way story lines are shaped, this will not occur at the expense of Paramount reneging creative control, or involve introducing material that may adversely affect sponsorship or syndication deals.

Again, the Internet provides an interesting challenge to such attempts at corporate control. Encouraged by increasingly affordable equipment, various fan films have been distributed on the Web, with narratives that have included the gay story line fans have long campaigned for. The fan-created Web series, *Star Trek: New Voyages,* has been running since 2004 and has even featured original series actors such as Nichelle Nichols and Walter Koenig reprising their roles as Uhura and Chekhov (see chapter 11 on fan produced episodes). With the involvement of such established stars, scripts written by contributors to *Deep Space Nine,* and costumes and sets designed by series insiders, the line between amateur and professional, "fannish" and officially sanctioned, becomes difficult to ascertain. Admittedly, *New Voyages* is allowed to continue its operations because it does not seek a profit and is freely available to download, and it can also be seen, like the other fan sites tolerated by Paramount, as another means of free publicity helping to generate continued interest in a franchise that they have themselves largely allowed to flounder. Nevertheless, this Web series also refutes the notion of fans as passive viewers, or even that fans merely comprise viewers alone, with the show utilizing professionals who have been involved with *Star Trek* and who evidently wish to express their continued interest and enthusiasm by donating their time and skills.

It is a measure of the increased prominence fans are taking, with the franchise seemingly in trouble once again, that they have been left to uphold its legacy, and to create new work for themselves now that the last of the spin-offs, *Enterprise*, has been cancelled. As its 40th anniversary approached, a digital miniseries, *Of Gods and Men*, directed by Tuvok actor Tim Russ and starring a variety of *Star Trek* characters from over the years, was being made to commemorate the event, with the actors involved describing it as a "gift" to the fans. As Walter Koenig has commented on the project, "The original series was in danger of being cancelled after the second season, and the fans came through. Once again—after 40 years—with the support and enthusiasm of the fans—*Star Trek* will have another life on the Internet—and I'm very pleased to be part of it." Clearly inspired by *New Voyages*, shot partly on its set, and obviously encouraged by the continued commitment of fans, *Of Gods and Men* offers an apt example of what Jenkins has referred to as "convergence" between the industry and the people, and is testimony to the debt the franchise has always owed its followers in providing creative inspiration, and a much-needed sense of direction.

The relationship between fans and the industry is often fractious, yet another interesting acknowledgment of fans seemingly occurred with the creation of a character that debuted in *The Next Generation* and later starred in *Voyager*. Lieutenant Reg Barclay (Dwight Schultz) appears very much as a "Betty Sue" character—the conventional term used in fan fiction when the narrator inserts themselves into a *Star Trek* environment— thereby fulfilling a common fan fantasy. While he may not initially seem to be a progressive depiction, with his lack of social skills, various neuroses, and tendency to live in a dreamworld, Barclay is finally proven to be a commendable nod to the investment fans have made in the show, and an affirmation of their underlying qualities.

Barclay is first introduced in the episode "Hollow Pursuits" (1990) as a shy engineer who prefers life in the computer-simulated holodeck rather than interacting with crew members who largely undermine him. In many ways he seems to be the archetypal Trek-nerd, opting to exist in a fantasy world due to inadequacies that prevent him from fully engaging with the real one. In fact, it is just such a stigmatized figure that Gwenllian-Jones seemingly has in mind when she describes fans as exhibiting "a deep-seated compulsion to build, enter and uphold a virtual reality" (167). The fan as psychologically disordered, or dangerously delusional, is thus corroborated in Barclay's initial characterization, and by the end of the episode he is encouraged to relinquish his seeming dependence on holo-programs, deciding to delete all but a few from the ship's computer. The ability to act as a fully functional member of the *Enterprise* cannot coexist, supposedly, with being a socially inept loner, and Barclay must forgo these constructs in order to conform to accepted protocol. Ironically however, and most significantly, his imaginative capacities are ultimately championed towards the end of *Voyager*, as it is his refusal to comply with the status quo, and abandon the lost crew, that finally helps to recover them in the series finale.

Always the most improbable member of Starfleet in his awkward manner, predilection for daydreaming, and preference for solitary pursuits, Barclay ultimately demonstrates that it is by thinking outside the box, and not fitting in with the crowd, that one can triumph, thereby overcoming the narrow confines through which others may judge us. He may be derided by the crew at the outset of his career, unkindly referred to as "Lt. Broccoli" even by the captain, yet Barclay becomes the unlikely hero in *Voyager*'s finale when his faith wins out against the odds. He consequently articulates many of the contradictions by which *Star Trek* fans have come to be understood. Intelligent and creative, yet socially awkward and emotionally erratic, Barclay initially compensates for his supposed inadequacies through a fantasy world in which he imaginatively reshapes existing crew members to boost his self-esteem. He is consequently reprimanded for using their images for his own ends (precisely the activity Jenkins terms as "poaching," activities which are continuously threatened by electronic copyright laws in terms of appropriating characters supposedly owned by Paramount).

Barclay struggles to overcome his "neuroses" and comply with Starfleet requirements, yet his emotional difficulties continue to define and stigmatize him. Reassigned to Earth in *Star Trek: Voyager* he is declared unfit for work by his commanding officers in the episode "Pathfinder" (1999) because of an overriding obsession with contacting the *Voyager*, which is at large in the Delta Quadrant. Although his interest in this seemingly "lost cause" is misread as a symptom of his former "holodiction," Barclay proves himself, and is reinstated, when he discovers a micro-wormhole through which contact with the crew is finally made possible. In the series finale, "Endgame" (2001), he ultimately acquires heroic status by detecting a transwarp aperture that allows the ship to get home while averting a potential Borg invasion through the same portal. Barclay triumphs, on his own terms, when his imaginative tendencies reach into the depths of space and eventually help return *Voyager*'s lost crew—personnel that have notably been forfeited by his superior officers. In doing so, far from being derided as a Trek-nerd warranting little respect, or reprimanded as a poacher stealing images that do not rightly belong to him, Barclay might stand as an idealized representative of the fan community at large, one whose faith in the franchise has seemingly surpassed production figureheads such as Brannon Braga and Rick Berman in continuing to conceive possibilities for saving another seemingly lost cause, *Trek* itself, and proving capable of doing so. Barclay is never fully assimilated into Starfleet, yet is honored nonetheless, his skills, despite being undervalued at times, finally shown to be invaluable to an organization that largely misunderstands him. Fans may be similarly derided within popular culture, distrusted or disregarded by the industry, yet are a vital means of keeping the show alive through their faith and a degree of loyalty that remains, for the most part, relatively intact.

Barclay was, understandably, a big hit with fans, with a number of Websites created in his honor, and it seems only reasonable to assume that if we can love the series for such outsider heroes, there is no reason to think that we will necessarily buy into the "preferred" ideology *Star Trek* offers, any more than we will indiscriminately buy up any available merchandise. Indeed, despite the films having earned $1.76 billion globally at the box office, and a further $4 billion gained world wide from related products, limited ticket sales for its most recent film, *Star Trek Nemesis* (2002), and low ratings for *Enterprise* amply indicate that fan approval cannot be taken for granted. In online discussions fans frequently take issue with select episodes and story lines, showing a canny awareness of ideological subterfuges that are often as insightful (and in many cases more accessible) as those given by academics. The Internet has extended the reach of former fanzines in sharing these ideas, yet corporate censorship has also limited such practices, and although many discussion boards are tolerated sites also disappear on a daily basis with nary a comment. Nonetheless, while "Web wars" remain a concern, it is also online that *Star Trek* has ironically acquired a new lease on life, for both the show and its fans. James Carley, executive producer of *New Voyages*, in graduating from an avid collector of *Trek* memorabilia to key figure behind the show's resurgence on the Web, invites us to look more closely at the stereotypes surrounding *Trek* fans and their relationship to the industry. If the "Trek-nerd" is a largely derogatory evaluation the "Textual Poacher" is guilty of an equally simplistic charge. The fact of the matter, as with all such polarizations, is that the truth lies somewhere in the middle.

The future of one of the most successful franchises in the world is equally insecure, particularly at the time of its 40th anniversary. The fact that *Nemesis* made less money than any other *Trek* film and that no more television series are planned after *Enterprise* suggests that the franchise is running out of steam, with no new series in production for the first time in 18 years. The likelihood that Paramount will jettison *Star Trek* completely seems unwarranted, particularly given the money that is still potentially to be made from it, yet its future arguably rests with its fans and the engagement they continue to have with its characters and narrative possibilities.

Their importance lies not simply in terms of providing a ready market for any new ventures or ancillary products, but in keeping the faith, as they did when NBC was first persuaded to stake the original series for a further two seasons, and again in the 1970s when fans continued to maintain interest in the show long before the franchise existed. Paramount may prefer it if we simply play the newest game version of *Star Trek*, or visit their adventure park in Las Vegas, spending wads of cash on rides, enjoying refreshments at Quark's Bar and Restaurant, and purchasing a souvenir photo of ourselves in the captain's chair, but the unofficial and illicit pleasures we prefer to make up for ourselves will always be a bigger draw. They cost nothing, after all, yet afford so much. Clearly, if *Star Trek* is going to survive it will have to take fan interests further into account. The franchise may have lost sight of these recently, but to quote a Rule of Acquisition: Even a blind man can recognize the glow of latinum.

Notes

1. Available at http://www.web.mit.edu/cms/People/henry3/consume/html/.
2. See Jenkins' *Textual Poachers* (1992), with Paramount refuting the idea that Data has emotions (38) and writing the relationship off as a one-night stand (230), despite episode elements that contradict these claims, and Michelle Erica Green's Web article "TV Fans Connect and Create Online."

Works Cited

Bacon-Smith, Camille. *Enterprising Women: Television Fandom and the Creation of Popular Myth.* Philadelphia: University of Pennsylvania Press, 1992.
Fiske, John. *Understanding Popular Culture.* London: Routledge, 1989.
Green, Michelle Erica. "The Selling Out of *Star Trek.*" Littlereview.com (1991). http://www.littlereview.com/getcritical/trek/selltrek.htm.
_____. "TV Fans Connect and Create Online." Littlereview.com. http://www.littlereview.com/getcritical/xfiles/msnbc.htm.
Greenwald, Jeff. *Future Perfect: How "Star Trek" Conquered the World.* New York: Viking Press, 1998.
Gwenllian-Jones, Sara . "Web Wars: Resistance, Online Fandom and Studio Censorship." *Quality Popular Television: Cult TV, the Industry and Fans.* Edited by Mark Jancovich and James Lyons. London: BFI, 2003: 163–177.
Jenkins, Henry. *Textual Poachers: Television Fans and Participatory Culture.* London: Routledge, 1992.
_____. "The Poachers and the Stormtroopers: Cultural Convergence in the Digital Age." *Les Cultes Médiatiques: Culture Fan et Oeuvres Cultes.* Edited by Philippe Le Guern. Rennes, France: Presses Universitaires de Rennes, 2002: 343–378.
_____. "Digital Land Grab." Techreview.com. http://www.techreview.com/articles/00/03/viewpoint0300.asp?p=1.
Jindra, Michael. "*Star Trek* Fandom as a Religious Phenomenon." *Sociology of Religion* 55, no.1 (1994): 27–51.
"Paramount's Book Warpath." Vidiot.com (2001). http://www.vidiot.com/bookwar.html (accessed on 22 July 2006).
Short, Sue. "The Federation and Borg Value Systems in *Star Trek.*" *Foundation: The International Review of Science Fiction* 92 (Autumn 2004): 31–50.

11

Fan Culture and the Recentering of *Star Trek*

Justin Everett

Ownership is a funny thing. I technically own my property, but I cannot raise an oil well upon it, nor can I expand it or build a deck without the permission of my township. I may own stocks but have no control over the corporations they represent. Legally, I own my dog, but this does not give me license to abuse her, as I could an inanimate object.

Technically, Paramount "owns" the Star Trek[1] franchise. Paramount has the right, as it recently demonstrated with the cancellation of *Star Trek: Enterprise*, to support one of its properties by funding its continuation or killing it outright. However, in spite of these rights, it has become blazingly apparent to me that Paramount does not "own" the greater cultural text that is Star Trek. It owns the franchise and it is the only entity allowed to profit from Trek's existence, but the universe created by *Star Trek*'s many incarnations extends beyond legal borders. This includes not only films, television series, books, and other official products, but unofficial products as well, such as fan clubs, Web sites, costumes, conventions, props, and mountains and mountains of fan fiction. It spills over into territory that is neither created nor owned by Paramount, but is "owned" by fans. This ownership may not meet the full legal definition of the term, as Paramount can control and limit anything bearing a close resemblance to the *Star Trek* name or its universe. It is perhaps best to consider Star Trek a shared possession, one that has both legal and social aspects.[2] This fan ownership likely existed even before Bjo Trimble fired off her first letter to NBC in an effort to save the original series, and has grown through the years to provide a fan base that could be counted upon to purchase the multitude of officially licensed products produced or endorsed by Paramount. But something has happened in recent years, beginning, perhaps, even before *The Next Generation* (*TNG*) went off the

186

air. There was a sense, a noted observation at first, beginning with the first episode of *Deep Space Nine* (*DS9*) (and perhaps even before), that *Star Trek* the official franchise had somehow, inexplicably, crept away from its center and had ceased to be "Star Trek," the ideological universe (see chapter 3 on the decline of the franchise after *TNG*).

Dissatisfaction can manifest itself in many ways. Fans could simply turn off the television, stop attending club meetings, attending conventions, and buying fan-created products. To a degree, some of this has happened, as the cancellation of *Enterprise* indicates. However, fans can also react to their dissatisfaction by taking possession of the greater cultural text that surrounds Star Trek. One way that fans have taken possession of Trek is by producing their own "Internet series." Easy access to technology, and a means of distributing fan-made films via the Internet, has made this task more personally rewarding and less daunting than it once was. Fan-made films are particularly interesting because they represent Trek not as produced, but as fans would like it to be. While a number of groups have taken on the task of creating "new" Trek series, one in particular, producing under the title of *Star Trek: New Voyages*, is intriguing because of its bold attempt to faithfully recreate the original series and, in so doing, return Star Trek to its mythical and ideological roots. This, to my mind, represents a *recentering* of Star Trek.

I

This dissatisfaction with the official franchise began with grumblings in fan circles and on the Internet, but eventually manifested itself in a decline in viewership that likely began with *DS9*, continued with *Voyager*, and finally plummeted when *Enterprise* debuted and presented fans with a prehistory that, in the minds of the fans, did not mesh with the details of the original show and the partially fan-created universe. (It is noteworthy that the name of the ship, and the name of the show, thumbed its nose at this much-revered continuity since the United Space Ship *Enterprise, NCC-1701*, was deemed to be the first ship to bear that name.) Though the show did much to explain its anachronisms and its sometimes wild, and seemingly desperate, attempts to create dramatic plot situations that would bring the fans back—the transparent "9/11" scenario created in *Enterprise*'s third season "Xindi" arc is perhaps the best example—still they leaked away. The show had knocked the Vulcans off their pedestal and made liars and spies out of them. The stories, mostly weak recycles of episodes that had been done again and again, indicated perhaps that Star Trek had said all it had to say and that the franchise had run its course. In response to this, the producers brought on board Manny Coto in its final season. His tactic, which seemed to represent a sensitivity to the fans' desires to return to the old order, was to inject as many references as possible to the original series (TOS).

Though Coto made serious attempts to resurrect the show with its nostalgic references to TOS, the fan base had been largely lost. When *Star Trek: The Next Generation* was in its first season, it brought in 8.5 million viewers; at its height in 1992, it brought in 11.5 million. Viewership through the next two series declined to 4 million by 1999 (Fuller). When *Enterprise* premiered, it brought in over 12 million viewers. By the time it was cancelled four years later, the viewership had dropped to 3 million, and had dipped as low as 2.5 million ("List of *Star Trek: Enterprise* Episodes"). It is worth noting that the shows that did acknowledge the original series sometimes did better in terms of viewership. *TNG* brought back Scotty and the original bridge, Spock, and Sarek. *Deep Space Nine* paid homage to "The Trouble with Tribbles" (1967) by blending its characters into the original episode. By comparison, the attempts on *Enterprise* seemed vain and haphazard. Though Brent Spiner's appearance provided a ratings spike, the attempts to explain the absence of Klingon cranial ridges in the twenty-third century, the recreation of the mirror universe, and the soft porn provided by an Orion slave girl were less than spectacular.

If the Internet fan traffic is to be believed, then the fault lies squarely on the shoulders of the producers. The final episode of the series, "These are the Voyages..." (2005), was received as an insult. *Trekweb*'s mysterious reviewer, "O. Deus," while inexorably critical and demanding, was unquestionably an advocate for the show he hoped it would become. His weekly reviews were filled with a longing for the *Enterprise* he eventually hoped to see, but the producers never, well, *produced*. He writes that the final episode:

> ... might have been intriguing at any other point in the show's history, but as a finale it is a dismissal of ENT....."Voyages" reduces ENT and its crew to nothing more than characters in a holodeck simulation whom Riker and Troi can switch off an on at will [O. Deus, "These are the Voyages..."].

It is ironic that this is exactly what Riker and Troi do. They walk away from the simulation much as the fan base has abandoned *Enterprise*. If nothing else, the holodeck simulation drew even more attention to the artificiality of *Enterprise*. To many fans, this show was not a natural part of the Star Trek universe they had helped create and had grown to love.

The fans, certainly, were not the only ones to reject *Enterprise*. SF (science fiction) author Orson Scott Card wrote a scathing commentary for the *Los Angeles Times* in which, after disparaging the fans for resurrecting a show that was "bad in every way that a science fiction television show could be bad," called TOS (The Original Series) "grade school for those who had let the whole science fiction revolution pass them by." Of course, Card is correct in a certain sense. Reminiscent of *Forbidden Planet* (1956), which itself throws a backward glace to the childlike space operas of "Doc" Smith and his contemporaries, *Star Trek* reflects a time when SF was oversimplified by the tastes of Hugo Gernsback and other editors of the early pulp era. Trek does not, except in a few shining moments, even reflect the sophistication of the Golden Age, when John Campbell's leadership brought science fiction into the realm of respectability. It certainly does not reflect the artistic grit of New Wave, nor the movements that have come and gone since.

Still, Card misses the point. Star Trek, in its essence, is not about quality SF. It is "sci-fi"[3] in every sense that the term represents for the serious writer. If Star Trek is sci-fi, which it certainly is, this does not mean that it does not have a place in American popular culture. Gary Wolfe, for instance, has suggested that "'sci-fi' may have a legitimate use in describing highly formulaic mass-audience entertainments" (2005: 21). Few would question the impact that sci-fi, including Star Trek and *Star Wars* (1977), has had on popular culture. Its simplistic and formulaic nature does not neutralize its cultural legitimacy. Star Trek was never intended to be profound. It is trite, flashy, superficial, and has wide appeal with its own particular, and very loyal, audience. It never presumed to arise to the level of Asimov, Clarke, Le Guin, Delany, or Butler.[4] It serves a different audience for a very different purpose.

Though many fans reacted to Card's scathing critique, perhaps one particular example will suffice to illustrate the general sentiment. In a letter to the editors of the *LA Times*, one fan, who claims to have worked on *DS9* and to have hosted Card's family on set, responded to Card's essay:

> "Star Trek" fans are those who ask that question [what if?] on a daily basis. What if people were that kind, that brave, that respectful? What if we went out there? What would we find? Who [*sic*] would we meet? Will we survive it? ... I believe that as long as mankind strives to better itself, there will be a place for "Star Trek." ... Because to me, it shows there is always a place to grow to, a behavior to strive toward, a new goal to look for ... a respect for beliefs different from one's own ["Card Trek"].

This response to Card's critique is not interesting for what it tells us about Star Trek as quality science fiction. In fact, the letter would seem to confirm Card's complaint regarding Trek's superficiality. The writer, in parts of the letter not excerpted here, does little more than defend Trek's forward-looking multiculturalism and rattle off the names of some if its more significant writers. What the letter does accomplish, and does demonstrate in the excerpt above, is that the fan base is not so much motivated by the quality of the science-fictional ideas but by the forward-looking idealism represented by the cultural microcosm encapsulated within the hull of the ship—or ships—called *Enterprise*.

The expectations Card articulates—which he believes, rightly, that Star Trek has failed to provide—fall within the purview of what Eric S.

Rabkin (2004) has called a "cultural system," meaning "a set of typical dramatic situations, recurring elements, even themes and styles" (462). SF he sees as particularly influential at present for its propensity to help us deal with technological change (462). It is these conditions which Card believes Star Trek has not met at a sufficient level of quality. In most cases he would be correct. However, one of the widely recognized forces that drives SF, and drives Star Trek, is its adolescent optimism. Brian Aldiss (2004), one of the few writers known equally well for his literary criticism of the genre as for his fiction, observes that SF writers—a sentiment I would extend to the fan base—"are really sweet men and women, boys and girls, carrying the innocence of early youth into middle age" (511). In stating that "the real Golden Age of science fiction is twelve," David Hartwell (2005: 269) notes the uniqueness of the SF fan as a person "who always lives in the SF world, but under cover of normality most of the time—except while attending a gathering of like minds" (272), which points to the uniqueness and insularity of the SF community as one distinct from the rest of the world in its childlike wonder about what the future may bring.

That the Star Trek community shares common points of connection to the greater science fiction community cannot be denied. However, it is a distinct subgroup, consisting, as Card points out, of some individuals who do not read mainstream science fiction or participate in the broader life of science fiction fandom in any other way. These individuals may be drawn as much by the idealism that the anonymous writer of the letter above points out as by any science-fictional ideas that may be present. In his study of the relationship between Star Trek and the Heaven's Gate cult, Jeffrey Sconce (2004) points out that "fans were far more interested in the *continuing community* of the story world than in the isolated (and often quite ridiculous) plots of individual episodes" (212; italics in original). This interest in continuity, Sconce continues, contributes to a developing fabric of an "extratextual metaverse" that becomes "a psychic structure one can choose to inhabit at will" (215). This structure, he contends, becomes a kind of "coping mechanism for enduring the daily grind of contemporary life," which he sees as approaching religion (218).

Michael Jindra shares this view, arguing that Star Trek creates a belief system built upon the American myths of progress and discovery empowered by science: "The generalized beliefs involved in ST fandom consist ... in putting faith in science, humanity, and a positive future" (49). Lincoln Geraghty views this as an "American monomyth" that "combines the lone hero motif with an inherent urge to do good and be redeemed, to bring about salvation to the less fortunate" (2005: 193), which has religious connotations of its own. In directing its fans toward a better world built upon these ideas, Jindra argues that Star Trek fandom can be understood as a religion, or at least religion-like, in that the activities engaged in by the fans serve to reinforce the stability of the community and its worldview (48–49). Similarly, Robert Kozinets has noted a utopian ethic built up around the IDIC (Infinite Diversity in Infinite Combinations) ideology (2001: 77). More importantly, Kozinets noted fans' awareness of the disparity between the "sacred text" of Star Trek's anticapitalist utopian ideology and Paramount's motive of maximizing profit (81). Finally, Kozinets observes that his study suggests that "to find the extraordinary or sacred, a special effort or *even a retreat away* from mainstream forms of entertainment may be required" (85; italics mine). This may suggest that the abandonment of *Enterprise,* and the investment in fan-created texts, may be essential to recentering the mythico-religious ideology represented by Star Trek. This, if nothing else, may serve to validate the centralization of fan ownership of the greater ideological text.

II

While its role as religion may be questionable, at least for healthy-minded individuals, that Star Trek, through the two-way textual interchange between the fan community and the official products released by Paramount, is a communally-created "megatext"—to borrow a term from Daniel Bernardi (1998: 7)—cannot easily be questioned. The existence of Star Trek as a megatext is as dependent on the approval and cocreation of the fan base as the fan community is dependent on the regular release of licensed products upon which to feed. Jindra, who sees the Star Trek megatext[5] as a legitimate, communally created mythology, describes the process of megatext creation as:

> ... the process of creating mythology where [the fans] ... use the available "tools" and "materials" of the culture to create a mythological structure over a period of time. In this situation, the [fans] ... act not on their own culture; but on the alternative one they have constructed (but which of course cannot be totally separated). The creation of new plots and stories and the ironing out of existing ones is essentially the mediating of contradictions in the story (universe). In this universe, the contradictions are an affront to the consistent universe the fans so desperately want to see created [Jindra, 1992: 46].

The "tools" and "materials" refer not only to the primary texts of the Star Trek universe, the television episodes and films, but its ancillary products in the form of technical manuals, novels, and megatextually accurate props, costumes, and the like. It is when the cocreators fall out of line with one another, with Paramount releasing one product while the fan community demands another, that the greater megatext begins to falter, decay, and die. It is this transgression that may have been committed by Paramount as television episodes, and in particular those associated with

Enterprise, began to violate the mythic megatext as the fans were willing to accept it. It was as if the Pope had rewritten the books of the Bible and had been excommunicated by the faithful.

Many who were involved with *Enterprise* were mystified by their abandonment by the fan base. One of the most prevalent answers has been that Star Trek has just seen too much airtime. In an interview following the cancellation of the show, *Enterprise*'s executive producer, Rick Berman, said with a verbal shrug, "Climates have changed. I think you can just squeeze so many eggs out of the old golden goose" ("Berman Reacts," SciFi Wire). Producer Ronald D. Moore, however, has commented that Star Trek is not "dead," but that it has "entered into an interregnum" from which it will eventually emerge ("Ronald D. Moore Says"). The online fan community has expressed its reasons for the demise of the show. One predominant view cites creative burnout or some variation of Berman's comments, noting that eighteen years of continuous production is enough, if not too much. A second view espoused by the fan community indicates that Star Trek has passed its time, with calls for a "reinvented" and "grittier" Trek along the lines of Moore's new *Battlestar Galactica*. This viewpoint is echoed by *Babylon 5*'s Bruce Boxleitner, who, reflecting on the demise of this Trek-like space opera, believes that today's SF audience— at least those who watch television space operas—prefer a heavier and less idealistic postapocalyptic fare (Philpot).

This shift seems logical in the post 9/11 world. The current popularity of an (almost) R-rated *Battlestar Galactica* would seem to confirm this. However, Star Trek was born, and thrived within the fan base, in a world threatened with nuclear war and social upheaval. The 1980s and 1990s, periods of relative prosperity, brought the SF world apocalyptic visions like *Blade Runner* (1982) and the *Terminator* series. *The X-Files*, one of the most paranoid television series to ever exist, was at the height of its popularity during perhaps the giddiest and most indulgent years of the tech boom. While an uncertain world is bound to breed a certain amount of uncertain literature, it is also bound to produce its opposite. It is bound to produce the literature of denial in the form of escapism, fantasy, and the literature of utopia.

Star Trek, in its original incarnation, and certainly in *TNG*, evolved into utopic literature. Roddenberry's original series proposal contains several summaries of projected episodes—of which some were produced for TOS—which can be read as commentaries on the unlikelihood of a perfect society. Roddenberry makes a point in this document of indicating that *Star Trek* will consist of "...continuing characters ... fully identifiable as people like us" (Roddenberry, 1964: 3). Though Roddenberry later indicated that he had always intended for *Star Trek* to depict an improved humanity (Kozinets, 2001: 72), it was only as episodes progressed that utopist elements unfolded, and were emphasized after cancellation by vast collections of fan fiction and licensed novels. This evolved gradually in the shows of the original series within the cultural milieu of the 1960s. Further, it became a mythos within the fan base, and as the twin mythologies endorsed by the fans and the officially licensed products coevolved, a collective megatext[6] became the shared property of Paramount, those who added to the "text" through its officially licensed products, and the fans who added to it with their own costumes, props, art, songs, stories, plays, and fan-created movies and episodes.

III

The Star Trek mythology may be seen as a communally created megatext shared by Paramount and the fan base. The loss of viewership over the years, and particularly the cancellation of *Enterprise*, may have as much to do with a schism between the fans and Paramount in terms of the nature of the mythological canon as it has to do with an overexposure or a leaking off of the fan base. The megatext is a compilation of individual mythologies into two broad textual groups, one created "officially" by Paramount, and the other supplied by the fans. For many years, these twin mythologies have both fed and fed off of one another. Fans complained about discontinuities and supplied explanations for their existence. (The Klingon ridges and the distinct TOS types of Klingon makeup described as racial characteristics provide one benign example.) Eventually, the discontinuities between what the fans wanted to believe and what Paramount put before them grew greater, eventually resulting in a schism which caused the viewership to leak away so profoundly that *Enterprise* was cancelled. However, the fans did not go away. They have turned to their own community and their own talents to correct the direction of Star Trek's future history. From a mythico-semiotic perspective, what has happened is extremely interesting and requires some explanation.

Ferdinand de Saussure (1986) described language in terms of two essential elements: a linguistic system and the individual signs that compose that system. The language system provides the rules and structure that allow meaning to take place. However, since all members of a particular linguistic community share in the creation, alteration, and maintenance of a system of signs (74), it can be altered over time by the collective force of the members of a linguistic community (78). The system of signs may be said to be relatively stable as long as the signs entering to compose the system and the signs leaving as new utterances are made are within the agreement of the overall community. This does not mean that the overall sign-system complex does not fluctuate, but that it maintains itself in a state of "linguistic continuity" (81). As Saussure notes, language changes and evolves as individuals within the community contribute new signs to the system and react to the system as a whole (19) which allows for changes or variations within the system.

In the present argument, the Star Trek megatext may be perceived as the overall system, with the licensed and unofficial products of two distinct communities—the "official" producers at Paramount and the consumers in the fan community. Because these two communities can be seen as connected but distinct, then it is possible for each to view the megatext differently, just as two communities speaking the same language, when separated, will diverge over time. Since the two communities generally do not communicate directly (except through the media of television and film), but within their own communities (on Paramount's lot or in fan clubs, for instance), then it is reasonable to assume that some divergence would occur over time. This divergence, I believe, is what has resulted in the devaluation of *Enterprise*, and now that there is no series on television or film in the works, the fans have taken over as the unofficial producers and consumers. The fans have effectively taken over the megatext that is Star Trek. This has resulted not only in numerous clubs and conventions, but also in a series of fan films which have become more professional with time, and have begun to effectively replace the "official" products. One effort worth considering in some depth is the fan "series" *Star Trek: New Voyages* (*NV*), which, distributed free on the Internet, has taken on the enormous task of continuing the original series. It has done so with great success, and in this effort has attracted many talents associated with various series and films, from the original series to *Star Trek: Voyager.*

Though *NV* remains a fan effort in its genesis and continues to be fan driven as it evolves, it is distinctly different from other efforts. This is not because *NV* came upon a new idea. Fan fiction—from the often female-authored "slash" fiction to innumerable attempts at home movies—has been a prevalent force in the Star Trek megatext since the cancellation of the original series. As a teenager, I remember hearing about a fan-created film entitled "One Cube or Two" featuring cube-headed aliens, and hearing at conventions about numerous other efforts. However, the availability of computer technology (and the ability to create computer-generated special effects) has put creating a reasonable facsimile of a Star Trek episode within reach of dedicated and talented fans. Additionally, the Internet has given fan filmmakers a means for advertising and distributing their efforts.

This does not mean that the results have been particularly impressive, or that they have attracted much dedication or attention from other fans. The most notable of these efforts, other than *NV*, is the *Starship Exeter* "series," which produces "episodes" set in TOS time period. Though the makers of *Exeter* are owed good language for their contributions, their "episodes" are more reminiscent of the fan films that made the rounds of conventions and fan clubs in the 1970s and 1980s than something that approached a level of professionalism and slickness characteristic of a studio-produced series.

One way in which *NV* has been different from the other attempts has been its boldness. Instead, as with the other "series," of attempting to create a new story with a new ship and a new cast, *NV* has sought to recreate—and continue—TOS from the moment of its cancellation in 1966, with the goal of continuing into *Star Trek: Phase II*, which was scrapped in order to begin the series of feature films. Secondly, *NV* has had the good fortune of attracting—gratis—the talents of a number of individuals associated with the original series and others. Their first attempt, "Come What May," contained acting and writing clearly on a par with the *Exeter* series. However, *NV* had the good fortune of obtaining the services of a special effects expert and other professionals to its mission. Had this not happened, *NV* might have attracted little attention outside of the online Star Trek fan community. The *NV* family followed its initial success with "In Harm's Way," an episode that involved the first of a number of TOS veterans, and allowed the *NV* organization to demonstrate its talent for high-quality special effects as well as duplicating TOS in loving detail. (The level of this detail is worth mentioning. Paramount borrowed the *NV* "gooseneck" viewer for one of its episodes, and the crew appealed to the online community in order to locate coffee cups and a decanter that would match those used in TOS.) As of this writing, another episode, "To Serve All My Days," was in the editing stage and due for release sometime in 2006, and features Walter Koenig reprising his role as Pavel Chekov. Though the list of other *Star Trek* veterans who have volunteered their time to make *NV* a reality are too numerous to mention, among them are actors George Takei and Grace Lee Whitney; science-fiction authors and TOS writers David Gerrold and D.C. Fontana; Marc Scott Zicree and Michael Reaves, who have written for *TNG* and *DS9*; and Ron D. Moore, who spent 18 years as a *Star Trek* special effects supervisor. The list could go on.

Something is going on here.

What is "going on," in my view, is the reclamation of Star Trek by its fan base (which must now be redefined to contain many former Trek professionals). It is nothing less than the recentering of Star Trek.

With time, the megatext shared by the linguistic communities formed by Paramount and the fans diverged. As Saussure notes, it is impossible to study a linguistic structure directly, it is possible to infer some elements of that structure by examining some of the individual signs produced by the system: "Since changes are never made to the system as a whole, but only to its individual elements, they must be studied independently of the system" (1986: 86). Consequently, it is difficult, if not impossible, to tell at what point the ideological systems and fictional histories supporting Star Trek as a television and movie megatext diverged from the fan megatext; it is equally difficult to ascertain to what extent, and for how long, these two texts commingled during the slow process of their divergence.

However, it is evident, from the falling ratings and eventual abandonment of *Enterprise*, that this divergence did occur. Secondly, even as *Enterprise* was falling to cancellation, *NV* was increasing in popularity, and eventually resulted in over six million downloads[7] of "In Harm's Way," if unofficial estimates are to be believed.

While much of this interest in *Star Trek: New Voyages* may be due to the lack of an "official" show being currently on the air, the fan interest, plus the interest of the professional community formerly associated with Trek, seems to point to something more substantial and compelling. There is "something" at the core of Star Trek that will not go away. That "something" draws not only fans, but fan-professionals who have flocked to the show. That "something" is an ideology and a future history that exceeds the textual boundaries that had surrounded the original show. This megatextual growth is something that Gene Roddenberry had likely never anticipated. What is particularly compelling is the draw that the original series represents for fans and professionals alike. In spite of the poor quality of the writing, the neon sets, the superficial characters, and the unimaginative plots, Star Trek in general, and TOS in particular, created a center of meaning, a place to which people could point and say, "Yes, that is what we want to be." It was childlike in its genesis, and it continues to be juvenile in its simplicity and its optimism to this day. In spite of this, it is a collective idea that certain people are not willing to let go. In looking back at TOS, the fans are experiencing nostalgia, certainly. They are looking back toward the 1960s, and beyond that, toward the pulp period of SF, toward the simple, clear-cut adventures of "Doc" Smith and Burroughs. But at the same time, the fans are looking forward to the future with optimism. They are not just looking for utopia. They are planning for it.

That is why *New Voyages* has become so popular, and that is why it represents the recentering of the collective megatext known as Star Trek. May there be much more to come.

Notes

1. I have used "Star Trek" without italics to refer to the shared cultural text. With italics, *Star Trek* refers to the Paramount property.

2. The legal issues surrounding Paramount's ownership, and the extent to which it will and will not allow fan communities to create products that are based upon the shows, situations, and characters of the official franchise, go beyond the purpose of this essay. However, Paramount's standard practice has been to allow such products as long as those products are not made for profit. Paramount licenses certain things officially (costumes, prop replicas), for which the makers must pay a portion of their earnings. However, Paramount has not, as of this writing, licensed fan films or other dramatic productions.

3. Brian Aldiss refers to "sci-fi" as "demeaningly downmarket" (2004: 511). However, Aldiss is elusive in his definition of what identifies quality SF: "Popularity is no guarantee of worth, nor is its opposite.... Nor can what is popular or what is designedly obscure

be condemned as entirely worthless" (511). Yet there seems to be some consensus on the part of SF authors who consider themselves "serious" about SF to distance themselves from Trek. This is reflective of conversations I have had with Nancy Kress and Tom Purdom on separate occasions when they used "sci-fi" to describe much of the popular fare on television that is passed off as science fiction. I would only point out that this distancing is similar to that which the literati—those whom Aldiss calls "snooty higher echelons of literature" (511)—employed in rejecting SF as literature. This practice continues even today.

4. It should be noted that there were exceptions, even though most of these, such as Harlan Ellison's script for "City on the Edge of Forever" (1967), hearkened back to Golden Age themes. Other episodes were written by notable writers, although their contributions to Trek did not rise to the level of their other work.

5. Jindra uses the term *mythology* to refer to the fan-created products of the Star Trek universe. I have substituted the term "megatext" for the sake of consistency.

6. I am using the term *text* loosely here, and mean the products of the greater Star Trek community. This may include episodes of the various series, movies, fan films, licensed novels, slash fiction, costumes (licensed or fan-created), and so on. I see these "texts" as rising out of the greater "cultural system," to employ Rabkin's term.

7. Jack Marshall, former coproducer of *New Voyages*, estimated the downloads from official sites to be six million, though actual exchange through file sharing programs might actually be much higher. The downloads are legal since Paramount allows *New Voyages* to operate as long as it does not profit from its work. As such, the episodes are "unlicensed" fan products.

Works Cited

Aldiss, Brian. "Oh, No, Not More Sci-Fi!" *PMLA* 119.3 (2204): 509–512.

Answers.com. "List of *Star Trek: Enterprise* Episodes." http:// www.answers.com (accessed on 27 February 2006).

Bernardi, Daniel. *"Star Trek" and History: Race-ing Toward a White Future.* New Bunswick: Rutgers University Press, 1998.

Card, Orson Scott. "Strange New World: No 'Star Trek.'" *Los Angeles Times,* 3 May 2005. Also available at http://www.LATimes.com.Latimes.com/news/opinion/ commentary/la-oe-card3may03,0,6007802.story?coll=la-news-comment-opinions (accessed on 5 May 2005).

"Card Trek." *WriterGroupie.com.* http://www.writergroupie.com/columns/cardtrekcolumn.htm (accessed on 5 May 2005).

de Saussure, Ferdinand. *Course in General Linguistics.* Edited by Charles Bally and Albert Sechehaye. Translated by Roy Harris. La Salle, IL: Open Court, 1986.

Fuller, Greg. "*Star Trek* Ratings History." *Trek Nation.* http://www.treknation.com/articles/ratings_history.shtml (accessed on 26 February 2006).

Geraghty, Lincoln. "Creating and Comparing Myth in Twentieth-Century Science Fiction: *Star Trek* and *Star Wars.*" *Literature/Film Quarterly* 33, no. 3 (2005): 191–200.

Hartwell, David. "The Golden Age of Science Fiction is Twelve." *Speculations on Speculation: Theories of Science Fiction.* Edited by James Gunn and Matthew Candelaria. Lanham, MD, Toronto and Oxford: Scarecrow Press, 2005: 269–288.

Jindra, Michael. "*Star Trek* Fandom as a Religious Phenomenon." *Sociology of Religion* 55, no. 1 (1994): 27–51.

Kozinets, Robert V. "Utopian Enterprise: Articulating the Meanings of *Star Trek*'s Culture of Consumption." *Journal of Consumer Research* 28, no.1 (2001): 67–88.

O. Deus [pseudonym]. "'These are the Voyages...' Ends it All." *Trekweb.* http://www.trek web.com/articles/2005/05/16/4288f58ad5204.shtml (accessed on 16 May 2005).

Philpot, Graham. "Bruce Boxleitner Is the Star of the Hit U.S. TV Show *Babylon 5*." *Red Zone.* http:// www.area51radiostation.com/zredzone.html (accessed on 21 February 2006).

Rabkin, Eric S. "Science Fiction and the Future of Criticism." *PMLA* 119, no. 3 (2004): 457–473.

Roddenberry, Gene. "Star Trek." Unpublished manuscript, 11 March 1964.
Sci Fi Wire. "Berman Reacts to *Enterprise.*" http://www.scifi.com /scifiwire2005 (accessed
    on 3 February 2005).
Sconce, Jeffrey. "*Star Trek, Heaven's Gate,* and Textual Transcendence." *Cult Television.*
    Edited by Sara Gwenllian-Jones and Roberta E. Pearson. Minneapolis and London:
    University of Minnesota Press, 2004: 199–222.
Trekweb. "Ronald D. Moore Says Future of STAR TREK Franchise Now in Care 'Of Its
    Fans.'"   http://www.trekweb.com/articles/2005/02/07/4207d45461a95.shtml
    (accessed 7 February 2005).
Wolf, Gary K. "Coming to Terms." *Speculations on Speculation: Theories of Science Fiction.*
    Edited by James Gunn and Matthew Candelaria. Lanham, MD, Toronto and Oxford:
    Scarecrow Press, 2005: 13–22.

12

Locating the
"*Star Trek* Experience"

ANGELINA I. KARPOVICH

Fandom finds many ways to express itself. From the collection of trivia and merchandise, through the production of creative materials inspired by the original text, to pilgrimage: that is, cultural tourism motivated by fandom, which can take the form of attendance of fan conventions or of tourism focused on geographical sites associated with the object of fandom, sites which are variously deemed the locations of "symbolic pilgrimages" (Aden, 1999: 93), "media tourist sites" (Couldry, 2000: 65), and "cult geographies" (Hills, 2002: 144). Although this aspect of the fan experience has received significantly less academic attention than that of fans' textual productivity, most types of fandom can in fact be seen as dependant on at least a fleeting sense of physical "presence" at a particular geographic location. For example, it is considered *de rigueur* for many sports fans to be physically present at sporting events (indeed, it is this quality of "presence" that often marks a sporting competition as an "event" for sports spectators). Similarly, in popular music fandom, attending live performances is recognized as an intrinsic, often a somewhat more "authentic," aspect of being a fan. Somewhat paradoxically, despite the fact that recorded or transmitted versions of sporting events and music concerts usually offer both a better vantage point and a more comfortable viewing experience than actual attendance of the event, these fandoms place a premium on physical presence rather than mediated spectatorship, a premium which for Sandvoss (2005) is motivated by "a search for unmediated experience, of putting oneself, literally, in the place of the fan text and thus creating a relationship between the object of fandom and the self that goes beyond mere consumption and fantasy" (61).

Certain sites associated with fandom have taken on a metonymic role,

in which the geographical site, as object of fan pilgrimage, becomes prac-
tically interchangeable with the particular fandom. Indeed, the idea of
the metonymy of space is by no means new. For example, in his seminal
analysis of the creation and development of moral panics, Stanley Cohen
referred to the symbolic power of words and place-names in communi-
cating stereotypes: "Neutral words such as place-names can be made to
symbolize complex ideas and emotions, for example, Pearl Harbor,
Hiroshima, Dallas and Aberfan" (Cohen, 1980: 40).

Popular music fandom offers many examples of metonymic spaces, of
which Graceland is perhaps one of the most immediately obvious. The experience of Graceland as a metonym for Elvis fandom is enhanced by the
apparent completeness, or "intermediality" (Adamowsky, 2003), of the visitors' immersion. The entirety of the Graceland experience features continuous visual and audio reminders of Elvis Presley's career. As well as being
able to tour the Graceland mansion and the associated exhibits, the visitors
are presented with numerous merchandise shops, a diner serving Elvis'
favorite foods, and photo booths which allow the visitors to appear in the
same photographs as Elvis. Next door to the Graceland complex, the Heart-
break Hotel is open for business, and features a TV channel dedicated solely
to showing round-the-clock Elvis films. Given this proliferation of commercial services for fans, Graceland is perhaps the prime example of what
Sandvoss terms "the crudest display of commercialism, commodification
and a society based on an economy of signs, simulation and spectacle"
(Sandvoss, 2005: 53). Yet Sandvoss admits that the commercialization of
sites of fan pilgrimage can go hand in hand with the "appropriation of
popular culture as well as ... interaction between and among fans" (Ibid.).
In the case of Graceland, there is no doubt that the completeness of the
experience, expressed through both its intermediality and the fact that
the site is dedicated solely to Elvis Presley, allows Graceland to take on a
metonymic quality, which has enabled it to become the undisputed pre-
mier site of Elvis fandom, despite the significant roles played in his life
and career by other locations, such as, for example, Hawaii or Las Vegas.
Other examples of metonymy in music fandom are sites associated with
particular genres or periods, rather than individual performers, such as
the immediate associations between New York's CBGB's and mid–1970s
punk rock, or between Manchester's Hacienda and 1980s rave music.

Sports fandom also allows for a degree of metonymy in relation to
geographical sites. Followers of individual teams often attribute a particular significance to their team's "home ground" arena, and, just as in
music fandom, certain geographical sites become associated not just with
a particular team but with a sport in general. For example, the title of
the 2004 film *Wimbledon* (dir. Richard Loncraine) relies precisely on the
general audience's awareness of the metonymic quality of the association
between a southwest London suburb and world-class tennis.

Within this framework, fans of films and television shows initially posit a paradox, since the objects of their fandom are always-already mediated through the screen. Media fans seemingly have no comparable access to the experience of watching unmediated action, which characterizes sport and music fandom. However, media fans are by no means exempt from the fannish emphasis on proximity to the geographical sites associated with fandom. Pilgrimages to geographical locations have long been a feature of film and television fandom. In fact, fan pilgrimages are so characteristic of this fandom that certain distinctions between types of experience can be observed. Whereas Couldry seems to define the spectrum which spans from "highly commercialised, organised sites with museum-like displays and theme park entertainment" to "not fully commercial leisure sites (entry is free) [which] are visited simply because they have been sites of media production" (Ibid.) primarily in terms of commercial status, I would suggest that the same spectrum can also be conceptualized in terms of the degree of autonomy afforded to the visitors, following Combs's (1989) distinction between "official," "semi-official," and "unofficial and even counter-official" sites of popular celebration. Thus, the official studio tour, such as those offered by a variety of Hollywood studios, or the Granada Studios Tour (Couldry, 2000), offers a highly structured, infinitely repeatable experience, in which the fans may at times seemingly be positioned as participants, all the while remaining as spectators. The next type of experience is the fan-organized tour, such as *The Third Man* Tour of Vienna or the *Avengers* Walking Tour (Miller, 1997), which shares a degree of structure with the studio tours, but posits different hierarchical relationships between the tourists and the tour guide. The presumption that devotion to the object of fandom is "shared" by the tour guide and the tourists allows for a greater degree of interaction on the part of the tourists; in contrast to the official studio tours, fan-organized tours allow the fan tourist the possibility of immediate intervention, interjection, challenge, or addition to the narrative presented by the fan tour guide. Finally, the unofficial tour, such as *The X-Files* tour of Vancouver, can dispense with both a defined structure and a tour guide. Such a tour is both an "'underground' activity" (Hills, 2002: 147) and, more importantly, an individualized, often unique, "quest narrative" (148).

Such range and diversity of potential experiences available to media fans may illustrate the importance of pilgrimage within media fandom. Yet, as well as potential gains, are there potential disappointments lying in store for the media fan? Unlike the adherents of sport and popular music, media fans traditionally tend to follow fictionalized worlds, and every instance of physical proximity brings with it a potential demystification and disavowal. Indeed, tour guides often delight in revealing the nuances and the mechanics of the creative process, and in pointing out the subtle inconsistencies in the finished products (although fans themselves are frequently sufficiently knowledgeable about production processes to be able to speculate about the technicalities of filming [see Couldry, 2000: 98]). Such knowledge adds to the valuable resources of information at the fan's disposal, but at the same time may alter the ways in which fans will watch the film or program from this point on.

There is a further difficulty associated with being a fan of a particular genre. While fans of contemporary or historical texts have comparatively few problems with locating the physical sites associated with their fandom (even visiting foreign locations is not outside the realms of possibility), fans of texts set in the future are confronted with trying to locate sites which, technically speaking, may not yet exist. In their place, it is suggested (Rodman, 1996), science fiction fans use community gatherings at fan conventions, thus replacing a fixed geographical space with a transient social space as a focal point of fandom—a point which is corroborated by Jindra's (2000) claim that fan conventions are "an opportunity to immerse oneself in the *Star Trek* 'experience'" (171). However, Rodman's dismissal of *Star Trek* fans as lacking geographical sites of "significance" (1996: 124) not only overlooked the case of Riverside, Iowa, which proclaimed itself the "future birthplace of James T. Kirk" and has been hosting an annual *Star Trek* festival since 1985 (McPherson, 2004: 79), but has since been made redundant by the opening of two official *Star Trek* installations: the permanent *Star Trek: The Experience* at the Las Vegas Hilton, and the temporary *Star Trek Adventure* in London's Hyde Park in 2002–2003. Although the latter two official installations present useful case studies of the relationship between the fan tourist and licensed attraction, I intend to focus on the notion of metonymy of geographical sites to explore the relationships between the two *Star Trek* installations and their immediate geographical contexts.

Star Trek: *The Experience, Las Vegas, June 2005*

In popular culture, Las Vegas is the city of the Rat Pack, of Bugsy Siegel, and of *CSI*. Its nickname, reflecting its mafia-connected origins and its past and perhaps even current excesses, is Sin City. It is not, then, at first (or even second or third) glance, a city in which the noble ideals of the United Federation of Planets have the slightest bit of resonance. Yet the history of Las Vegas is also closely associated with spectacular, often visually excessive, live entertainment provided by the likes of Frank Sinatra, Elvis Presley, Siegfried and Roy, and Cirque de Soleil. The addition of *Star Trek: The Experience* to the ever-multiplying array of the city's attractions yet again illustrates Las Vegas' ability to absorb, reinterpret, and reproduce almost any form of cultural expression, by using "decontextualized history and art to create sites where culture and commerce mix to expand [the casinos'] markets" (McCombie, 2001: 60). Thus, according to Adamowsky (2003), the main concepts represented in *The Experience*, such as "expedition, exhibition, and a space of infinite distances," can easily be seen in Las Vegas terms as "mass tourism, theme parks and the logic of games" (2003: 1).

In other words, the undeniable artificiality of Las Vegas could in fact serve to verify the potential reality of the world of *Star Trek*. Located firmly within the contexts of reproduced spectacle, artificiality, and playfulness, which extend and overlap throughout the city, *Star Trek* is of course still fictional and unreal, but, crucially, in this particular context it is no more and no less fictional and unreal than ancient Egypt, or medieval Camelot, or, for that matter, the iconographic representations of supposedly contemporary Paris, Venice, or New York. And if some of these "fictional" spaces can spontaneously become "stand-ins" for the "real" spaces which they represent (as in the case of the New York, New York hotel, which, in the aftermath of the September 11 bombings, became an instant shrine to the real New York, providing visitors with a direct focus for the outpouring of their emotions [Rothman, 2003: 36]), then by extension, such a possibility of closely approximating "reality" is encoded into each and every public site in Las Vegas, including the *Star Trek Experience*. As Miles and Miles (2005) argue, "Las Vegas presents to the consumer what is a fantastical out-of this-world [*sic*] experience, something that does not appear to be real, but which at the same time is packaged as being the most readily available and natural of experiences" (115). Thus, a city with no discernible history, and a city which routinely imports historical ephemera from elsewhere and blows up its own landmarks to make space for new buildings, becomes "a good place to experience the blur between entertainment in the media and an increasingly ephemeral built environment" (Davies and Cook, 2004) and as such, may in fact be ideally suited to imagining the future.

Star Trek: The Experience is located on the ground floor of the Las Vegas Hilton. Unlike the more central, more recently built hotels, the Hilton does not have an exotic "theme" or an array of spectacular attractions which would serve the twin purposes of luring visitors and giving the hotel a unique identity. In contrast with the often outlandish, even frivolous, decors of other Las Vegas hotels, the Hilton appears generic and purpose-built for serious gambling. The presence of a permanent official *Star Trek* installation within the setting of a large casino initially appears to run contrary to the spirit of *Star Trek*, which has traditionally portrayed get-rich-quick schemes and extravagant acquisition as both futile and immoral (see for example the episode "Mudd's Women" (1966) from the first season of the original series and *The Next Generation* 1990 episode "The Most Toys"). Indeed Porter (1999) quotes a fan's general and heartfelt hope for "[L]ess materialism. [The crew of the starship *Enterprise*] weren't shown to amass riches" (1999: 254). However, as Kozinets (2001) points out, the reality of *Star Trek*'s "socially utopian and anticapitalist text" has, from its earliest origins, been "produced by and firmly situated within a commercial and commercializing culture" (80). While Roberts (2001) describes the entirety of the *Star Trek Experience* as "a long commercial for Paramount products" (354), Kozinets presents a much earlier example, citing William Shatner's memoirs on the origins of IDIC (see chapter 2 for further discussion of this event):

> As *Star Trek*'s original series drew to a close, Roddenberry opened a mail-order business called Lincoln Enterprises in order to sell a small line of *Star Trek* merchandise directly to fans.... At the same time, Roddenberry—who had not rewritten any scripts that season—imposed a script rewrite on a current episode. The rewrite contained what Shatner terms a "pointless" speech in which Captain Kirk "speaks the praises of a medal of honor known as the 'IDIC,' which stands for 'Infinite Diversity From [*sic*] Infinite Combinations." Shatner calls this scene's inclusion "Gene's rather thinly veiled commercial" for the IDIC medallions that would soon be marketed by Roddenberry's Lincoln Enterprises [2001: 81].

Despite (or perhaps because of) such early precedents of commercialization of the *Star Trek* mythos, *Star Trek: The Experience* is carefully designed to integrate with its immediate surroundings, without positing a challenge to them. The refreshment area, which is named after, and replicates the interior of, Quark's Bar from *Deep Space Nine*, is, along with numerous gift shops and a section of the casino, one of several *Star Trek*-themed areas which surround *The Experience* but do not charge for admission. As the only character to have a significant part of the installation named after him, Quark arguably gains greater immediate symbolic prominence within *The Experience* than any other character from the series. *Star Trek*'s most famous Ferengi thus provides a thematic, and indeed a physically tangible, link between the series and a Las Vegas casino hotel; after all, no other place on Earth would seem to follow The Rules of Acquisition quite so faithfully.

While Roberts (2001) interprets *The Experience* as foregrounding the "masculine" aspect of military conflict and thus disenfranchising female fans, I would argue that an equally valid interpretation of persistent themes and signifiers within *The Experience* can show that it is primarily designed to rationalize its own presence within its particular location. For example, the museum part of installation contains large screens which show clips from various episodes of *Star Trek*. Instead of focusing on visually spectacular scenes of military conflict, or on memorable scenes with great narrative significance, most if not all of these clips seem to show the crew together, relaxed, and playing poker. Needless to say, while the brief poker-playing scenes, which frequently featured in the opening or closing scenes of *The Next Generation,* are neither visually exciting nor narratively significant, they appear entirely appropriate in the context of the location. Indeed, spectators who turn away from the monitors will find themselves looking back, past the entrance to *The Experience,* at a fully functional, futuristic, and to all intents and purposes *Star Trek*-themed casino, which actively invites their participation.

The museum section combines a *Star Trek* timeline with displays of costumes and props from the series. While the displayed items are cross-referenced with the episodes or films in which they featured, the timeline interweaves actual events related to the development of space travel technology with notable events from all five television series and the ten feature films, thus closely approximating Combs's (1989) discussion of sites such as the NASA Museum, the Museum of Science and Technology, and the Epcot Center as "shrines that celebrate the future, however conceived" (74). Although Combs draws a clear distinction between traditional elite institutions which "build shrines to symbols of faith, patriotism, and knowledge" and "popular shrines" which "communicate the legitimacy of popular experience, even if it is lurid, frivolous, or downright kitsch" (Ibid.), in practice, such distinctions increasingly appear somewhat eroded, if not outdated. In an era when science museums emphasize their need to employ interactive entertainment techniques in order to make their subject matter accessible to a wider audience (McCombie, 2001: 61), an installation dedicated to a fictional story-world reproduces the form and structure of a science museum in order to verify the central premise of the story-world: that the kind of space exploration portrayed in *Star Trek* is almost within humanity's grasp. As Roberts puts it, "The museum ... provides an interpretation of the *Star Trek* world that prepares the audience member for the actual narrative of the ride. The museum-style presentation provides verification for the idea, essential to the rest of *The Experience,* that the *Star Trek* world is real and palpable" (2001: 352).

However, the museum remains a simulacrum, perhaps more of a simulacrum than the rest of *The Experience.* Beyond the exhibits themselves and the barest amount of explanatory notes which accompany them, the museum makes no attempt to approximate the depth and variety of detail which characterize most modern museum exhibitions. The absence of additional media which one would expect in a museum, such as a printed or audio-guide to the exhibits, underlines the utilitarian premise of the museum section, as outlined by Roberts: the museum is designed merely as a preamble to the interactive rides, rather than an attraction in its own right. Moreover, the exhibits and the interactive elements of *The Experience* necessarily privilege the later incarnations of the *Star Trek* franchise over the original series by giving them, and their characters, far greater prominence within both the museum area and the narrative of the interactive rides. As if the notion of a "museum of the future" was not paradoxical enough, this museum actively avoids indications of the passage of time, which would have included references to the obviously dated original series. Just like the casinos, which deliberately remove indicators of time, such as clocks or natural light, in order to encourage the gambler to spend both time and money, *The Experience* appears to be designed as a liminal space, "a dream-like world in which time loses its significance" (Miles and Miles, 2004: 109), in which the boundaries between reality and fiction (as well as perhaps those between idealism and consumerism) are eroded. It is worth noting that a sense of liminality is also central to Porter's (1999) account of the significance which some *Star Trek* fans place on attendance at conventions, which represent a "place and moment in and out of time" (1999: 245). Although I am not suggesting that the liminality of fan conventions deliberately echoes that of casinos, the parallels between them, as sites and moments which are set apart from the everyday experience of most visitors, are both obvious and striking.

In a further example of the integration of the *Star Trek* installation within Las Vegas, *The Experience* is not the city's only, or indeed the first, instance of a museum-as-simulacrum. While the majority of the casino interiors which offer reproductions of recognizable artifacts from around the globe are presented as a straightforward pastiche, they are occasionally positioned alongside more "genuine" signs, and this juxtaposition undermines the very notion of authenticity. For example, McCombie (2001) noted the case of the collection of original art formerly on display at the Bellagio Hotel, which charged $12 for admission and often required long waits to enter, "just like blockbuster art shows at conventional museums" (McCombie, 2001: 61).

The museum part of *The Experience* leads to the two rides, the original "Klingon Encounter" and the recently opened "Borg Invasion 4D." The "Klingon Encounter" ride, unchanged since *The Experience* opened in 1998, illustrates how prominently the concept of integrating the immediate surroundings of the installation featured in the initial overall design of *The Experience*.

A group of 26 visitors is led into a turbo lift by an attendant, who is dressed in the uniform of a junior Starfleet officer. From this point, the visitors adopt the hybrid position of the participant spectator, as they are inserted into a narrative of time- and space-travel. However, the attempt to make the narrative more "plausible" by anchoring it so firmly, so literally, to contemporary Las Vegas has actually undermined the verisimilitude of the ride. The group of visitors is informed that one of them is an ancestor of Captain Picard, which leads to a military encounter with the Klingons before the group is returned to its original location, following a spectacular simulated ride over the Las Vegas skyline. While Captain

Jean-Luc Picard is more consistently central to the narrative of *Star Trek: The Next Generation* than any other character, his identity as a Frenchman, frequently referred to in the series, seems to preclude the possibility of him being a descendant of the vast majority of visitors to *Star Trek: The Experience*, never mind one in every 26 who take the ride. Less than 10 percent of the total annual number of visitors to Las Vegas are foreign nationals, a figure which dropped significantly following the September 11 attacks (Mihailovich, 2004). Given the frosty relations between the U.S. and France in the aftermath of the Iraq War, the central narrative premise of the ride becomes less and less plausible. In fact, as the only European in my tour group, I was in absolutely no doubt as to which of us held the key to the planet's future. The Las Vegas skyline portion of the ride, once a faithful representation of the topography of the area, is no longer accurate; several of the landmark hotels have been demolished and replaced with newer, larger, more spectacular buildings. While this portion of *The Experience* was apparently designed to recall and perhaps surpass the thrills offered by the rooftop roller coasters which serve as attractions in many other Las Vegas hotels, the outdated virtual experience increasingly seems inferior to the ever-modernizing array of real-life thrills on offer elsewhere in the city.

An awareness of the constant process of modernization taking place within the city may have informed the publicity for the much newer "Borg Invasion" ride, which is promoted as much on its use of cutting-edge technologies as on its narrative: "This is ... the first Star Trek production to be shot totally digitally, the first multiple angle 3-D production, and the first attraction to use 2K digital cinema projection, which produces the highest-resolution digital projection commercially available" (Whiteside, 2004: 1).

The intermediality of the "Borg Invasion," achieved through the technical combination of 3D, motion stimulator, surround sound, and other contemporary technologies as well as the aesthetic combination of performative and spectatorship elements, leads the participants to experience what Adamowsky terms the collapse of the "culturally established boundaries between the senses.... The pictures feel, the sounds have a taste, shock and excitement surpass oppositions between the visible and the unseen" (2003: 1–2). Meanwhile, Roberts describes a more conscious, but similarly complex, reaction to another part of *The Experience*, that of coming face to face with a performer dressed as a Klingon: "I *knew* that despite his appearance, I was not being confronted by a 'real' Klingon; yet an immersion in the *Star Trek* world made his Klingonness palpable and threatening to me" (2001: 350).

The problem with such accounts of the successful illusion of a simulated reality created by *Star Trek: The Experience* is that they do not consider the extent to which the visitors themselves participate in creating their own experience. As a visitor to *The Experience,* my first reaction to a performer dressed as a Borg drone was very similar to Roberts' description of her reaction to a Klingon. Although intellectually I knew that the Borg approaching me was not "real," and indeed that the Borg in general are not "real," my knowledge of the role of the Borg within the *Star Trek* universe made the figure terrifying on a primal level. However, this reaction was dependent not only on my knowledge of the Borg, but also on my knowledge that the Borg was an official part of *The Experience,* rather than a fellow visitor. Although *The Experience* hosts many specialist fan events (including, this being Las Vegas, *Star Trek*-themed weddings), it is relatively rare to encounter a fan dressed in full *Star Trek* regalia on an ordinary day. For example, out of over two hundred visitors observed in the course of my visit to *The Experience,* only one was wearing an item displaying affiliation to *Star Trek*—an official *Deep Space Nine* merchandise T-shirt. In general, then, the environment of *The Experience* equates the wearing of elaborate costumes with the official permanent participants, be they the Starfleet uniforms, Borg costumes, or a janitor's uniform worn by the performers, or the Starfleet Academy Cadet uniforms worn by ticket collectors, official photographers, and other staff at *The Experience.*

In a discussion of what he calls "uniform debates," Kozinets describes the wearing of the *Star Trek* uniforms by fans as a frequent source of unease for outsiders, for whom uniforms may reinforce the "stigmatic mainstream perceptions of *Star Trek* fans as (1) immature (the association with Halloween, thus costumes rather than uniforms) and (2) mentally unstable (engaging in inappropriate dress/behaviour, confusing fantasy with reality)" (2001: 76). In contrast, Porter again focuses on the liminal qualities of the uniforms and other signs of allegiance:

> [M]any ... don the mark of fandom by wearing *Star Trek*-inspired T-shirts, badges, or jewelry, thereby clearly demarcating themselves as "fans" and distinguishing or separating themselves from their everyday social statuses and roles.... Through the donning of *Star Trek*-inspired costumes, fans can abandon their adherence to social structural personas and construct or adopt liminal personas that leave them free to explore aspects of their humanity and personality repressed or ridiculed in mainstream social contexts [1999: 249–250].

Instead of functioning as a sanctuary where fans can freely express their allegiance, *Star Trek: The Experience* seems to place a proprietary restriction on the wearing of *Star Trek* costumes. However, the danger posed by costumed visitors within the context of *The Experience* is not that they may be confusing fantasy with reality, but that their own presence may be confusing the other visitors' and perhaps also the performers' perception of the internal logic of *Star Trek: The Experience.* As Miles and Miles note in a general discussion of the iconography of Las Vegas, "Las Vegas may be full to the brim of [*sic*] consumers of culture, but those consumers are not, ultimately, creative players in control of this process. They can only be creative players *within* the process" (2005: 126). The general lack of official *Star Trek* merchandise on display among visitors to *The Experience* may in fact also serve to preserve the illusion that the story-world of *Star Trek* is real, as opposed to a fictional narrative with extensive merchandising spin-offs. In other words, by not wearing explicit signs of allegiance to *Star Trek*, most visitors are, consciously or otherwise, helping to maintain the illusion of verisimilitude which *The Experience* constantly strives to create.

Moreover, simply by being present at the site of *The Experience*, each of the visitors unconsciously ensures that their experience is collective, which renders it more meaningful for each participant. Each of the individual visitors to *The Experience* serve a complex array of functions for their fellow visitors; they become part of the performance in which each participant spectator observes not only the actions of the official performers but the reactions of the visitors around them, and they simultaneously serve as witnesses to each other's unique experiences. This phenomenon is described by Reader (1993) in his analysis of fan pilgrimages to graves of deceased idols:

> [D]espite their different motivations, they could find common ground in their shared, yet individual, participation in the same event.... [H]ere, indeed, was a form of *communitas*: on an individualised level pilgrims found a common bond in that they were apart from their ordinary lives, in an entirely different situation, on their journey yet realising that those around them were doing the same thing, and perhaps sharing similar feelings.... This enabled them to accept the differences and get on with their own pilgrimages, while letting everyone else get on with theirs [1993: 243–4].

Urry (1995) extends Reader's observation to suggest that the need to share an event is a common, if not essential, part of the tourist experience:

> [A]t least part of the social experience involved in many tourist contexts is to be able to consume particular commodities in the company of others. Part of what people buy is in effect a particular social composition of other consumers, and this is difficult for the providers of the services to ensure.... The satisfaction is derived not from the individual act of consumption but from the fact that all sorts of other people are also consumers of the service and these people are deemed appropriate to the particular consumption in question [1995: 131].

To put it simply, the success of *Star Trek: The Experience* depends in part on the visitors adequately performing their roles as fans, spectators, and participants. For a comparative examination of what happens when these roles are not performed satisfactorily, I turn now to the temporary *Star Trek Adventure* installation in central London. Although the following section was not initially designed as an auto-ethnography, the circumstances of my visit dictated that there were simply no other responses to record apart from my own.

Star Trek Adventure, *London, March 2003*

The eagerly anticipated opening of the temporary *Star Trek Adventure* installation in London's Hyde Park was designed to coincide with the London premiere of the tenth feature film of the *Star Trek* franchise, *Star Trek Nemesis* (dir. Stuart Baird, 2002). Featuring props, sets, and interactive elements as well as the largest selection of *Star Trek* merchandise available under one roof, the *Adventure* proved so popular with visitors that its run was extended by two months. The installation closed on 31 March 2003, rather than on 31 January, as was initially planned. I visited the *Adventure* in its penultimate week, on an entirely unremarkable weekday afternoon. By this time, *Nemesis* had finished its run in the major cinemas, and the Hyde Park *Adventure* seemed to have satisfied most fans' desire for pilgrimage. In contrast with the opening weeks of the installation, which were marked by large crowds, special events, and the apparently frequent appearance of fans dressed in *Star Trek* costumes, in its closing weeks, the *Star Trek Adventure* seemed highly subdued.

Located within walking distance of some of London's most popular tourist attractions, Hyde Park offers a respite from the crowds and traffic which lie just outside its gates. Over the years, it has regularly been the location of various exhibitions and open-air music concerts. The *Star Trek Adventure* is the latest in a long line of popular large-scale entertainment events to have taken place on this site. From the outside, the *Adventure* looks simply like a very large white tent. As I circle the exterior of the tent trying to find the entrance, I can't help noticing all the generators, the cables, the very literal tears in the fabric which holds the show together. The exterior of the *Adventure* also appears hugely incongruous with the rest of Hyde Park. It is almost the beginning of summer, visitors to the park are cautiously attempting to enjoy the sunshine, and there is a tent in the corner, which was not there before and will not be there for much longer. "*Star Trek*: The Experience" is written on the large banner outside (since like the Las Vegas *Experience*, the London *Adventure* also has an interactive element), and, as I look at my ticket which, bought half an hour into the designated time slot and has the number "17" printed on it, I remember the last time I had an Experience in a large tent on a sunny day.

* * *

As a teenager, I used to go to a summer church camp. The church itself was re-created as a tent, which I and the other children would pile into for communal prayers first thing in the morning and last thing at night. (In between, there were prayers before and after each meal, and almost-daily religious study sessions held in the same tent.) I was questioning religion at the time: a part of me really wanted to believe, and, perhaps more importantly, to connect with a common heritage through religion. Another part of me floundered. But every summer, for two weeks, I was brought back, because there was something magical about the experience of being in that tent. Not in the sermons, or in the icons, or in the ringing of the church bell, or in the smell of the candles, although they were all hugely atmospheric and sometimes even now, when I come across those elements by chance, they still stir something in me. The magic of the place was in the communal experience. Standing side by side with friends, saying and singing the same words at the same time— hearing your own voice as a component of a loud mass of individual voices— there was something in it which got through even to a cynic-in-training like me. And there was something else there, too, something about the congregation being young, and made up entirely of people you were living with—and therefore of fitting in within the community; and there was a regularity to the event which was actually very reassuring—the comfort of repetition, of knowing which words would come next and the whole event therefore becoming a performance, in which everyone had a role, however small—so you could be a spectator and a participant all at once.

Did I digress? We didn't just pray all day every day for two weeks; we would also have excursions and campfires and mini-Olympics and themed dress-up days. One year, the theme was science fiction.

I dressed up as Mr. Spock.

* * *

"Are you a Trekkie?" asks the security guard.

"Why, do I look like a Trekkie?" I parry. I know I don't. My appearance fits so neatly into another pigeonhole that the box office clerk had said, "Sorry, unfortunately we don't do a student discount" before I even had a chance to ask for one. But back to the security guard.

"Nah, I guess you don't." He warms to his theme: "Some of them though, the Trekkies, they just go mad for all this stuff."

"Really?"

"Oh yeah, totally. Some come in all dressed up and stuff."

"So, have *you* been inside?" I ask.

"Yeah, loads of times. It's good, you know, if you're into that sort of thing, I suppose. Enjoy!"

Unlike the Las Vegas *Experience,* the London *Adventure* offers an audio guided tour of the museum section for an additional fee. The design of the audio console somehow manages to look simultaneously retro and hi-tech, so apt for this exhibition that I momentarily wonder if it was made especially for it.

The first thing I notice, and then almost immediately *stop* noticing, when I enter the exhibition area itself is the music. Incidental music from the shows and the films plays constantly, both immersing the visitors in the totality of the *Star Trek* experience and, at this stage, masking the fact that there are so few actual visitors around. I move on, through the first room which contains models of starships and various props from the series, and in which I am the only visitor, to the main exhibition space. Here, too, the visitors are outnumbered by about 4 to 1 by the exhibition staff. I try to take some photos of people looking at the exhibits, and fail, as there are almost no people around.

The *Star Trek* general knowledge quiz, with a touch-screen and a big screen overhead on which the questions and results are displayed, is a well-chosen interactive element. I can imagine how people would have crowded around it during the exhibition's peak, possibly working collaboratively, possibly pitting their knowledge against each other.

I move around the corner, to the costume displays. The costumes are impressive, but close-up they lose some of the luster. If the mannequins are the same size as the actors, then they somehow seem small and fragile and nothing like the stature I had always associated with the characters. Close-up, the weave on the uniforms seems too crude to have been produced four centuries from now (although it might be highly functional special Starfleet-issue weave, it is still not what I had imagined it would be like, and therefore a disappointment).

Next to the costumes is a full-scale mock-up of the bridge from the original series. Here, I see my first crowd, if four people can be called a crowd. The bridge is large enough not to be disappointing, and, in a nice moment of consistency, illuminated so that the color scheme is the same as in the show, but it is fenced off, so all we can do is take pictures. In the absence of being able to touch, or even to walk around the set, flashes are going off rapidly. It is strange to see an empty set; it looks just like it did on the show, obviously, but on the show it was almost never empty. Indeed, an entirely empty bridge would usually signify some kind of danger. So, although it is here—tangible and almost within touching distance—and although it is THE REAL THING (or as close to it as we—behind the barrier with our cameras—are going to get), at the same time it is not. It is a nice, very well-displayed prop, but although it looks very much like the bridge from the original series, and despite the *Star Trek* memorabilia which surrounds it, it could almost be a prop from any science-fiction show.

The cafeteria section of the exhibition also looks well-designed, seemingly replicating the canteen from *The Next Generation*. The metallic décor and the painted "stars" in the painted "windows" seem to invite another interactive experience, although the sandwiches on sale bring me back to Earth.

I walk past the transporters, where, for yet another additional fee, you can get a picture of yourself in the transporter. I pass. Instead, I go for a ride in one of the runabouts, which jolts along to a film of a bumpy ride through the galaxy. I am the only passenger. "Are they all the same?" I ask the attendant, gesturing at the row of runabouts. "Yep, they're all the same. Enjoy the rest of the exhibition." Next to the runabouts is a recreation of Quark's bar from *Deep Space Nine*, featuring many vividly colored liquids in unusually shaped bottles. Just like the set of the bridge, the bar is cordoned off to visitors and appears eerily empty.

Then another set—the torpedo room. Once again, it is very impressive in its scale. But also, to an extent, it looks like any futuristic weapons room, somehow oddly more reminiscent of a Bond villain's cave than of *Star Trek*.

The *Enterprise* part of the exhibition follows. The investment in the audio guided tour pays off with the only interesting bit of information it has provided all afternoon: the Starfleet guns in *Enterprise* are actually recycled Bajoran guns from the earlier series. I am not entirely sure why, but possessing this new item of insider knowledge seems impressive. Also, looking at the tiny cardboard scale models of the bridge is very satisfying, as I had just looked at the finished product of the same process.

An attendant comes over to tell me that it is very nearly time for the last "Experience" of the day. This, and the large notices outside which tell you that those taking the Experience will not be readmitted to the main exhibition, builds up the impression that the Experience is the only possible worthwhile culmination to the exhibition. The group taking part in the Experience consists of me and two couples, one in their thirties, the other in their fifties; all of us have our cameras at the ready. A young girl ushers us in. The doors slide along with a satisfying *whoosh*. We are in the engine room. A voice welcomes us to the Experience, and points out that, while at the moment this is just a set, exciting things can be achieved with a few effects. On cue, the music changes, the lights dim and flicker, smoke starts coming out of the engine. Sirens go off. We are hurriedly "evacuated" by another attendant.

We are in a turbolift. As I wonder what exciting things can possibly happen in a fake lift, it starts to jolt slightly and side panels light up in sequence, doing a pretty realistic imitation of actual lift movement. Warnings are sounded, the lights dim, smoke comes out. My companions and I look at each other embarrassedly. I look at the wall of the lift and see that it is covered in a grey carpet. I bought exactly the same carpet once, because it was the cheapest carpet I could get. "Most offices use it," the sales assistant told me at the time, "it's so cheap that it doesn't even matter if you spill stuff on it." This is most definitely not the kind of interior I envision when I think of *Star Trek*.

The lift stops and we are at the Holiest of Holy: the bridge from *The Next Generation*. Amazingly, it doesn't have any barriers around it. "Walk around, but DO NOT sit in the Captain's chair," says the attendant. The set is quite dark and my camera does not work without a flash. My fellow visitors take pictures of each other, but appear distinctly underwhelmed. We are ushered out, through another empty refreshment area, and left to our own devices in the gift shop.

The gift shop takes up a lot of space, but offers a relatively limited variety of merchandise. It seems to sell mostly T-shirts and baseball caps, which commemorate not the television show, or the newly released film, but only the exhibition itself. When I heard the exhibition contained possibly the largest-ever collection of merchandise for sale under one roof, I was actually looking forward to the gift shop more than the exhibition itself. I was expecting endless model kits, and action figures, and replica phasers which made cool sounds and maybe even lit up. Instead, the only merchandise on offer associated with the series appears to consist of mountains of Tribbles.

On the way out of the gift shop, there is a supplementary gift shop. This one sells videos and books. Here, for the first time, I actually see more than a dozen people together in one place, looking through the books, discussing them, recommending them to each other. It is no coincidence that the supplementary gift shop is also one of the smallest areas of the exhibition; a space small enough for the few visitors to interact with each other.

An attendant collects my audio-guide console as I leave. Staff around the foyer of the exhibition outnumber the visitors by about 7 to 1. I want to ask the attendant what the atmosphere was like when there were large crowds of visitors going through the exhibition, but she looks so bored I decide to leave her alone.

My two-hour slot is still not over by the time I step outside. It is still sunny. And from the outside, it still looks like a big tent.

Conclusion

There are a number of structural differences between the two *Star Trek* installations. The absence of an audio guide or guidebook at the Las Vegas museum can be explained simply by the fact that it is both significantly smaller and has far fewer exhibits than the London site. It is unlikely that the absence of extensive explanatory materials is due to the lack of interest from visitors; rather, as the names of the two installations suggest, they have different emphases. The Las Vegas *Experience* is centered on the innovative and spectacular interactive rides. While the museum section is a superficially accurate simulation of a "real" museum, space constraints mean that exhibits are not displayed to their full potential, while a close reading of the *Star Trek* timeline reveals at least one error in the spelling of a major character's name. Instead, emphasis on polished professionalism is placed on both the technological spectacle and the actors' performances in the interactive elements of *The Experience.*

The London *Adventure* appears as almost a direct reversal of the Las Vegas formula. Perhaps as a result of the technological constraints of staging the installation in a park, the interactive elements were neither spectacular nor imaginative, while the extensive museum area offered genuine factual information about the world of *Star Trek.* Notably, staff at the London installation did not wear anything which might have resembled *Star Trek* uniforms. Since the *Adventure* did not make any attempt to "immerse" its visitors in the *Star Trek* story-world, there was no danger of costumed fans disrupting the boundary between performers and spectators, which may have explained the reportedly high number of visitors who did indeed wear their uniforms to the *Adventure.* The far less structured nature of the *Adventure* thus resulted in accounts which praised it as a "suitable vehicle to release fans' creativity and to create a sense of personal identity" (Geraghty, 2003: 21).

The more "traditional," less interactive, content of the *Adventure* also allows for a more straightforward comparison with other, entirely different, sites of fan pilgrimage. Both Sellars and Walter (1993) and Couldry (2000) note that a visit to a location (or, in the case of the *Star Trek Adventure,* a set) which is familiar from repeated watching on television may mark a return, rather than an exploration: "People pay to visit a location they have already watched free on television for years; part of the pleasure is not seeing something different, but confirming that the set is the same as something already seen" (Couldry, 2000: 69). Couldry draws a distinction between "watching" the location on television and "seeing" it in person: "Being on the set therefore connects two normally separate sites of discourse: the home and the site of media production" (84). The highly interactive Las Vegas *Experience* may allow the visitor to momentarily become a participant in the *Star Trek* story-world, but the London *Adventure* allowed the visitor to explore, at leisure, how *Star Trek* was created.

While neither installation site is metonymic, or intrinsically connected with *Star Trek,* the Las Vegas site is deeply integrated within its immediate surroundings; it is this thematic integration, rather than the permanent status of the installation, which lends it a far greater sense of congruity than that of the temporary London site. More than anything else, though, my own experience as a visitor to both sites illustrates the essential, although commonly overlooked, role played by the visitors themselves in creating an overall impression of a site of pilgrimage. Rod-man's (1996) prioritizing of geographical "sites of significance" over non-specific convention sites which bring together fans of media texts, in particular *Star Trek*, seems particularly shortsighted in this context. The "significance" of sites is in fact rarely completely intrinsic; rather, as this comparison between the two official *Star Trek* experiences has shown, it is created, accumulated, and maintained by the continuing collective experience of those who actually visit them, or desire to make such a pilgrimage.

Works Cited

Adamowsky, Natascha. "See You on the Holodeck! Morphing into New Dimensions." *Transforming Spaces: The Topological Turn in Technology Studies.* Edited by Mikael Hård, Andreas Lösch, Dirk Vericchio. N.p., 2003. http://cms.ifs.tu-darmstadt.de/file admin/gradkoll//Publikationen/space-folder/pdf/Adamowsky.pdf (accessed 30 June 2006).
Aden, Roger C. *Popular Stories and Promised Lands: Fan Cultures and Symbolic Pilgrimages.* Tuscaloosa: University of Alabama Press, 1999.
Cohen, Stanley. *Folk Devils and Moral Panics: The Creation of the Mods and Rockers.* 2nd ed. Oxford: Martin Robertson, 1980.
Combs, James. "Celebrations: Rituals of Popular Veneration." *Journal of Popular Culture* 22, no. 4 (1989): 71–77.
Couldry, Nick. *The Place of Media Power: Pilgrims and Witnesses of the Media Age.* London: Routledge, 2000.
Davies, Paul, and Julie Cook. "The Algiers Motel." *Stripping Las Vegas: A Contextual Review of Casino Resort Architecture.* Edited by Karin Jaschke and Silke Ötsch. Weimar: University of Weimar Press, 2004.
Eade, John. *Placing London: From Imperial Capital to Global City.* Oxford: Berghahn Books, 2000.
Geraghty, Lincoln. "*Star Trek*: The Adventure." *Vector: The Critical Journal of the BSFA* 228 (March/April 2003): 20–21.
Hills, Matt. *Fan Cultures.* London: Routledge, 2002.
Jindra, Michael. "'It's About Our Faith in Our Future: *Star Trek* Fandom as Cultural Religion." *Religion and Popular Culture in America.* Edited by Bruce David Forbes and Jeffrey Mahan. Berkeley: University of California Press, 2000: 165–179.
Kozinets, Robert V. "Utopian Enterprise: Articulating the Meanings of *Star Trek*'s Culture of Consumption." *Journal of Consumer Research* 28, no. 1 (2001): 67–88.
McCombie, Mel. "Art Appreciation at Caesar's Palace." *Popular Culture: Production and Consumption.* Edited by C. Lee Harrington and Denise D. Bielby. Oxford: Blackwell, 2001: 53–63.
McPherson, James Alan. "'Beam Me Up, Scotty.'" *Prime Times: Writers on Their Favorite TV Shows.* Edited by Douglas Bauer. New York: Three Rivers Press, 2004.
Mihailovich. "Foreign tourists get set to play with cheaper dollars." *Las Vegas Business Press,* 2 April 2004.
Miles, Steven, and Malcolm Miles. *Consuming Cities.* New York: Palgrave, 2004.
Miller, Toby. *The Avengers.* London: BFI, 1997.
Porter, Jennifer E. "To Boldly Go: *Star Trek* Convention Attendance as Pilgrimage." *"Star Trek" and Sacred Ground: Explorations of "Star Trek," Religion, and American Culture.* Edited by Jennifer E. Porter and Darcee L. McLaren. Albany: State University of New York Press, 1999: 245–270.
Reader, Ian, and Tony Walter, eds. *Pilgrimage in Popular Culture.* London: Macmillan, 1993.
Roberts, Robin. "Performing Science Fiction: Television, Theatre, and Gender in *Star Trek: The Experience.*" *Extrapolation* 42, no. 4 (2001): 340–356.

Rodman, Gilbert B. *Elvis after Elvis: The Posthumous Career of a Living Legend.* London: Routledge, 1996.

Rothman, Hal. *Neon Metropolis: How Las Vegas Started the Twenty-First Century.* London and New York: Routledge, 2003.

Sandvoss, Cornel. *Fans: The Mirror of Consumption.* London: Polity Press, 2005.

Urry, John. *Consuming Places.* London: Routledge, 1995.

Whiteside, Lee. "The Borg Invade Las Vegas." *ConNotations* 14, no. 2, (April/May 2004): 1, 9.

13

A Very *Trek* Christmas

Goodbye

KAREN ANIJAR

40 Years on the Final Frontier

I have been watching *Star Trek* ever since the first episode aired in 1966. The first ballet I ever choreographed was based on *Star Trek* (it was awful). I wrote my dissertation on Trekker teachers. My first book came out of my dissertation (again, *Star Trek*). I thought it was going to be a simple task writing a chapter about the *Trek* franchise at this very critical moment in history. I was wrong.

In this chapter I use an autobiographical form of narrative intertextualized with informal interviews with family and close friends (something I have referred to in the past as "kitchen table methodology"). I also utilize what I loosely term as net narratives emanating from a variety of sources in the public domain (which include blogs, bulletin board postings and Web pages). In addition, the popular media (newsletters, newspapers, magazines, commercials and television) acts as a text. All names except for my own and those of family members have been given pseudonyms. The *Star Trek* franchise is floundering (as was I trying to write this chapter) and is trying to find a way to make itself appear relevant.

Captain's Log Star Date 11111.88: The Tooth Fairy May Cometh

I have a broken tooth on the right side of my mouth. Sometimes, it hurts a great deal. On other occasions it does not bother me at all. When it hurts, my husband (Scott) says in Vulcan monotone, "Well, Karen you better get it checked." And, I respond, "Yeah, okay, soon." I am terrified of dentists.

Josh (my son) is home from graduate school for the holidays. I notice his teeth are stained, the last thing he wants to do is to go to the dentist, something I do understand. Scott does not want to go to the dentist, either. "Ugh," I grunt and shut myself into a room that is quiet. There is no television; the only things are a bunch of catalogs and magazines. I pick up the Florida AAA monthly member guide, which is a magazine about cars, roads and special events in Florida, and then I see an article on Starship Dental. I look up the Website and e-mail the commander about insurance and go ask Josh if he wants to go to get his teeth done. There is no response. He is sleeping on the sofa. I will ask Caroline (my stepdaughter, who is a freshman at Arizona State University) when she comes home from a date or Scott when he comes home this evening. I have to finish this chapter and so many thoughts surrounding *Star Trek* are flooding in and out of my mind that I need to focus on something. Maybe I will focus on Starship Dental.

When Josh, Scott and Caroline were all together at the dinner table I ask, "Want to go to Starship Dental? You know the place that was in *Trekkies* (1998)." We all agree to make appointments, but then decide it is too much effort. But, my tooth still hurts; I make an appointment at the dentist near our house. He asks, "What are you writing about?" I tell him *Star Trek.* He tells me he loves the program. He does not wear a Starfleet uniform but he does have a picture of Jesus watching over his dental chair.[1]

Vignette Two: The Holiday Gifts and the Trek *Tree*

Chrismahanakwanzakah[2] arrived and everyone is home: Scott and I do not believe in organized religion. The holidays for Scott are an excuse to consume. Joshua is anticonsumerist and does not buy presents, Caroline has been busy for the past month buying and wrapping gifts. I did not protest the Christmas tree (even though it makes my Jewish genes quiver). Scott must have seen me wince at the thought of *it* in my house: "Karen, look at the Seven of Nine and the *NCC-1701* ornaments." I groan.

I have to finish the *Star Trek* chapter soon and I still need to focus on something, maybe it will be on the tree. "If there is a tree I have to buy gifts," I thought to myself. What could I possibly buy for Scott? It is not as if we are lacking in anything at all. If anything we have far more than we could ever want and certainly way more than we need. Focus on the chapter: don't think about presents. But, I can't focus. I log on to e-Bay. I think to myself: *What if I buy something* "Trek"? *After all I need to write this chapter! I could write it on weird* "Trek" *things people sell on e-Bay.*" I order a Captain Picard tie, and a Borg bank. Then I find William Shatner's authentic (faux) kidney stone. Resistance would be futile, it is only $2.99! Scott is a pediatric cardiologist. Kidney, heart, both are body parts, close enough—not perfect but a pretty good match. Too bad they don't have Picard's prosthetic heart for sale. What does it mean to buy an authentic faux kidney? Yes, I know hyper-reality.... tell me something new that I haven't lived before.

Vignette Three: The New Show

Sitting at my computer, looking at *Trek* Websites—which are both mourning and celebrating the end of *Trek*—I come across a Website which discussed *Star Trek: New Voyages*:

> We believe in the type of future envisioned by Gene Roddenberry. "New Voyages" is our vision of *Star Trek*. A *Star Trek* set in the 23rd century and created in the 21st. It's a *Star Trek* with a familiar look, a familiar crew, but something new, and we think, something special.
> There are other fan films—some want to imitate the 60s' look and feel of the show—some are focused on other parts of Roddenberry's universe, and all are made with love and passion.
> However, *New Voyages* is not the *Trek* of the 60s. It is the *Trek* of the future; a *Trek* that looks modern and flows as fast as any action adventure show on TV today.
> *New Voyages* was created in April of 2003 by James Cawley and Jack Marshall. Our goal is to tell stories that fall within the 4th and 5th year of the five year mission. These "short films" continue the original 5-year mission of the *Enterprise* and are produced currently at a rate of 2 per year. As such we consider each short film an "event" not merely a new episode of a weekly TV show. Enjoy the show—and enjoy the science fiction! [Anonymous, n.d.].

I call Scott, I call Caroline, and I wake Josh up. I download the different components of the episodes that are available online. I watch the show. Nobody else really seems that excited about it. I discuss who is involved but it falls on deaf ears. Scott promises he will watch the show; two weeks later he has not. I chatter (trying to prod someone to watch the show): "Do you know Walter Koenig is on the show? And, that Gene Rodenberry's son is involved?" I call David, my writing partner and coeditor of a Web based journal entitled *Public Resistance*. He is far more into *Star Wars* and really does not get *Star Trek*.

So, I try to watch it myself, and I try to enjoy it ... but, I cannot. I call out again: "Does anyone want to see the show?" Nobody does. I understand: "Like the *Star Wars* films, the *Star Trek* franchise doesn't have a place in the new century. "Bye bye, Kirk and Spock and Bones and the guys, bye bye new pretenders. For a brief while anyway, it's been ... fun" (Lileks, 2005: 53). As I live in a theocratic fascist state, even the xenophobic program *Enterprise*[3] seems like a quaint artifact from a bygone era.

Warp Forward to April 2006: A Trek *Interlude*

George Takei came out of the closet and made an appearance on *Will and Grace.* *Will and Grace* stars Eric McCormack, who was also in the movie *Free Enterprise* (1999), about several *Trek* geeks who become friends with William Shatner (and his attendant overbearing ego). William Shatner (and his attendant overbearing ego as parody) stars as Denny Crane on *Boston Legal* along with Rene Auberjonois (Odo), and Jeri Ryan (Seven of Nine) will guest star on the season finale. Many of the episodes reference *Star Trek* (the show often feels like a veritable intergenerational *Trek* fest featuring actors from all the *Trek* series). For example, on one episode Denny Crane takes his friend and fellow attorney, Alan Shore (played by James Spader), to Nimmo Bay in Canada, where they spend the night in a cabin. Alan reads a book on sea lice and explains to Denny that the lice are called "cling-ons." Denny queries: "Did you say 'Klingons?'" William Shatner (who has won an Emmy for his performance on *Boston Legal*) still does Priceline commercials. On occasion former costar Leonard Nimoy has appeared with Shatner on Priceline ads.

Nimoy recently appeared *sans* Shatner in a commercial for Aleve (an arthritis drug) which premiered during the Superbowl. In the Aleve spot Nimoy can't make the Vulcan hand sign (*it hurts him*). He has to appear at a *Trek* convention. Nimoy's agent tells him to try Aleve. He does, and can make the Vulcan live long and prosper sign (to thunderous applause from Trekkers at the mock convention).

As I contemplate recent *Trek* alumni enterprises, and what they might mean to *Trek* fans, Joshua calls me from Massachusetts. "Mom, they are making a new *Trek* movie, it was just announced, go look it up!" I did. But several days later it turned out that at least part of the rumor which made its way into several news sources was not entirely true. The incorrect portion: the movie will be a prequel featuring younger versions of Kirk and Spock. The correct part of the news story is that J.J. Abrams, creator of the television series *Lost* and director of the movie *Mission: Impossible III* (2006), will be involved. The television series *Mission: Impossible* featured Leonard Nimoy who replaced academy award winner (and old friend of my mother) Martin Landau. Landau turned down the role of Spock for the original *Star Trek* series. I am not really playing a form of six degrees from Kevin Bacon game, rather all of this strip-like self-preferentiality in which the entire text and context of *Star Trek* is grounded in nothing beyond *Trek* itself further blurs the distinction between reality and hyper-reality while concurrently making nostalgic a future which has already passed. Self-preferentiality becomes another commodity fetish in a long capitalist chain of objectification.

One culture jammer has suggested, "Where critique is no longer a possibility, parody is always an alternative response." But, then again, what happens when parody itself is also thrown into the commodified matrix and marketed as a product such as William Shatner Inc? The blurring of the boundaries between Shatner and Kirk transforms the person into a product of mass consumption to be bought and sold in a world where everybody and everything becomes associated with one brand name or another. Shatner has his William Shatner DVD club (for sci-fi videos) and the *TekWar* series (among other enterprises) and neither are associated (in the Trekker imaginary) so much with Shatner as with James T. Kirk.

Spring came (and I am still not finished with the chapter). The documentary *How William Shatner Changed the World* premiered on the History Channel featuring Shatner examining the ways *Star Trek* technology inspired real-life innovators. At the same time TV Nation premiered *Shatner Living in TV Land* featuring Shatner singing (including his song "Has-Been"). I think back to Shatner's 2005 *Invasion Iowa* reality television program shot in Captain Kirk's future birthplace of Riverside, Iowa (where every year a festival is held in Kirk's honor). The location itself is a hyper-real version of future nostalgia, a terrain in which faded and fading future simulacra, "nostalgia for nostalgia's sake, without a deep sense of history" (Wang, 2002: 669), or a sense of any history at all, intermingle with a sense of loss for what never did exist.

In *Invasion Iowa*, Shatner "pretends" that he is making a science fiction movie and uses local townspeople for different parts, neglecting to tell them that *Invasion Iowa* is a reality television show and the process of making the movie is both the text and context. It is funny. The townspeople (the butt of the joke) seem genuinely nice in comparison with the Hollywood types, both during the filming of the ersatz film and after the ruse is revealed. Ruse is the operative term here since reality television can be seen as a form of democratized television (anyone can be a star) but it is illusory in the same way we live under the illusion of the incredibly empty signifier "freedom" in the United States.

Everything Old Is New Again

New Voyages, the fan based project (see also chapters 10 and 11 in this volume), boasts "authentic *Star Trek* luminaries" such as Grace Lee Whitney, D.C. Fontana, George Takei, Ron Moore, and David Gerrold, among others. I think back to the authentic William Shatner faux kidney stone

I bought for Scott for Christmas. As life, art, and fantasy become intertwined, and all three are increasingly the products of market researchers and corporate planners. Fantasy goes on the market (Fjellman, 1992). Baudrillard wrote (and I am paraphrasing here) that the moment we invoke the authentic we already exist in a world of simulacra. The locus of authenticity simulates something else, as if there ever was something else, a place, a time, a tradition that remains unmediated and uncommodified. Choice in the market place of existence becomes nothing more or less than the range of commodities available. The fake authentic seen in the episodes of *New Voyages* (that I screened) begins with "brought to you in living color on NBC" (with the peacock), attempting to recapture the moment in time in which the original *Star Trek* was produced (the production company is even called retro-productions). Messages of authenticity and legitimization (after all, the show is approved by the Rodenberry family) are part of a "historic imaginary" in which the references create and sustain an association with an idealized past (the fake authentic). Time itself becomes a commodity transformed, imagined, and sold. It is no different than living here in Orlando in the wonderful world of Disney with its Main Street USA. It is no different than the hordes of SUV, truck and Suburban drivers on the expressway pretending that the oil supply is not going to dry up.

Part Two: Star Trek *Goes to War and It Is a Lot of Fun, Too*

I went inside the mountain at NORAD, one of the most top secret defense locations in the Strategic Air Command in Colorado. And they were, at that time, in the process of redesigning their situation room to look and feel more like the bridge of the *Enterprise*:

> I'm a *DS9* type myself. The Neocon ideology seems to be fairly similar to the Dominion's, to me, at least: maintain permanent hegemony. Substitute "Iraq" for "Cardassia" and "God" for "The Founders" and George W. Bush would have made a fine Vorta.
>   The question is, why aren't the Bushies interested in creating a cloned Jem'Hadar army? You can't be a paranoid empire without the cloned army, damnit.
>
>   —*Star Trek* fan

> *Star Trek* is a picture of military life ... such a life is ordinary and permanent for its members [Ross, 2006].

Every day on television I can watch approximately eleven hours of *Star Trek* (not counting the movies). Two cable networks provide the majority of "*Trek* time"; the first is Spike Television, "the first television network for men" (Spike made the *Invasion Iowa* program), and the second is G4, the video game network. Both networks seek to market to the same demographic: 18–35 year old males. G4 has created a new-old *Star Trek* using "classic" *Trek* episodes with interactive formatting (in an attempt to make *Trek* attractive to the sought after demographic). Although the demographic is sought after for marketing, ephebiphobia (fear of youth) has reached a crescendo, becoming a full-blown media panic. "Images of 'ordinary' teenagers besieging grown-up havens are everywhere.... Today's ephebiphobia is the latest installment of a history of bogus moral panics targeting unpopular subgroups to obscure an unsettling reality: Our worst social crisis is middle-Americans own misdirected fear" (Males, 2004). Ron Powers in an article for *Atlantic Monthly* entitled "The Apocalypse of Adolescence" (2002) writes: "Violence by 'ordinary teens' from 'ordinary communities' constitutes a 'new mutation in the evolution of the murderous American adolescent.... while we sleep, go about our business, leave our doors unlocked, children are prowling the landscape with knives."

Michel Foucault (1980) wrote, "bodies are the battlefield," something that may well be a double entendre in a war without end (Bush's war on terror) combined with our hatred for America's young people. The No Child Left Behind Act contains a provision, if you attend a public high school, that your school system is required to turn over your private information to the U.S. military unless you opt out. Most people (parents, children and teachers) are unaware that they can "opt out," or that the military is using schools to recruit and to maintain a database of 30 million 16- to 25-year-olds. Opting out requires a form, signed by a guardian or a parent, stating that you do not want the military to have your private information. The army specifically targets schools in poor areas (both urban and rural) with disproportionate numbers of recruits being Blacks and Latinos. White households with incomes over $60,000 are underrepresented in recruitment efforts. Military recruiters outnumber college recruiters in inner city high schools (Laporte and Boyle, 2006).

America's Army is a free online game with over "6.5 million registered players" (Vargas, 2006: A-1). The game is being used by the U.S. military as a recruiting tool. A version of *America's Army* will be available on cell phones this summer (Vargas, 2006: A-1). The game has been such a hit that the Army "has recently gone one step further with the game, organizing video-game parties around the country ... the Army estimates that nearly a third of all young people of prime recruitment age have been exposed to it" (Downing, 2004), the same demographics G4 targets in its marketing efforts:

"The technology in games has facilitated a revolution in the art of warfare," says David Bartlett, the former chief of operations at the Defense Modeling and Simulation Office, a high-level office within the Defense Department and the focal point for computer-generated training at the Pentagon.... Lt. Col. Scott Sutton, director of the technology division at Quantico Marine Base, where the mock-up M16s are used, says soldiers in this generation "probably feel less inhibited, down in their primal level, pointing their weapons at somebody." That, in effect, "provides a better foundation for us to work with," he adds.... Retired Marine Col. Gary W. Anderson, former chief of staff of the Marine Corps Warfighting Lab, agrees. And he takes it a step further: Today's soldiers, having grown up with first-person shooter games long before they joined the military, are the new Spartans, he says [Vargas, 2006: A-1].

Spartans were designed to serve the state, quintessential soldiers trained in endurance and conformity to unquestioningly obey orders without critique or ethical deliberation; they "just do it!" I recall something a Trekker who was also a teacher said to me way back in 1993 (while I was writing my dissertation):

> Of course, I respect Starfleet, and believe in it.... Yes, the future is military. There is nothing wrong with the military. It is a world where respect prevails, and where everyone can rise to his or her ability. But, to make it happen you need the tools to drive the future; that is where technology comes in.[4]

Star Trek 2.0: *And Now For Your Proto-Retro* Trek *Commercial*

YouTube is a user generated site for distributing video content. Recently G4 created a partnership with youtube.com to market its commercials for *Star Trek 2.0*. YouTube began featuring a short promotional clip for *Star Trek 2.0*, a new series that features action figures reenacting classic episodes of the 1960s sci-fi series in a contemporary urban setting, infused with irreverent, interactive commentary. Dubbed "*Star Trek* Karaoke," the clip is currently being housed in the top spot on YouTube's featured videos section on its home page, bordered by an adjacent "provided by G4" logo (Shelids, 2006). Three other commercials have now been uploaded. What is meant by contemporary urban settings? Well, Spock is a hip-hop rap artist. White appropriation of rap music and black signifiers has been well documented. I show the commercials to Scott. I ask him what he thinks. His face contorts a bit at the sight of Spock speaking in a hip hop vernacular. Urban in the science fiction vernacular is racially coded. The urban sci-fi future uses images of decomposition (literally moving the jungle into the city). Machinery and computers in the techno-bleak landscape interface and intertwine with metaphors of the primeval jungle. A jungle where "Asians, Hispanics, Blacks and Eastern

Europeans swarm the streets; most Caucasian Americans seem to have departed for off-world colonies. A paramilitary police force maintains order and enormous corporate headquarters dominate the skyline" (Lev, 1998: 30).

The setting may have changed but the ideology remains. Predators, particularly young predators and mutant predators, wander the street preying on anyone "normal" who should happen to stumble into these forbidding zones. Given our intense hatred for young people the entire generational cohort of postmillennials are the first generation in history to be positioned as "mutants," as "predatory," as "inhuman" and "devolved" (Giroux, 2001: 92). As one young man explained on his Web page:

> Modern-day America is a bad place to be young. We have an increasing multitude of insulting age-laws confining youth to second-class citizenship: curfew laws, graduated driver's licenses, age-limits on buying nicotine gum?! We also have courts enforcing a double-standard of justice. Our whole society seethes with hatred for the young. I can count a hundred movies I've seen where an adult hits a child or teenager and the youth simply accepts it rather than hitting back or pressing charges.... Rapists who prey on children are cheered-on by porno mags (*Barely Legal*), rock stars (Queen, George Michael, Sonic Youth, The Cherry-Popping Daddies), and novelists (Joseph Hanson, Vladimir Nabokov). In supposedly Christian churches, preachers impress upon their followers that children are to be viewed as property of their parents who deserve physical punishment if they disobey....

Young people are far more like X-Men than they are like the stalwart crew of the *Enterprise*:

> For many, it is hard not to identify with the plight of the X-Men. They were a group of tightly-knit individuals, made outcasts by a society bent on hate and consumption, who employed their advanced powers to defend the marginalized and continue the struggle for justice. Likewise, the members of FMTM [post-rock band From Monument to Masses] possess their own superpowers. They too, use them to encourage and fuel and inspire those who fight against inequality, exploitation, and hate [Barreto, 2005].

The X-Men, who were born as mutations, "as if the sins of the fathers had been visited upon the children," negotiate a world that hates and fears them (Morrison, 2003: 1). The X-Men's world is apocalyptic, a battlefield in which homosapiens disparage and attempt to destroy their mutant progeny (homosuperior), who eventually become outcast from the homosapiens' oppressive social order. As Ehrenrich (2000: 5) noted:

> What has happened, in the last thirty years, to separate the idealistic young so radically from their responsible liberal elders, if not from civilization itself? ... Thirty years ago, the ... young might be denounced as spoiled

products of affluence, but they still represented "our future." Today, kids in general ... are targeted as "superpredators" and gang members, subject to curfews, anti-gang injunctions, high school drug war harassment, imprisonment along with adults, even execution the dark apocalyptic vibe: a society that destroys its own young, whether by poverty or beatings, is doomed.

As another young man explained on his blog:

> There is a war on America's youth. Our generation has personally witnessed and experienced the birth, maturation, manipulation and degradation of all of us who were born out of injustice and adopted as the quintessential voice to those for whom justice and equality has turned a blind eye. Like government, religion and all other institutions, hijacked by a corporate machine engaged in a war against all of Humanity, bent on dividing us from other cultures, fueling our mistrust and hatred towards one another, and ultimately controlling us through fear. Fear is a weapon of mass destruction in which the young are considered collateral damage.

The generation with the short attention span are the new "Spartans," the generation which has begun to recognize that class warfare is being waged in our culture. All young people are an age cohort "dispossessed of a future" (Giroux, 2001: 92). As Matthew Klickstein (2003) so eloquently wrote for an Alter Net article:

> I'm fine, thanks. Actually, on second thought, I'm petrified. I'm 21 years old, in three months I will be graduating college, and I have absolutely no idea what the future holds in store for me. Oh, yeah: also, we're going to War. Geepers—before, it was a matter of finding a reasonable job that I could both enjoy and contribute my skills, passion and time. Now, well, maybe I'll be dead before I have to worry about finding my first "real-life" paycheck. In case you were wondering, America, my joints are in great stress pain, ... I've been throwing up ... panic attacks are rampant, and drug use is a much more abundant part of my life these days.

This brings me to the point of this chapter: the *Star Trek* franchise in its current incarnation does not make much sense:

> ... the show was born in the LBJ years. Fans have cut *Trek* so much slack the shears are dull. They accept that the communicators of the future are larger than modern cell phones. They accept that most species in the galaxy speak English and look like us, aside from odd nasal prostheses. They accept almost anything—even the decision to let William Shatner direct the fifth movie. And most accept the end. Perhaps it's time to set it aside for a while. *Star Trek* has always mirrored the era in which it was made, and perhaps we live in times whose stark fears don't really translate well [Lileks, 2005: 52].

Jason, one of my son's friends, flatly noted: "I cannot think about going to the stars when I do not think I am going to live long enough or have enough money to see a glacier before we are all fried." Another of Joshua's friends remarked, "*Star Trek* is really a white man's game."

The Spartan-Disposed Ritalin Generation Enters the Symbolic Capital Market?

> I didn't know what I was watching, I was flipping channels and then boom here is this bizarre border with text moving in every direction. I didn't know where to direct my focus. Should I be watching the show? Or the counter that tells the number of times that Uhura walks by or Spock uses the neck pinch. There was chat room like thread at the bottom; I found the whole thing fucking stupid. *Star Trek* can be made into a game and that game could be campy and funny reflecting the time in which it was made. It could be great cheese. Repackaging it this way well I think it is trying to be sort of quasi Japanese anime (but that is apocalyptic) it does not go well with *Trek*. All of that on the screen at once ... well, I was rather scared.
>
> —Joshua Anijar

G4's addition of interactive formats, including a live chat (in which viewers' comments will run across the screen much like a 24 hour news show), an accumulating tally of *Trek* statistics (highlighting *Star Trek* quirks and plot devices), as well as something known as the Spock Market:

> A stock market simulation that turns the experience of watching *Star Trek* Classic into a real-time, interactive game. During the airing of each show, viewers who register on www.g4tv.com/trek2.0 are given "credits" with which to buy and sell stock in "companies," commodities and characters associated with the show. Stocks include:
> - Captain Kirk (ticker symbol JTK)
> - Spock (SPK)
> - Uhura (UHU)
> - Dr. McCoy (MDM)
> - Nurse Chapel (CHP)
> - Sulu (SLU)
> - Scotty (SCT)
> - Starship Phaser and Photon (PHP)
> - United Federation of Planets (FED)
> A real-time stock ticker running on the right-hand side of the TV screen shows the gains and losses of each stock as they are affected by the events in each episode—and by the increase or decrease in demand for that stock on the part of other players [Krutzler, 2006].

Practicing hyper intensified capitalism on the real or symbolic (cultural) market in itself is laden with a specific yet invisible matrix of privilege. Who plays the stock market, after all? It is not the Black population, who represent only a tiny fraction more than 11 percent of all workers (but they do represent nearly half of the prison population). Maybe *Trek* is a baby boomer or Gen X game and a white one at that, since that is whose posts I read in the chat rooms.

Boldly Going Nowhere at All

Many years ago psychologist Robert J. Lifton wrote that Americans are far more like survivors of Hiroshima than they "care to realize ... living ... in a world dominated by Holocaust past, contemporary and anticipated" (Lifton, 1967: 361); he coined the phrase "psychic numbing" to describe what he saw as a profound cultural shift, a chronic social condition mandating a complete reorientation of the "self." Admittedly, Lifton's thesis essentializes the complexity of the post-World War Two universe in which the fragile veneer of business as usual betrays the apocalyptic anxiety simmering just below the surface. Suffice to say cataclysm has become a chronic cultural condition, a tradition or form of "ontological hysteria: a prolonged fear of imminent annihilation [and] panic over the insecurity of existence" (Giroux, 2001: 197).

Flaschenpost, a metaphor coined by Adorno, signifies a message thrown into a bottle for future generations to open. The Genie has been let out of the bottle, and the message that has been sent is the result of almost 60 years of nuclear knowledge, combined with the ever-present Western religious subtext of the apocalypse. Exacerbating this further is a pronounced "generation gap" occurring in the text and context of how various age cohorts negotiate the (post)apocalyptic terrain. Yet for the postmillennial generation who came into adulthood as we entered into the "new normal" the universe seems tinged with horrific absurdity. In the transformation from the "unthinkable to the banal" (Brown, 1988), apocalypse has become something normalized, just one more hazard of life in the twenty-first century. There has been a shift in consciousness. The *Star Trek* franchise is out of step, out of touch. *Star Trek* speaks to a modern narrative of progress that may never have existed but certainly can no longer exist.[5]

I was driving with Scott in the Arizona desert; it was a beautiful evening. I asked him if he wanted to live forever. He said "No!" He said no because he feels things are only going to get harder and harder and the world is going to be unrecognizable in two generations. John (a friend of Joshua's) said forcefully, "There is nothing left. We sit on the ruins of this empire." Thomas, another young man, feels that:

> While they will sit there and smirk and lie ... using Orwellian language like "Healthy Forests" to promote clear cutting, and "Clear skies" to promote more pollution, "No Child Left Behind" to promote not giving schools what they need ... I fear for the state of the world, it isn't one event that's causing everything ... it's the loss of civil liberties, it's the rape of the

environment in the name of profit, it's the wholesale slaughter of people across the world for corporate greed, it's the rollback of a woman's right to choose to have a baby or not. Is this the end of the world? Probably!

An anonymous (student) blogger writes:

> The earth shakes in Asia and a generation of children is lost. The wind flails America and a city is destroyed. A giant wave rises in the Indian Ocean and whole islands are drowned along with swathes of coastland.... Bush and his cronies (the four horsemen of the apocalypse) lied us into an unnecessary, illegal war on false pretenses. Administration apologists will tell you that there's no better place to live, that "the U.S. is a beacon of light in a dark and twisted world." Bushists do nothing but darken said beacon of light. What meaning do the ideals of freedom and justice hold when our leadership continually lies to us and to the world? It is Orwellian to suggest that the "perception management" campaign—a fancy term for lying—unleashed by the Bush administration somehow serves to strengthen our democracy. Our freedom is the right to be lied to; justice is ... by Presidential fiat, not a legal system. These things are not supposed to happen in a democracy.... The sea is turning to acid, the air is choking us, the polar ice caps are melting. Famine, pestilence and plague used to be dread words from the Bible; now they are everyday events. Bush is going to probably kill us all anyway.

Anachronisms on the Final Frontier

Star Trek was created:

> during a time when America was consumed by the Cold War, a time when humankind seemed bent on destroying itself, a little optimism went a long way. At a 25th anniversary celebration for the original series, Roddenberry, who passed away in 1991, had this to say: "It speaks to some basic human needs: that there is a tomorrow, it's not all going to be over with a big splash and a bomb, that the human race is improving, that we have things to be proud of as humans" [NPR, 2002].

Contrast that with:

> The 2005 Fall television show line-up presents a whole series of programs with dense worlds of secrets and threats, in which our protagonists are seemingly the only barrier between everyday life and Armageddon. Moreover, each also centered on a complex, dark federal government.... Aesthetically, each show offered a grim, doom-laden atmosphere of darkened rooms and grisly deaths [Kompare, 2005].

Reality echoing both Wittgenstein and Niels Bohr is just a word in a particular game of science. Reality, echoing Janis Joplin, is just another word for nothing left to lose. There is nothing left to lose because our children live in a time where apocalyptic fears translate into a cataclysmic consciousness. As some of the young people I have known their entire lives have said to me:

> The American dream is dead. We are in the age of corporate control, a soulless entity that does not need people to survive. What the capitalists need are mindless drones who are dead but don't even know it.
>
> Ever since I was a child everything that I have seen had to do with the end of the world, teenage mutant ninja turtles, The Transformers, *ID4*, He-men and She-Ra and of course the X-men, and *The Matrix*, but not *Star Trek.*
>
> We desperately desire a different tomorrow, one that we can't fully articulate. I am not sure if I will ever make it to 30 or 40. Although I still fantasize about change... But, I cannot mourn for a future that is not mine to have. Space travel? *Star Trek?* Ummm, how are you going to get the fuel? My reality is George Bush and New Orleans and what does that future hold?

I finish this chapter where I started: in the dentist's chair. I was having my gums examined by a specialist who asked me what I was writing. "Something on *Star Trek*," I answered. He responded, "I used to watch it all the time growing up. Seems kind of ridiculous now; we aren't going to reach the stars. We are not going to solve our problems: not everything is a techno-fix." *Star Trek* used to feel like what might happen in the future. I guess I have grown up and as a parent with four daughters my incredible lack of optimism is really sad. Roddenberry did not get it right. We boomers really messed it all up. I think as he scaled my irritated gums, *What is left for the* "Enterprise" *franchise? Well, what is left for any of us?*

Notes

1. As I argued in *Teaching Toward the 24th Century: "Star Trek" as Social Curriculum* (2000) there is a synthesis of the technological and the spiritual which has a complex enigmatic relationship with the rational.

2. Rumor has it that the term was originally coined by Richard Branson. I have found evidence of the term being used but not who created it.

3. *Enterprise*, it seems, was the least favorite of the *Star Trek* shows, according to all with whom I spoke. Comments were often harsh: "urinating on Rodenberry's grave and fornicating with his corpse," "I hated the portrayal of the crack whore Vulcan and what the fuck happened to the Vulcans? I thought they were our friends." Others were more thoughtful, discussing "the lack of direction just bumbling around some planets and then when the time stuff was brought in you knew they were desperate, also the Rod Stewart theme song—please ... I do not recognize the mythical universe I loved."

4. *Star Trek*'s links with the U.S. military are brought into stark relief on the "*Trek* to the Troops" Website (trektothetroops.com) founded by Christopher Mulrooney. Mulrooney is a member of the Arizona National Guard. He spent a year in Iraq and after returning home he began "*Trek* to the Troops," whose goal is to bring *Star Trek* personalities and a bit of fun to our *Trek*-loving troops overseas. Understanding the military legacy of *Star Trek*, they have embarked on creating a *Trek* tour in Iraq. Fans in the military are appreciative; for example, one letter on the site stated:

I'm a sergeant first class in the active army; 19 yr vet of desert storm and went to OIF the first 15 months of this conflict as an engineer platoon sergeant. I love my job, and I am a huge sci-fi fan, and *Star Trek* fan. Honestly I think it was *Star Trek* that gave me the sense of being part of something like the US Army, I watched it when I was a kid and even now, I'm now trying to get my eight year old to watch *Enterprise* with me. You guy's are doing a great job and thank you for your service to OUR nation! It really makes you feel good that there are fellow Trekkies out there that appreciate our troops and love *Star Trek* too. (trektothetroops.com—note: I corrected the spelling errors.)

5. The modernist narrative, I believe, came to an end in World War Two (in the ovens of Auschwitz and Dachau and with the dropping of the atomic bomb on Hiroshima and Nagasaki). We began to realize that the logical end of a technology that moves ever forward could well be genocidal. It was at that time that an apocalyptic consciousness emerged. Most young people I spoke with do believe the world will end in their lifetimes. And not for religious reasons. But they accept it and go on. Among the young people I spoke to, who also watch *Star Trek* at all, thought *Deep Space Nine* was the only *Trek* with meaning: "I liked the characters and the conflict." "It wasn't the oh we are so happy *Star Trek*, or the *Star Trek* with Captain Kirk fucking everything in the Universe or Captain Picard giving some lame paternalistic speech about justice and goodness and how humans have evolved.... Sisko kicked ass and the themes with the dark apocalyptic vibe felt more realistic."

Works Cited

Anijar, K. *Teaching Toward the 24th Century: "Star Trek" as Social Curriculum.* New York: Falmer Press, 2000.
Anonymous. *"Star Trek: New Voyages."* http://www.newvoyages.com (n.d.).
Barreto, M. "From Monument to Masses." *WireTap,* January 10, 2005. http://www.alternet.org/wiretap/20945.
Bennelli Brothers Blog. http://bennellibrothers.com/blog/archives/2005/03/william_shatner_1.php (2005).
Brown, J. "A is for Atom, B is for Bomb: Civil Defense in American Public Education, 1948–1963." *The Journal of American History* 75, no. 1 (1988): 68–90.
Downing, J. "Army to Potential Recruits: Wanna play?" *Seattle Times,* December 7, 2004. http://seattletimes.nwsource.com/html/localnews/2002111412_wargames07e.html.
Fjellman, Stephen. *Vinyl Leaves: Walt Disney World and America.* New York, Westview Press, 1992.
Giroux, H. "Mis/Education and Zero Tolerance: Disposable Youth and the Politics of Domestic Militarization." *boundary 2* 28, no. 3 (2001): 61–94.
Klickstein, M. "The Things We Fear." *WireTap,* March 17, 2003. http://www.alternet.org/story/15389/ (accessed June 4, 2006).
Kompare, D. "We Are So Screwed: Invasion TV." *Flow: A Critical Forum on Television and Media Culture* 3, no. 6 (2005). http://jot.communication.utexas.edu/flow/?jot=view&id=1304.
Krutzler, S. "G4 Planning *Star Trek 2.0* Interactive Viewing, Plus 'Uncut' Marathons." *Features* (2006). http://www.trekweb.com/articles/2006/03/08/440f8315dc674.shtml.
Laporte, J., and M. Boyle. "'War on Terror' from a race/class perspective." (2006). http://www.csun.edu/Faculty/Sheena.Malhotra/GRCS%20Files/Final %20Projects/military-recruitment.htm.
Lev, P. "Whose Future? *Star Wars, Alien,* and *Blade Runner.*" *Literature Film Quarterly* 26, no. 1 (1998): 30–38.
Lifton, R. *Death in Life: Survivors of Hiroshima.* New York: Random House, 1967.
Lileks, James. "*Star Trek* Warps to an End." *American Enterprise* (June 2005): 52–53.
Males, M. "Coming of Age in America." *Youth Today* (February 2004). http://www.home.earthlink.net/~mmales/yt-mead.htm.
Morrison, G. *The New X-Men* 123. "Testament." New York: Marvel Comics, 2003.

NPR. "*Star Trek* Present at the Creation." http://www.npr.org/programs/ morning/fea tures/patc/startrek/ (2003).

Powers, R. "The Apocalypse of Adolescence." *The Atlantic Monthly.* (2002) http://www.the atlantic.com/ doc/prem/200203/powers.

Ross, K. "The Fascist Ideology of *Star Trek*: Militarism, Collectivism, & Atheism." *Friesian.* http://www.friesian.com/trek.htm (2006).

Shelids, M. "G4 Partners with YouTube." http://www.mediaweek.com/mw/news/inter active/article_display.jsp?vnu_content_id =1002276962 (accessed April 14, 2006).

Vargas, J.A. "Virtual reality prepares soldiers for real war young warriors say video shooter games helped hone their skills." *Washington Post,* February 14, 2006, A-1.

Wang, Ban. "Love at Last Sight: Nostalgia, Commodity, and Temporality in Wang Anyi's *Song of Unending Sorrow.*" *position: east asia cultures critique* 10, no. 3 (2002): 669–694.

Notes on Contributors

Karen Anijar is associate professor in curriculum and cultural studies at Arizona State University in Tempe, Arizona. She also serves on the faculty of bioethics and is a fellow in the Center for the Study of Religion and Conflict. Her three most recent books are *Teaching Towards the 24th Century: The Social Curriculum of "Star Trek"*; *Science Fiction Curriculum: Cyborg Teachers and Youth Cultures* (with John Weaver and Toby Daspit); and *The Curriculum and the Culture of the Condom* (with Thuy Dao-Jensen). She serves on the international editorial advisory board for both the *Journal of Curriculum and Pedagogy* and the *Journal of Critical Educational Policy Studies*.

Elizabeth D. Blum received her bachelor's degree from the University of Texas in 1991. After several years of working as a paralegal for a prominent Houston law firm, Blum enrolled in the graduate history program at the University of Houston, where she completed both her master's degree (1997) and her doctorate (2000) in American history. Dr. Martin V. Melosi directed her dissertation, entitled "Pink and Green: A Comparative Study of Black and White Women's Environmental Activism in the Twentieth Century." Since graduation, Dr. Blum has been teaching at Troy University in Troy, Alabama. Dr. Blum has several publications, including articles in *Women's Studies*, *Pollution A to Z*, chapters in various works including *To Love the Wind and the Rain*, a volume on African-American environmentalism, and several book reviews. Her book, *God, Gold and Family*, a gendered examination of activism at Love Canal, is currently under contract to the University Press of Kansas.

Wei Ming Dariotis is assistant professor of Asian American studies in the College of Ethnic Studies at San Francisco State University. Her specialties include Asian Americans of mixed heritage and Asian American literature, art and culture. She serves on the boards of the Asian American Theater Company and of iPride—a mixed heritage family organization. She is an advisory board member of Pacific Fusion TV, Kearny Street Workshop, and the Asian American Women Artists Association. Publications include "Developing a Kin-Aesthetic: Mixed Heritage in Asian and Native North American Literature," in *Mixed Race Literatures*, edited by Jonathan Brennan, and "Becoming a Bi-Bi Girl," in *Restoried Selves: Autobiographies of Queer Asian American Activists*, edited by Kevin Kumashiro.

235

Michael S. Duffy completed his PhD in film studies in the Institute of Film and Television Studies, School of American and Canadian Studies, at the University of Nottingham. His thesis focused on the regional acquisition of digital technology, visual effects aesthetics and industrial change in 1990s cinema. His interests include special effects, music video, animation, fan discourse, and East Asian cinema. He has published in *Scope: An Online Journal of Film Studies*.

Justin Everett holds MA and PhD degrees from the University of Oklahoma, where he specialized in composition studies and English Renaissance literature. Both his MA thesis and PhD dissertation focused on Peircian semiotics. He has published papers in *Linguistica Antverpiensia, Reader Response*, and other refereed journals. A textbook, *Dynamic Argument*, is due to be published by Houghton Mifflin in 2006. He has worked for the University of Oklahoma, the University of Central Oklahoma, and Tulsa Community College, and is currently an assistant professor of English at the University of the Sciences in Philadelphia, where he directs the writing center and teaches courses in writing and in science fiction and fantasy literature. He holds memberships in the National Council of Teachers of English, the Modern Language Association, and the Science Fiction Research Association.

Lincoln Geraghty is principal lecturer in film studies and subject leader in media studies in the School of Creative Arts, Film and Media at the University of Portsmouth, with a PhD in American studies from the University of Nottingham. He is on the editorial boards of *The Journal of Popular Culture*; *Atlantis: A Journal of the Spanish Association for Anglo-American Studies*; and the online journal *Reconstruction: Studies in Contemporary Culture*. He has published widely on all series of *Star Trek*, science fiction television, and collecting *Star Wars* toys. His first book, *Living with "Star Trek": American Culture and the "Star Trek" Universe*, was published with I.B. Tauris in 2007 and he is currently coediting a collection with Mark Jancovich entitled *The Shifting Definitions of Genre: Essays on Labelling Films, Television Shows, and Media*.

Ina Rae Hark is professor of English and film studies at the University of South Carolina. She is the editor of *Screening the Male, The Road Movie Book, Exhibition, The Film Reader*, and *Screen Decades: the 1930s*. She has published over forty articles and book chapters and has been concentrating during the last decade on science fiction film and television. She is currently writing the BFI Television Classics volume on *Star Trek*.

Dave Hipple is a PhD student at the University of Reading, researching science fiction on television. He holds a first degree in English from St. Andrews, and MAs from the Open University (education) and Reading (science fiction). He has reverted full-time to academia after a career in university administration.

Angelina I. Karpovich is lecturer in broadcasting and multimedia technology at Brunel University. Her research concerns media fandom and the social issues of media texts and technologies. She no longer cross-dresses as *Star Trek* characters.

Donald E. Palumbo received an AB in English from the University of Chicago and a PhD from the University of Michigan. He is professor of English at East Carolina University, former president of the International Association for the Fantastic in the Arts, member of *The Journal of Popular Culture* and *The Journal of the Fantastic in the Arts* editorial advisory boards, and Film Area chair for the national PCA conference. Formerly advisor to Greenwood's "Contributions to the Study of Science Fiction and Fantasy" and now co-editor of McFarland's "Critical Explorations in Science Fiction and Fantasy" series, he has also published four books and over sixty articles on science fiction and fantasy, existential literature and philosophy, comic books, and film. He is currently completing a book on the monomyth in American science fiction.

Paul Rixon is a senior lecturer in media and cultural studies at Roehampton University, UK. He has published in a number of areas, including the rise of the information city, new media coverage on the Iraq War and, recently, he has published a book entitled *American Television on British Screens: A Story of Cultural Interaction* (Palgrave, 2006).

Sue Short lectures in media and film studies at Birkbeck College–University of London and the University of Hertfordshire. She has published work on a range of SF-related subjects, including two essays on *Star Trek* printed in the academic journals *Foundation* and *Extrapolation*. Her latest book is on the subject of supernatural women in contemporary horror, to be published by Palgrave.

Barbara A. Silliman earned her PhD at the University of Rhode Island, with her dissertation on the propagandistic elements in Frank Herbert's science fiction novel *Dune*. She is active in the Popular Culture Association's Science Fiction and Fantasy and Jewish Studies areas. Her interests also include the application of Carl Jung's psychological theories to literature, film, and television, specifically the science fiction genre. She is a founding member of the Jungian Society for Scholarly Studies and a member of the Delegate Assembly of the Modern Language Association. She currently is coeditor of a text of critical essays on the new *Battlestar Galactica*, to be published in 2008.

Index

Aaron, Hank 102
ABC (TV channel) 49
Abrams, J.J. 221
acting 159–160
adoption 76–79
African Americans 63–79, 82, 97, 181
American Monomyth 190
"Amok Time" 67–68
The Andromeda Strain 34
Apollo 11 18, 157
Apollo 14 17
Archer, Jonathan 53, 55–56
Asian Americans 63–79
Asimov, Isaac 23, 28, 178, 189
Auberjonois, Rene 221
The Avengers 155, 201

B-4 125–135
Babe Ruth 101
Babylon 5 24, 44, 46, 49, 51, 192
Bacon-Smith, Camille 174
Bajorans 63, 76–79, 101–109
Ba'ku 92, 94, 117–135
Bakula, Scott 53
"Balance of Terror" 89
Barclay, Lt. Reg 182–185
Barrett, Duncan 4, 158
Barrett, Michèle 4, 158
Barrett-Roddenberry, Majel 28–30, 64
baseball 5, 55, 100–110
Bashir, Julian 107
Battlestar Galactica 4, 43, 49, 51, 56, 192
Baudrillard, J.S. 223
BBC (TV channel) 6, 26, 153–168
Beastmaster 46
Beauty and the Beast 49
"The Begotten" 76–77
Behr, Ira Steven 50–53
Bell X-1 17
Berman, Rick 2–3, 41–57, 146, 184, 192
Bernardi, Daniel 12, 191
The Bionic Woman 43

The Bitter Tea of General Yen 68
Black, John 12–13
Blade Runner 4, 141, 192
Blake's 7 43–44
Blalock, Jolene 54
Blish, James 32
The Borg 54, 63, 70–76, 102, 118–119, 123, 180, 183
Borg Invasion 4D (ride) 206–207
Boston Legal 221
Bounty (HMS) 134
Braga, Brannon 48–57, 184
"Broken Bow" 54
Buck Rogers 43
Buffy the Vampire Slayer 4, 46, 49
Bukatman, Scott 141, 149
Bush, George W. 223–224
Butler, Octavia 189

"The Cage" 64, 84
California Institute of Technology 31
"A Call to Arms" 103
Campbell, Joseph 6, 102–110, 115–135
cancellation 2, 22, 187–188, 192–193
Cardassians 101
Carson, David 15
Carson, Rachel 93
Cartmell, Deborah 18
CBS (TV channel) 48
Chapel, Nurse Christine 66–68, 228
Charlie's Angels 153
"The Chase" 75
Chekov, Pavel 93, 181, 195
"Chimera" 78
Christianity 83–84, 91, 104
Christmas 219
Citizen Kane 34
Civil Rights 82–83
Clarke, Arthur C. 189
Close Encounters of the Third Kind 33, 141
Cochrane, Zefram 54
Cohen, Stanley 200

Cold War 50, 119
community 7, 12, 19, 174, 190, 193–194
computer games 223–231
Conquest of Space 141
continuity 25, 142–143
"The Corbomite Maneuver" 14
conventions 2, 57, 203–209
Coto, Manny 55, 187–188
creativity 7, 174–175, 199
Crusher, Beverly 147
C.S.I. 202
cult fandom 44, 162, 190

Data 4, 15, 124–135, 181
Dax, Curzon 103
Dax, Ezri 107
Dax, Jadzia 103
The Day the Earth Stood Still 34
de Certeau, Michel 176
Decker, Willard 116, 120–135
deixis 14
Delany, Samuel R. 189
de Saussure, Ferdinand 193, 195
DiMaggio, Joe 101
Discovery (space shuttle) 18
Disney World 223
Doctor Who 1, 43, 153, 157, 165
The Dominion 70, 78, 101, 103
Doohan, James 159, 165
Dragnet 160
Dukat, Gul 103–110

Earhart, Amelia 17
Earth 16
Earth: Final Conflict 24, 46
Ellison, Harlan 29–30, 178
Emerson, Ralph Waldo 85–86
"Emissary" 104
"Encounter at Farpoint" 37
"Endgame" 183
Engel, Joel 29, 32, 35–36, 43
Enterprise (HMS) 17
Enterprise (NX 01) 18
Enterprise (space shuttle) 17
Enterprise (starship) 6, 13, 25, 35, 118,
    139–150, 157–158, 187
Enterprise-B (starship) 121, 123
Enterprise-D (starship) 17, 121, 123
Enterprise-E (starship) 147–150
environment 4, 83–97
Excelsior (starship) 145
"Explorers" 106
extinction 5
"Extreme Measures" 79

"Family Business" 106
fan culture 173–185
fan mail 30, 163

fan websites 179–182, 192, 220–223
fans 6–8, 44, 138, 199–216
Farscape 46
The Federation 30, 44, 54, 56, 70, 102,
    180, 228
Ferengi 54, 65, 204
Fern, Yvonne 26
filk songs 176
film 1, 5, 115–135, 138–150
Firefly 50
Fiske, John 155–156, 177
Flash Gordon 68
Fontana, D.C. 195, 222
Forbidden Planet 188
The 4400 49
Foucault, Michel 224
The Founders 70, 76–79
Fox Network 45–46
Frakes, Jonathan 37, 56
Free Enterprise 221
freedom 50, 57, 222
From the Earth to the Moon 82
Fry, Philip J. 1
The Fugitive 15
Futurama 1

G4 (TV channel) 224–229
Galaxy Quest 173
"The Galileo Seven" 87
Galipeau, Steven 15
Gene Roddenberry's Andromeda 24, 46
Genesis (planet) 69, 91–93, 121
Gernsback, Hugo 189
Gerrold, David 195, 222
Glenn, John 18
Goddard, Robert H. 18
Graceland 200
Grand Canyon 88
Great Britain 6, 153–168
Greenwald, Jeff 173
Gregory, Chris 1
Gwenllian-Jones, Sara 45, 48, 178

Hawthorn, J. 13
Heaven's Gate 190
Heinlein, Robert 50
Hercules 101
Hercules: The Legendary Journeys 46
The Hero with a Thousand Faces 6, 115
Highlander 46
Hills, Matt 11–12, 199–201
"Hollow Pursuits" 182–183
holodeck 56, 106–110, 183
"Homefront" 78
Homer 106
homosexuality 181
"Honor Among Thieves" 103
How William Shatner Changed the World 23

humpback whales 94–95
Hunter, I.Q. 18
Hyde Park 202, 210–214

IDIC (Infinite Diversity in Infinite Com-
  binations) 12, 30, 63–79, 191, 204
ILM (Industrial Light and Magic) 145
"Image in the Sand" 103
Imperialism 70–79
"In a Mirror, Darkly" 25
International Space Station 18
Internet 2, 44, 184–185, 188–196, 218,
  225–231
interracial kiss 65, 82
intertextuality 137–150
Invasion Iowa 222, 224
Iraq War 74, 207, 223–225
"Is There in Truth No Beauty?" 29
ITV (TV channel) 153

James, Clive 166–168
Jancovich, Mark 50
Janeway, Kathryn 72–74
Jefferies, Walter M. 159
Jenkins, Henry 7, 37, 138, 162, 174–176,
  180
jeremiad 4
Jindra, Michael 180, 190–191
Johnson-Smith, Jan 24, 56, 149
Jones, Miranda 29
"Journey to Babel" 67
Jurassic Park 145
Justman, Robert 12–13, 26, 32, 173

Kellogg, Robert 13
Kennedy, John F. 90
Kim, Ensign Harry 74–79
Kira, Colonel Nerys 78, 103–110, 181
Kirk, James T. 3–5, 7, 11, 24, 53, 65, 68,
  84–97, 100–101, 115–135, 141, 144–146,
  158–167, 202, 222, 228
Kitty Hawk, NC 17
Klingon Encounter (ride) 206–207
Klingons 54, 70, 91, 117, 121, 145, 174
Koenig, Walter 181–182, 195, 220
Kon-Tiki 17, 54
Koufax, Sandy 108
Kozinets, Robert 191–192, 204
Kozloff, Sarah 14

LaForge, Geordi 122, 126
Las Vegas Hilton Hotel 8, 177, 185, 199–
  216
Leeta 107
Le Guin, Ursula K. 189
letter campaign 30–33, 178
Lewis, C.S. 26
liberal humanism 3, 23, 44

Lichtenberg, Jacqueline 33
Lincoln Enterprises 27–30, 204
Lindbergh, Charles 17
Lost 49, 221
Lost in Space 43
Lunar Orbiter 18

"The Man Trap" 26, 84, 87
Manifest Destiny 71
Marshak, Sondra 33
"Masks" 101
The Matrix 4, 177
McCoy, Leonard 68–69, 84, 87, 116–135,
  228
mega-text 12, 37, 191, 193, 195
"The Menagerie" 25, 84, 89
merchandising 1–2, 6–7, 28–30, 174–175,
  190–191, 193, 204, 208–210, 214, 219–
  220, 222
metonymy 199–200, 202
"Mirror, Mirror" 25
Mission: Impossible (series) 221
Mission: Impossible III 221
mixed heritage identity 4, 63–79, 181
Monomyth 6, 102–110, 115–135
Montalban, Ricardo 35
Moon Landing 18, 157–158
Moore, Ronald D. 51–57, 192, 195, 222
"The Most Toys" 203
"Mudd's Women" 203
multiculturalism 76–79, 82, 158, 189
Murdoch, Rupert 45
Mutant X 46
myth 14–15, 100–110, 191–193

"The Naked Now" 37
"The Naked Time" 37, 89
narrative 13
NASA 17, 205
Nash, Roderick 83
Native Americans (Indians) 72, 83
NATO 50
NBC (TV channel) 22, 30–32, 64, 178,
  185, 223
New Frontier 83
New Hollywood 5
New York, NY 93, 203
Nichols, Nichelle 64–69, 159, 181
Nimoy, Leonard 30, 32, 146, 162–167, 221
Nog 107
novels 2, 32, 191
nuclear power 89–90

Odo 4, 63, 70, 76–79, 181, 221
Odysseus 101, 103, 106, 118
opening narration 3, 11–19
opening titles 16–18
Orientalism 66

"Paradise Lost" 78
"Parallels" 55
Paramount 2, 6–8, 22, 25–38, 41, 45,
  137–150, 174–185, 186–187, 193–196
"Pathfinder" 183
"Patterns of Force" 162
Pearson, Roberta 36, 146
"The Pegasus" 56
Penley, Constance 7, 68, 161
Phoenix (warp test ship) 18
Picard, Jean-Luc 6, 12, 70, 101, 115–135,
  146–150, 207
Piccard, Auguste and Jean 17
Pike, Captain Christopher 84
Pilgrimage 199, 201, 209
Piller, Michael 43, 50, 53
Planet of the Apes 4
"Plato's Stepchildren" 65
Pol, Dr Mora 76–79
Presley, Elvis 200, 202
Prime Directive 70–79, 119, 126
pulp magazines 24, 189, 196

Quantum Leap 15, 53
Quark 105–110

racism 63, 163, 173
Radio Times 26, 154–168
Reagan, Ronald 94
Reeves-Stevens, Judith and Garfield 33
Relic Hunter 46
religion 100–110, 190–191
retrovisions 18
"Return of the Archons" 100
"Revulsion" 74
Rhode Island 84
Richards, Thomas 70
Riker, William 56, 120, 188
Riverside, IA 202, 222
Roberts, Robin 204–205, 208
Roddenberry, Gene 1, 2–3, 12, 15, 19,
  22–38, 63–64, 82, 159–167, 173, 192,
  216
Rom 107
Romulans 25, 54, 89, 96, 103
Russ, Tim 182
Ryan, Jeri 221

Saavik 122
Sandvoss, Cornel 199–200
Sarah (Sisko's mother) 104–110
Sarek 67, 117, 188
Schilling, Curt 102
Scholes, Robert 13
Sci-Fi Channel 46–47
science fiction literature 23–38, 189–190,
  192
science fiction television 22–38, 189–190

Sconce, Jeffrey 190
"Scorpion, Part 1" 72–74
Scott, Montgomery (Scotty) 122, 159,
  188, 228
segregation 65–66
self-improvement 4
semiotics 193–196
September 11, 2001 8, 18, 55, 187, 192,
  203, 207
Seven of Nine 4, 63, 70–79, 219, 221
sexuality 4, 74–76
Sha Ka Ree 91–92, 123
Shadowlands 26
"Shadows and Symbols" 104
Shatner, William 23, 28–29, 31, 53,
  65–66, 159, 162–167, 204, 220–222
Shepard, Alan 17
Shinzon 96, 117–135, 148
"Shore Leave" 86
Short, Mick 14
Silent Spring 93
Singh, Khan Noonian 35, 91–93, 121–135
Sirtis, Marina 56
Sisko, Benjamin 100–110
Sisko, Jake 102–110
The Six Million Dollar Man 43
Sky One (TV channel) 25
Slash Fiction 7, 68, 161
Sobchack, Vivian 139, 148
Sojourner Mars Rover 18
Solow, Herbert 30, 173
Son'a 94
The Sound of Music 34
Soviet Union 18
space exploration/race 18
Space: 1999 43
space opera 51, 192
"Space Seed" 35
"Space the final frontier..." (opening
  line) 3, 12–14, 36
special effects 6, 137–150
Spike TV 224
Spiner, Brent 15, 188
Spinrad, Norman 24
Spirit of St Louis 17
Spock 4, 7, 29, 35, 63–70, 84, 89, 92,
  116–135, 144, 160–167, 188, 211, 228
Sport 5, 100–110, 199–200
"The Squire of Gothos" 85
Star Trek (Animated Series) 32
Star Trek (The Original Series) 2, 22
Star Trek Adventure 202, 210–216
Star Trek: Deep Space Nine 5, 16, 25, 41,
  45–53, 63, 76–79, 100–110, 181, 187,
  195, 204, 213
Star Trek: Enterprise 2, 4, 16–19, 22, 41, 47,
  53–57, 184, 187–196, 213
Star Trek Experience 2, 8, 177, 199–216

Star Trek Fact Files 178
Star Trek: First Contact 25, 116–135, 147
Star Trek Generations 116–135, 145–146
Star Trek: Insurrection 92, 94, 116–135, 147–148
Star Trek: The Motion Picture 25, 27, 32–34, 91, 116–135, 137, 139–142
Star Trek Nemesis 96, 116–135, 148–150, 184, 210
Star Trek: New Voyages 181–182, 187–196, 220–223
Star Trek: The Next Generation 2–3, 14, 22, 25, 35–37, 41–57, 75, 101, 119, 139, 145, 181, 186, 203, 205, 212
Star Trek: Phase II 33–35, 42, 140, 195
Star Trek: Voyager 16, 25, 41, 45–53, 63, 70–79, 145, 182–183
Star Trek II: The Wrath of Khan 11, 35, 68, 91–94, 116–135, 142
Star Trek III: The Search for Spock 35, 63, 68, 116–135, 142–143
Star Trek IV: The Voyage Home 5, 35, 91–95, 116–135, 144
Star Trek V: The Final Frontier 91–94, 116–135, 144–145
Star Trek VI: The Undiscovered Country 91, 116–135, 145
Star Wars 5, 6, 14, 33, 37, 43, 115, 140, 189
Starfleet 126, 206
Stargate: Atlantis 23, 47
Stargate SG-1 23, 47
Starship Dental 219
Straczynski, J.M. 24, 49, 51
Sulu, Hikaru 86, 145, 228
Sybok 91–93, 117–135
syndication 32, 43

"Take Me Out to the Holosuite" 106–110
Takei, George 145, 181, 195, 221–222
Taylor, Jeri 53
"Tears of the Prophets" 101
Teenagers 8, 218–231
TekWar (novels) 222
Television 1, 3, 6, 11–19, 37, 41–57, 153–168, 223–231
Terminator 2: Judgment Day 145, 192
textual poaching 7, 174–175, 183
"These Are the Voyages..." 17, 56
The Third Man 201
"The Tholian Web" 25
Thoreau, Henry David 85–86
tourism 201–216
toys 2
T'Pol 54
transcendentalism 85–86
Trekkies 173, 219

Trimble, Bjo 28–29, 31–32, 178, 186
Troi, Deanna 120, 188
"The Trouble with Tribbles" 188
"Turnabout Intruder" 32
Tuvok 182
TV Guide 1, 2, 23, 47, 56
2001: A Space Odyssey 140
Tyrrell, William B. 15

Uhura 64, 159, 181, 228
uniforms 25, 191, 208, 212
United Nations 50
U.S. Army 224–231
University of California, Los Angeles 19
University of Southern California 31
UPN (TV station) 41–42, 45, 48, 55, 57
utopia 12, 19, 180, 191–192, 196

V 43
Vampires 71
Vancouver, B.C. 46, 201
Verne, Jules 82
Viacom 48, 55
Vietnam War 70, 83, 119, 158, 163
"Vortex" 78
Vulcans 30, 54, 66, 91, 106–108, 187, 221

"Wagon Train to the Stars" 16
Warner Brothers 46
Warren, Diane 17
Watson, Russell 17
West Side Story 34
"What Are Little Girls Made Of?" 84
"What You Leave Behind" 79, 108–110
"Where My Heart Will Take Me" (theme song) 17, 54
"Where No Fan Has Gone Before" 1
Whitfield, Stephen 28, 30
Whitney, Grace Lee 195, 222
"Who Mourns for Adonis?" 100
"Who Watches the Watchers" 101
Wikipedia 26, 32, 36
wilderness 83–97
Will and Grace 221
Williams, Roger 84
Wilson, Harold 159
Wimbledon 200
Winston, Joan 33
Wise, Robert 34
Worf 70, 77
World War Two 93
Wright Brothers 17
Wyatt, Justin 5–6

The X-Files 45–46, 192, 201
The X-Men 226
Xena: Warrior Princess 46

xenophobia 77
The Xindi 55, 187

Yates (Sisko), Kasidy 103, 106–110
Yeager, Charles (Chuck) 17

Yellowstone National Park 86
Yosemite National Park 86, 92
YouTube 225–228